HUNGRY HILL

To the Patrons of the West Hartford Library...

Count the Connecticut references...

Best,
Carole O'Malley Gaunt

HUNGRY HILL

A Memoir

Carole O'Malley Gaunt

UNIVERSITY OF MASSACHUSETTS PRESS

Amherst

Copyright © 2007 by Carole O'Malley Gaunt

LC   2007002525

ISBN 978-1-55849-589-0 (paper); 588-3 (cloth)

Designed by Kristina Kachele Design, llc
Set in Fairfield with Lake Informal display
Printed and bound by The Maple-Vail Book Manufacturing Group, Inc.

Library of Congress Cataloging-in-Publication Data

Gaunt, Carole O'Malley.
Hungry Hill : a memoir / Carole O'Malley Gaunt.
p.   cm.
ISBN 978-1-55849-589-0 (pbk. : alk. paper) —
ISBN 978-1-55849-588-3 (alk. paper)
1. Gaunt, Carole O'Malley.   2. Dramatists, American—21st century—Biography.
3. Dramatists, American—21st century—Family relationships.
4. Women dramatists, American—Biography.   5. Alcoholism.   I. Title.
PS3607 .A97Z68   2007
812'.6—dc22   2007002525

British Library Cataloguing in Publication data are available.

Contents

THE AREA BOUNDED by the hillsides of Liberty Street, Carew Street, and Springfield Street in Springfield, Massachusetts, long home to the city's Irish, is known as "Hungry Hill." While the origins of the name have been lost in the shadows of history and folklore, the Connecticut Valley Historical Museum offers several theories. Since many of the Irish immigrants in Springfield hailed from County Cork, an area particularly hard hit by the Potato Famine, these hardscrabble newcomers in longing for a connection with the Old Country may have christened this section after a mountain in southwest Cork, which had itself received that alliterative name well before the nineteenth-century devastation. Another hypothesis is far more practical: the Irish Catholic families who settled here bought enormous quantities of groceries to feed their many children. The police in Springfield tell yet a different story; they claim the name arose because of a luxury the community lacked: restaurants. Policemen walking the beat on the "Hill" had to brownbag it. Whatever its origin, the name bespeaks times of tightened belts and growling bellies.

Back when I grew up on Hungry Hill, I was suffering from an emotional hunger.

HUNGRY HILL

Introduction

LIMELIGHT

"CAROLE, WHY DO you want to rake up all that family stuff?" Michael, my older brother, asked, gravel in his voice. "Isn't it enough you lived through it?" His bluntness was chilling, spiraling me back into the gray-tiled kitchen at 21 Lynwood Terrace where my brothers routinely dismissed me as the "crazy" one. But I had changed, and this time I would not back away from first-born Michael's harsh questions. Hadn't I raised my children, and didn't I know what a "family" could be? My daughters' passage into adulthood may have spurred me into writing this book. It was time for me, the only girl, to talk, to shred the cords of O'Malley silence binding me and my seven brothers to the terror and chaos of my mother's early death and my father's alcoholism. My long silence, the programmed silence of the "good girl," the silence of an alcoholic's daughter, was finally over.

When I was thirteen, my mother died from lymphatic cancer, a raging giant of a cancer, and I immediately became "different." My brothers were different too. We were motherless. Although it seems irrational and implausible now, I felt ashamed for not having a mother. But at that tender age, I knew no one else whose parent had died. At my mother's wake, where I brazenly eavesdropped on the whisperings of black-clad mourners—"Betty never even knew about the . . . ," "A blessing," "Well, at least, she was spared knowing"—I learned that my mother had never known she was dying of cancer. Silence itself can be a lie.

As I flailed about after her death, I decided that any mention of my mother would surely make others feel uncomfortable, saddened, or, worse yet, leave them with no idea what to say to me in my new, unwanted role as a "maternal" orphan. By that thinking, the way I ratcheted the feelings of others above my own, I crippled the sad and vulnerable parts of myself. Overnight I became hard and, bit by bit, I buried any of my needs. I kept quiet.

But my handsome father with his black Irish looks did not keep quiet. He was ever the scene stealer, taking center stage the way alcoholics and addicts seem to do. Glib and sentimental, my father grabbed the spotlight in our lives, and his children were bit players, cast in roles his disease had predetermined for us. As in many families of alcoholics, those surrounding him, my brothers and I, excelled at improvisational skills. In our chaotic home, there was never a formal script, never a sense of order for us. Everything completely depended on "how he was" that day.

In the field of alcohol or addiction literature, the focus generally is on the addict/alcoholic, and often scant consideration is given to the family members, the real victims, who are left frantically trying to hold things together. This is one of their stories. Each of my brothers has his own story. *Hungry Hill* is mine.

In western Massachusetts in 1959, John Fitzgerald Kennedy's budding presidential candidacy conferred on the people of Springfield a sprinkling of validity, glamour, and meaning we did not have on our own. With Kennedy's sandy-haired, blue-eyed movie-idol looks and his sharp yet endearing wit, the city of Springfield, and soon the nation, held him in an awe bordering on worship. Like many of Springfield's residents, JFK too was an Irish Catholic. The working-class city forgave him his eastern Massachusetts roots, his strange r's, and his Ivy League background.

The years 1959 through 1963 were a golden era for Massachusetts politics. The Kennedy dynasty was at the center of the national stage. The "pink" revolution was yet to come: Betty Friedan was stewing in the New

York suburbs; Gloria Steinem had not yet tossed the women's movement gauntlet down before the national psyche; and such miracles as birth control pills and panty hose were in their seedling phases.

As the only Negro in an entering class of 800 students, soft-mannered Yvonne Mullins avoided direct eye contact with her Cathedral High School peers, much in the manner of a subway-riding New Yorker.

With Elvis ensconced as the king of rock and roll, teenagers smirked at the big band, easy listening music of Frank Sinatra, Ella Fitzgerald, and Nat King Cole, their parents' choice.

Medically, cancer was a taboo subject, a word that could not be said aloud. A "spare the patient" dictum was in general use, as if the secrecy surrounding cancer was in itself a source of shame. While Alcoholics Anonymous meetings were finding their footings in the basements of Protestant churches, will power was the prescribed remedy of the day. Alcoholics were considered weak and flawed and a source of shame to family members. The treatment of addiction did not exist.

In the early 1960s, the world was, then as now, a frightening place: the Soviet Union and Cuba were in each other's beds; Communism was an ever-present threat to capitalism, religion, and democracy, and worse yet, Sputnik had orbited the earth.

But I was fighting my own battles of one kind or another over on Hungry Hill at 21 Lynwood Terrace.

1. Last Rites

LATER THAT SUMMER, I would resent that my older brother, Michael, knew all along my mother was dying. He had been told back in March, and I had not. I knew she was really sick. But as a thirteen-year-old, I believed in the magical power of miracles, believed in what the starched Sisters of Saint Joseph had told me: that a true miracle could occur at any time, if only I prayed hard enough. Either the nuns had lied to me, or I prayed the wrong prayers.

"Carole, I'm taking all the boys to Dombrowsky's to pick up cold cuts. Then I'll swing by the A&P to load up on groceries. I want the house quiet," my father says in a low voice, staring at his clenched hands. Ever since my mother came home from the hospital back in May, the week after Mother's Day, I have tried to keep the house quiet, even tomblike, ordering my brothers to play outside, day and night, in sun and pouring rain. My father's starting to treat me as an equal, as if he knows he can always depend on me. He pops two Alka-Seltzers into a jelly glass, and I wait for the familiar fizz and watch for the explosion of tiny bubbles.

"Rose should be here soon, kiddo, so hold the fort," he jokes, wiping white foam from his upper lip. At the door, nicked and scratched by the comings and goings of all my brothers, he hesitates. "The priest may come.

Do whatever he asks. I'll be back before the, the . . . Well, I'll be back," he says, leaving the door open behind him. When I walk over to close the door, I see my seven brothers packed into the 1958 Ford station wagon on a Saturday morning outing to the family butcher, and for half a second I wish that I were with them too, arguing and bickering and lobbying for the shotgun position. Yet I do like the responsibility, being singled out, the specialness of being in charge.

I pry a Hydrox cookie perfectly apart to glide my teeth over the sugary white filling and wonder whether my father said he had called the priest? Is that what he said? No, that's not what he said. He said the priest was coming. So did that mean the priest had called him? Why hadn't I asked my father? Because he wouldn't have answered me anyway? Besides, I already knew that the priest was coming to see my mother. Extreme Unction. Last Rites. Hocus-Pocus. I am licking crumbs of chocolate from my fingers when I hear a slight moan from my parents' bedroom, a moan I decide to ignore. On Wednesday night, my mother slipped into a coma, but she would slide in moans at the odd moment. Rose, the nurse, should be here any minute and she will know what to do. My mother, I think in some tiny scrap of my brain, may be dying.

When the front doorbell rings, my mind starts jumping, "No one's here. I'm all alone. Where is Rose? What's happened to her?" I know it's the parish priest because Rose would have come straight in the kitchen door. Anyone but the pastor, Father Power, I think as I hurry into the living room. I feel perspiration pooling under my arms, so I pull at my blouse. With a lurch, I open the living room door, scraping it over the carpet, and Father Miller, somber-faced, missal in his hand, is standing on the front porch. At church, Father Miller's sermons win for most boring—he never even tries to tell a joke in the first few minutes. I hope nosy Jay Vecchiarelli isn't watching from behind a shade across the street. I so want to hurry Father Miller in, but I hesitate, wordless, until after a moment he asks, "Where is your mother?"

As I lead him to the sickroom, my mother and father's bedroom, Father Miller asks me whether anyone else is home. Mechanically, he goes to the left side of the blond bookcase bed. Behind him, the drawn slats of the green venetian blind look like stripes neatly overlapping. As he studies my mother, whose pale, damp skin has a saint-like look, I shift from foot to foot. Although the sickness has made her, always a pretty woman, now ethereally beautiful, I can't make myself look at her. It's just too hard. With a confused expression on his face, Father Miller clears his throat and says, "You can't do this alone, Carole. We'll need someone else, another adult, since your father's not here." His words carry a pinprick of accusation—that I can't handle it—whatever *it* is.

"Rose, she's the nurse, well, really she's my uncle's sister, should be here any minute. My father told me that when he left," I explain, watching Father Miller set his prayer book on the end table.

"Is there a neighbor, anyone next door? Someone who could come over to be here?" he persists in the same monotone he uses in his Sunday sermons. Then, placing a purple stole around his neck, he directs me: "I want you to go next door to see if there is anyone there who could come over, Carole."

I stare at the speckled linoleum as I cross the kitchen floor wondering why I have to go get Mrs. Metzger to come over when my father didn't say anything about it. "I'm letting my dad down," I think as I cut through the opening in the hedges. I glance at the tar-cracked driveway and notice the deep scars winter has etched in its once smooth surface. I knock twice on the Metzgers' door and wait, secretly hoping no one is home. Dressed in a faded chenille robe, Mrs. Metzger scuffles to the door, her blond hair a smooth pith helmet.

"Yes, Carole, what is it?" she asks with a small smile.

"Father Miller's at the house for my mother and he wants you to come over, if you can," I say, the words rushing out while I point to Father Miller's black Chevrolet parked in front of the house.

"Just let me change. I'll only be a minute. Come in, come in. Wait here, Carole," she says, quickly disappearing down the hall. Mrs. Metzger bakes three days a week, and there is a fluted apple pie on a metal rack cooling on the counter. I breathe in the sugar-cinnamon smell of this kitchen, yet know from playing with the Metzger kids in the backyard that Mrs. Metzger has a vicious temper so I cannot be lulled into letting my guard down. In no time, Mrs. Metzger stands in the hallway in a beige wrap skirt with a matching blouse that she is still tucking in. As I follow her up the three back porch steps to my house, I study the tiny, even stitches in her skirt trying to figure out whether she has sewn this outfit or whether it's store-bought.

When we enter the sickroom, Father Miller nods slowly to Mrs. Metzger, and I keep my eyes on the hunter green goose-necked reading lamp attached to the blond bookcase bed, as if I have never seen it. My dad's *Time* magazine is spread open, and I move to close it when Father Miller's cough startles me.

"Carole, we're ready to begin. You stand next to Mrs. Metzger there at the foot of the bed," he directs in a soft confessional voice. Mrs. Metzger stands barely a foot from me, much too close. I begin playing with the gray line under my fingernails. Raising his eyebrows, Father Miller indicates he is satisfied with our bedside positions, and he begins reading solemnly from his black prayer book. I am trying to make out the gold lettering through his fingers when there is the tinny sound of the aluminum door closing. Rose's heels click across the kitchen floor, and in a minute she rushes into the bedroom, all out of breath.

"I'm so sorry. Jimmy needed a ride to his Little League game and Monty had to work. Hello, Father, I'm Rose Montanari from Holy Name parish," Rose says, slowing her voice as she talks to the priest. Masking his impatience, Father Miller mumbles that we will start again. Rose straightens the bed sheet and feels for my mother's hand. Reaching down, she places her handbag under the night table as if this was the signal for Father Miller to begin.

Father Miller recites the prayers in English as well as in Latin, but everything is a foreign language to me. I am tuning out, trying to envision the magical power of a miracle, wondering if a miracle has ever occurred in Springfield, Massachusetts. Now, the priest anoints my mother's high, unlined forehead with oil. So this is anointing, I think, wrapping one leg spaghetti-like around the other to test my balance and, half-smiling, I picture myself toppling to the floor. Father Miller moves his lips in prayer and asks us to make a response. If I have to talk, I might cry. A panic hits me because I have no idea what it is Mrs. Metzger, Rose, and I are supposed to repeat after him. Dustballs seem to climb up the sides of my throat. "I'll let them do it. I'll just move my lips. Maybe I'll mumble," I think.

Through the window, I can hear Jay and Joe Vecchiarelli yelling at each other outside on the street, fighting over a turn at bat. Father Miller winces, his link with divinity jarred, at the cracking noise of a bat hitting a baseball. In here, a heavy, slow-moving quiet spreads throughout the room. Suddenly, a miracle.

"Take care of my baby, take care of my baby, Tommy! Who will take care of my baby?" My mother lifts her head from the pillow, opens her eyes, sits bolt upright in bed with her arms extended heavenward, and, in a yelling-in-the-schoolyard voice, begs for my baby brother. Miracle or not, I hear myself screaming. Rose places her big hand on my mother's bony wrist and assures her firmly that they will take care of the baby, not to worry. I feel strong arms pinned around me and hear Mrs. Metzger's steady voice in my ear, saying, "Carole, Carole, there, there." My screaming fit ends, and I shake off her capable arms. Father Miller wipes some spit gathering in the corner of his mouth. My stomach flip-flops but, looking at my mother for the first time that day, I tell her, "I'll take care of the baby, Mom. I will, I promise." In a split second, she's gone again, lost. As mysteriously as the ghostlike flash of consciousness came in her, it disappears and her head falls back onto the pillow. Is this the miracle?

Tommy's barely two. What have I promised? Does my mother even know that I'm here? Funny, how my mom didn't say anything about my dad, mention his name, or me, standing right there. Then, needing a way for me to get through Father Miller's mumbo jumbo, needing the forms, the rite to end, I am imagining myself outside on the street running bases with Jay and Joe Vecchiarelli when Father Miller folds his purple stole, walks over to me, and extends his hands. Am I supposed to kiss his ring like Bishop Weldon's at Confirmation? Is he wearing a ring? He grips my sweaty palms and pats my shoulder, and I can see tears welling in the corners of his eyes. Priests can't cry. Please, Father, don't cry.

Rose begins lining up the medicines in alphabetical order and by volume on the night table. Mrs. Metzger pushes me toward the door, and I follow Father Miller down to the kitchen hallway.

"Tell your father that I was here, and that she can go to the hospital anytime now," Father Miller says to me in an almost kind way.

I am relieved to have directions to follow. But the next moment, barely breathing, I ask awkwardly:

"Father, in sixth-grade religion, Sister said that sometimes miracles occur when the Last Rites are given? Have you ever seen any miracles?" Can I go to hell for this? Asking the priest a question?

"Your sixth-grade teacher was Sister Mary Matthias?" Father says to me as I study the black dots of whiskers on his sunken cheeks.

"Yes, Father."

"I'll have to talk to Sister," he says, placing his hand on the kitchen doorknob. At that instant, Father Miller and I both know that there will be no more miracles. Maybe God knew that, despite my prayers and the good grades and the perfect conduct mark, it was all an act. Still, the rebel streak in me won't let me stop hoping.

Father Miller and Mrs. Metzger are outside at the edge of the driveway, their arms folded, their eyes on the house. For a minute, I stand there and then scrape specks of white paint from the brass doorknob with my fingernail until Father Miller drives off.

The sun is blazing down on the driveway with shiny bubbles of tar forcing themselves through the surface when our station wagon rounds the corner. My brothers pile out, slamming doors. My father implores them to be quiet, to stay out of the house until lunchtime, to think of "your sick mother."

My dad's carrying three brown bags brimming with groceries and shoves his broad shoulder against the door so that he can drop them on the kitchen table. I take the gallon of milk from his hand. His cheeks look red to me, and I think maybe it's the heat until I smell the whiskey on his breath.

"Hey, Princess, what's up, kid?" my dad asks, putting the neatly wrapped packages of meat into the freezer.

"He came," I say, pulling out a box of Rice Krispies.

"Who came?" my dad asks and hoists the milk into the refrigerator.

"Father Miller."

"Oh, he did?" My dad pauses with a quart of boysenberry ice cream, his favorite, in his hand.

"Yeah, I got Mrs. Metzger to come over. He made me get her."

"Well, that's good," he says, as if he didn't hear me and turns his back to open the freezer.

"He said to tell you Mom could go to the hospital anytime now. Dad, is she going?" Just this once, I want him to answer me, to be honest with me.

"I don't know, Carole." He knows, but he's not telling me.

"Di and Anne are waiting for me at Van Horn," I tell him. My brothers and I come and go as we please, never needing to ask permission.

"Shoot a little hoop with your friends?" he asks.

I shrug and say, "Rose is in there, with Mom." I show off some basketball tricks for him, pretend I'm dribbling, feint, and hang a hook shot. My dad smiles, and I jump down the porch stairs three at a time.

On my way to Van Horn Park, I picture myself a frenzy on the basketball court, making lay-ups, hook shots, jump shots, foul shots, shots from midcourt, and suddenly I'm shivering, with goosebumps popping up on my arms, as I realize how my dad had left me all alone.

Later, when I would try to figure out how our lives went so wrong, I marked my mother's death as the beginning of the end.

<hr/>

MOTHER'S DAY 1992

Joe O'Malley, Carole's father, looks around her apartment. He appraises the furniture, the draperies, and nods his head in a gesture of approval. Adjusting the sofa pillow behind him, he leans back and plants his feet.

JOE: Hey, Katsy, I wish your mother could see this apartment. God must be smiling at you these days.

CAROLE: You could say God's not so distracted these days. Do you still take milk and sugar in your tea?

JOE: I guess you're not offering me anything stronger. I'll have to settle for this weak sister tea.

CAROLE: Weak sister? Why not weak brother? Dad, that expression sounds to me like you're putting down women.

JOE: (*Placatingly.*) I'm sorry, Punkin. You seem defensive.

CAROLE: You're familiar with the word "sexist"?

JOE: (*Half jokingly.*) There was no women's movement in my day. (*His explanation sits in the air. He runs his fingers along the edge of the coffee table and picks up the cup and saucer. Without looking at Carole, he clears his throat.*) So how long has it been since you've banished the demon alcohol from your life?

CAROLE: Oh, so now it's a demon, I thought it was Irish Medicine. When Susie was two, I woke up on a Sunday morning with a pounding jackhammer in my head, and I knew I had a choice to make. I could either drink or be a mother—but I couldn't do both. And I stopped.

JOE: Just like that? (*Joe snaps his fingers.*)

CAROLE: Lucky I hadn't quite crossed over that line.

JOE: Your mother could drink and be a mother.

CAROLE: (*In a traitorous whisper.*) I wanted to outlive her. (*There is a moment of discomfort they both share, a moment of quiet. He breaks the silence and picks up the sugar bowl, spooning sugar into his tea.*)

JOE: What—no Tiffany silver service? No silver sugar tongs? No maid in uniform?

CAROLE: Mrs. Meade never wore a uniform.

JOE: We had the distinction of employing the only Jewish maid in Springfield. What a character she was.

CAROLE: Always throwing salt over her shoulder. (*Joe's face loses its smile when Carole picks up index cards. Inhaling deeply, she folds the index cards in half.*)

JOE: Pretty organized? If I didn't love you so much, I wouldn't have agreed to this, what is it, this inquisition of yours. Did some shrink put you up to this?

CAROLE: (*Exasperated with him.*) I'm sorry, Dad. But this is my interview. (*Carole pushes aside some family photos and reaches for a pair of glasses.*)

JOE: (*Changing the subject.*) How long have you been wearing glasses?

CAROLE: Dad, you're asking all the questions. You're throwing me off my game. (*Caving in.*) I guess I started wearing them right after Vicky was born.

JOE: Vicky—Abigail, Susan, and Victoria—not a Bridget, Maureen, or Kathleen in the bunch. That's what happens when you marry outside the faith. A WASP, no less.

CAROLE: Call me a rebel. Don't forget Father Power did marry us.

JOE: You looked so beautiful that day. Brought tears to these tired eyes.

CAROLE: (*Half teasingly.*) Dad, are you sweet-talking me? I asked you here because Abby will be fourteen next week.

JOE: She's a wonderful girl. Reminds me of you at that age.

CAROLE: That's what I'm trying to get at and why I invited you over today.

JOE: If it's not jewelry or flowers, I've always been weak at gift selection.

CAROLE: No, no, it's not that. Last week I would look at her, and a sadness so thick I could almost touch it crept into me. When Abby noticed how sad I was and asked me what was wrong, I began telling her how I was just her age when Mom received the sacrament of the Last Rites. Before I could finish, and I was as concise as possible, an O'Malley trait, she began crying. Here it was some thirty years later, but her reaching that same age had set me off.

JOE: (*Ignoring her.*) You seem all right now.

CAROLE: (*Angrily.*) I need to be all right, don't I? (*Joe picks up a cookie and breaks it in half. He scrapes the crumbs into a neat anthill.*) Anyway, Abby asked me not to tell her any more stories of my childhood. I was younger than she is now when you left me alone with the priest coming over to give Mom the Last Rites. I could not imagine doing that to Abby when I see how young thirteen is, barely a teenager.

(*Joe puts the tea cup down and straightens the cloth napkin over his knee.*)

JOE: Cloth napkins—there weren't many of these growing up, were there? (*An uncomfortable silence fills the room.*)

CAROLE: Why did you leave me in the house alone? You knew the priest was coming, but you were so nonchalant about his coming, so unclear to me about why Father Miller was coming. I was trapped.

JOE: Sad what happened to Father Miller. His alcoholism did him in.

CAROLE: (*Wearily.*) Dad, this isn't about Father Miller or the cloth napkins. (*With energy.*) I need to know why you left me there alone to face that passage through hell.

JOE: You were tough.

CAROLE: Tough?—did I have a choice? What? I was tough because I didn't faint. Mrs. Metzger grabbed my arm when I screamed.

JOE: After your mother got sick, you knew how I relied on you, counted on you to do whatever needed to be done. I thought if I let that moment seem as if it were just something you had to do, you could handle it better.

CAROLE: Dad, I was terrified, so scared. To cope, I had to click off a dial in my brain, my heart, my soul, my entire being. I'm just grateful

Father Miller had the sense to make me get Mrs. Metzger. Of course, at the time I thought that his making me get her meant that I was somehow letting you down.

JOE: Calm down.

CAROLE: (*Angrily.*) Calm down? Father Miller's rubbing oil on Mom's forehead, and she sits straight up in bed, begging, pleading, Who will take care of my baby? I screamed out loud. Once. One scream.

JOE: Mary told me you screamed.

CAROLE: (*Surprised.*) Wait, you talked about that afternoon with Mrs. Metzger?

JOE: Yes, she was a big help to me when Betty was dying.

CAROLE: So you knew what happened?

JOE: Yes, I did.

CAROLE: But, but, you never said anything to me.

JOE: What good would it have done?

CAROLE: That question is an excuse to do nothing. OK, it might have been hard for you but it might have helped me. I guess I wasn't the tough cookie you thought I was.

JOE: Maybe I misjudged you.

CAROLE: No, perhaps I misjudged you.

JOE: You know, Carole, I'm not sure this was such a good idea.

CAROLE: I'm almost done. Think of it as this year's Mother's Day gift.

JOE: Good.

(*Carole looks deep into his brown eyes, searching for clues.*)

CAROLE: (*Trying to control herself.*) When you came home from picking up the meats, Dad, you had whiskey on your breath.

JOE: So I had a shot of whiskey with Butch.

CAROLE: But, Dad, you must have had it in the morning.

JOE: Try to understand—I needed a crutch.

(*Carole brushes a speck off her skirt, avoiding his sad eyes.*)

CAROLE: What about a crutch for me? Running up the street? Playing basketball for hours on end? Were those my crutches?

JOE: How bad was that? It kept you out of trouble.

CAROLE: But, Dad, I needed you to be my crutch. I play-acted strong. I kept trying to be what you wanted me to be. When wasn't I trying to figure out a way to please you?

JOE: Well, if it makes you any happier, I'm not happy now seeing you like this.

CAROLE: I sensed you wanted a Pollyanna and that's what I tried to be.

JOE: Give me a little credit. I never said that.

CAROLE: No, you didn't, but I made up scenarios in my head, movie scenes of how I thought you wanted me to be.

JOE: (*Preying on her sympathy.*) I am sorry. I was weak.

CAROLE: (*She looks straight at him.*) When I needed you to be strong.

JOE: I don't want to stage a debate with you. How about a refill on the tea?

(*Carole exits, and Joe picks up a family photograph and studies it.*)

2. Gone

AFTER THE GAME, Anne, basketball under her arm, and Di head out of the park toward Penacook Street, and I wave goodbye, walking toward home, glad Anne always brought the basketball. The leaves on the trees sit still, watching me, warning me, Hurry home, hurry home. Hit by a need to get home, I start to run, reach the intersection of Liberty and Newbury, still running madly. Out of breath, I slow up at Marchese's when a car sidles up next to me. A Dion and the Belmonts song is blaring on the radio.

"Doll, we'll give you a ride. You don't need to run," the boys yell at me. I start running again and keep running, a twinge in my side, desperately wanting to reach home, picking up the sound of the boys' souped-up car racing away. Slamming the screen door behind me, I fall into a kitchen chair.

"She's gone," Michael says, his arms folded, leaning against the kitchen counter.

"Gone? Where? Where's Dad?" Gone, a lonesome word.

"He took Mom back to the hospital. Dr. Blackmer's meeting them there."

"When did they leave?"

"Twenty minutes ago, when you were at the park," Michael grunts at me.

"Is she coming back?" I ask, a question soaked with fear.

"Coming back? Weren't you in there with the priest? She's dying," Michael says in a whisper.

Dying. An explosion of scenes flashing in my mind one second, a shriveling, shrinking, wanting to hide under my bed, the next I want to pummel him. How dare he say this?

"Don't say that," I fight back. After a pause, I ask, "How do you know?"

"Mom has cancer, Carole, didn't you know?" Michael growls, licking his full lips.

"Dad said she had mononucleosis, the 'kissing disease,'" I answer, unsure of what's true, no longer safe.

"He just said that so people wouldn't talk. Dad told me back in March when Lew operated. The cancer had spread everywhere, and Lew just went ahead and sewed her back up." When had Michael started calling our family doctor Lew?

"So that's why Dad told me to keep the mononucleosis symptoms to myself?"

"Yeah, there you are in the library, poring over the encyclopedia. It gave him a laugh."

"Why did he tell you and not me?"

"Because I'm the oldest." It's a fact. I could no longer argue.

After a minute or two of silence, I drag myself over to the doorway of my parents' bedroom and can go no further, but from the safety of the hall, my eyes dart everywhere, collecting evidence: my mom gone, the sickbed all made up, the medicines disappeared, the windows wide open, and the blinds pulled up. A faint smell of the sickroom clings to the air, but it's the new sense of stillness and emptiness that makes my stomach cramp.

During a hot, sweltering night, at three thirty in the morning on June 9, 1959, with my father at her hospital bedside, my mother died.

If only I had prayed harder, I might have stopped the brutal madness headed our way.

* * *

"So, this means I don't get to go the eighth-grade class picnic at Look Park?" I make myself ask at breakfast, avoiding my dad's eyes.

"No," my dad answers with a sigh, "you'll have to skip it."

Upstairs, alone in my room, I stuff my bathing suit into my new watermelon beach bag and toss it across the room. I grab the new matching jersey and shorts set I wore in the fashion show, my outfit for the picnic, and study how the strawberries on the top match the strawberries on the shorts. I toss them in a heap on the rug, thinking how no one in my class will get to see them now. Why did my mother have to die the day of the class picnic? I've waited eight years for this day. A bony finger points at me—Carole, you are a terrible, selfish daughter to have even asked about a picnic. The mean part, deep inside of me, wishes my mother had waited to die until after the picnic.

From the bottom of the stairs, my dad yells up, "Carole, you better go downtown to buy some clothes to wear for the wake and funeral. And you better do it now," he orders when I get downstairs, "because I need you to be around this afternoon. The boys are all right wearing their Easter Sunday clothes, so they're all set, but you need to buy something black. Get in the car. I'll drop you off downtown on my way to pick up Mrs. Meade." It's final—no swimming at Look Park for me.

At the Armory Street light, my dad hands me a wad of bills and asks if I know what to buy.

"I wore this Mexican peasant blouse with a white and black print full skirt in the fashion show for the finale. I loved it. Dad, people even clapped," I answer, remembering how I pranced and strutted, my teeth in a permanent, frozen smile.

"I don't know about that outfit. Maybe you should check with Madeline," he suggests, then adds, "Your mother felt so bad that she couldn't see you in the fashion show. Betty was just too weak." As my dad clears his throat, I picture my aunts, Lee and Madeline and Stella in their gold-buttoned knit suits, clustered together at the rear of the auditorium. From backstage, I peeked out and realized that my aunts were not taking seats because they were not "mothers." Aunts—the second string.

"Dad, did Auntie Mad tell you about my military posture? During the tryouts, I threw my shoulders back and pulled my stomach in, and I think that's why the judges picked me." He's not listening, I can tell. There is a minute of silence until we reach Forbes, where the security guard is unlocking the front doors, and I jump out of the car and ride the escalator to the teen floor. Hoping that blackness will hide my perspiration, I buy the black peasant blouse with an elastic collar and three-quarter length sleeves and a new black straight skirt, spending twenty-four dollars in all.

3. God Takes the Saints Early

"GOD TAKES the saints early." John Dowd, a white-haired man with a crew cut, shakes my hand, looking directly at me with his pale, watery blue eyes as he canonizes my mother on the first night of her wake. The saint remark brings out a chill on the back of my neck, making me think of my mother always ordering me to do some chore and my yelling back at her to ask one of my brothers for a change. "Why me?" I'd shout. How does Mr. Dowd know my mother is a saint? She, Elizabeth Marie McCue O'Malley, mother of eight, has not had time even to perform the three miracles required by the Catholic Church for sainthood. Maybe Mr. Dowd, with his acne-scarred skin and his petite blonde wife waiting patiently behind him, has had a course in funeral remarks at Holy Cross, the Jesuit college that is sometimes called the Cross. Now, because of him, because of the saint remark, I have to pretend that my mother is a saint. I feel all tight inside because I am not ready to canonize my mother. For me, my mother was enemy territory. But now that she's dead I can no longer enter that mother-daughter minefield.

The Thomas P. Sampson Funeral Home, the Liberty Street branch, is crowded. All of Hungry Hill is here. The folding chairs are full, mostly with women. It seems as if the men are sneaking off. The evening has a party feel to it. My father has lined us up in age order, so I am standing at the head of the line between Michael and Danny. My father thanks people for coming, so I start to copy him, smiling until I remember this is a wake so I should try to look serious. The neck of my blouse has slipped down to my shoulder, and I'm pulling it up when my father leans over to me.

"Fix your blouse in the ladies' room and take care of your brother Joey on the way."

"I've already fixed my blouse."

"Well, go see to your brother, then." Joey stands on the side, where he is kicking the leg of a folding chair. Joey, seven and in second grade, has a fierce temper, making me, at thirteen, half-afraid he will kick me.

"Daddy wants you to stop kicking the chair."

"Make me."

"Look, Dad sent me over. He said that Mr. Sampson would ask you to leave," I say, improvising, though I think it could happen.

"You're lying." He kicks the chair again. A gray-haired woman in a folding chair looks at us, frown lines deepening between her eyebrows as she twists her head, her cap of tight curls staying perfectly still. She purses her lips, opens the clasp of her pocketbook, reaches in, and pulls out a crystal rosary.

"Joey, there are black scuff marks on the chair."

"So?" Joey puts his hands in his pockets.

"What about standing next to Gerry? Where Daddy asked you to stand?" I suggest. The lady with the rosary makes the sign of the cross and kisses the crucifix, a devotion I usually—no, always—forget. Joey tugs at the sleeve of my blouse, pulling it way below my elbow.

"What is it?" I ask, straightening my sleeve.

"I'm not standing next to him. He's a crybaby. Look, Carole." I turn to look at Gerry who is wiping tears from his cheeks with the back of his hand as Joey kicks the chair again.

"Joey, did you see the flowers from Cerago's, we, us kids, sent to Mom? Can you find them? I will give you a clue. Read the writing on the ribbon. Dad sent them for us, but all our names are on the card."

"Is my name on the card?"

"Yep. See if you can find which ones we sent and then you can show Gerry." He stops kicking the chair and races off to find his name. The flowers my dad sent from us kids are in the shape of a pink heart with a white satin ribbon with the word "MOTHER" in a gold-lettered script. The carnation heart makes me feel proud and, somehow, superior, so I hope my friends get to see it.

Mr. Sampson with his fleshy hands clasped over his stomach is standing in the entry to the room, as if he were guarding it from us. Across from him, Mr. and Mrs. Bigda, our next-door neighbors, are signing their names in a book. She hands him the pen and motions for him to sign. As usual, her hair is pinned up with neat curls in a nest. Mrs. Bigda is about six inches taller than her husband, and her hairdo doesn't help. There is a box of Kleenex right above the guest book. I need to grab three or four Kleenex for Gerry, but before I can get near the box, Rose Bigda crosses to me with her hands outstretched. Stanley, her husband with his stiff gray crew cut, shuffles along behind her.

"Carole, I am so sorry." She looks at me, waiting for me to say something. As I mumble the now familiar thank you, Stanley Bigda puts his arm around my shoulders. I can't hear what he is saying because Mrs. Bigda is making clucking sounds with her tongue, which leaves tiny little lines marring her bright red lipstick. Mr. Bigda puts his hand around his wife's elbow and guides her toward the open coffin. Mr. Sampson's eyes follow them as they walk up the aisle, cramped by the baskets of flowers perched on wire stands.

Safe knowing that Mr. Sampson isn't watching me, I lift a few Kleenex, stuff them in my skirt pocket, and glance down at the guest book, pleased to see that Rose Bigda began a new page as if her written entry were an endorsement of the O'Malley family's popularity.

Gerry is swiping under his nose with his index finger as I reach over and begin dabbing his cheeks with the Kleenex. He pushes my hand away.

"What are you doing?"

"Well, I was just helping."

"Well, don't. There's a girl in my class with her father waiting in the middle of the line." When I hand Gerry the tissue, he wipes his entire face, including his forehead as if there had been tears on his forehead. I start to walk away when he calls my name in a soft voice. I go back, and Gerry stares up at me, speechless. Impatient, I wait, thinking how I should get back to my place. Has he forgotten why he's called me? I don't have time. Lowering his head, Gerry looks to the front of the room, at my mother's coffin.

"Mommy looks so pretty, doesn't she?"

"She does." My mother's appearance has taken on a peculiar importance at the wake. "She's as beautiful as ever." "Your mother was so lovely, Carole. You have your father's dark Irish coloring, but your facial structure, the almond shape of your eyes, reminds me of Betty." "It looks just like Betty." Well, I would hope I would look like my mother. She *is* my mother. I steal a quick look at my mother and notice the set of crystal rosary beads wrapped around her fingers.

"Mom looks like she's sleeping. Is she really dead?" Gerry asks me with disbelief in his voice.

"Yeah, you know that."

"Who will take care of me?"

"Mrs. Meade." The talky housekeeper my father hired when my mom first got sick. Gerry curls up his lips, a sneer of dislike.

"Mrs. Meade throws salt over her shoulder. And she always says Joey is the apple of her eye, not me."

"Not me, either."

"You're thirteen. You're too old," Gerry says with a snicker.

"So? I'd still like to be the apple of someone's eye." I wonder why Mrs. Meade chose Joey, dark like me, and not blue-eyed, blonde Gerry. Mrs. Meade is a little crazy. My father told us that she has had a hard life. He wouldn't say more, but there is something about her thin, purple lips and black eyes that gives me the creeps.

"Well, I'll take care of you," I say.

"You're not a mother. You're a sister." Gerry smiles, smirks a little, and his eyes crinkle, his small shoulders relax. For the moment, he is happy that he has caught me, his big sister, in an error. His shoelace is untied, so I bend over to tie it.

"I can tie my own shoes."

"Ger, you're the apple of my eye," I say, relieved he has stopped crying.

While Gerry is tugging at his laces, I glance to the front of the room where Michael, my oldest brother, is squinting in my direction. Looking seems to pain him. He pushes his thick, bushy eyebrows together and moves his head slightly toward the coffin, glaring at me. I hand Gerry another Kleenex and walk off, telling him to get back in line, stand over by Danny.

Michael mutters at me, looking down at his special orthotic shoes for boys with flat feet. As if the shoes had a stickiness to them, Michael, unlike me, has been glued to his assigned spot.

"Dad said you're supposed to stand here next to me, so what do you think you're doing? You've been gone for ten minutes."

"Dad told me to . . ."

"He told you to stand here."

"Joey's kicking a chair, and Gerry's crying."

"You can't even respect our mother." Michael was always my mother's favorite. "Do you know how much she weighed when she died?" he asks me in an accusing tone as if I had been hiding pork chops from her. I can't remember the last time I saw my mother eat, the last time she ate supper with my father. "She weighed eighty pounds," he reports. I shudder. I didn't give her the cancer.

"I didn't even know she had cancer. Daddy only told you because you were the oldest. I kept thinking she'd get better. I kept making those stupid novenas."

"You were too young. I'm fifteen, sixteen next month. Dad said I'm getting my license as soon as I turn sixteen so I can help him with picking up Mrs. Meade." More news. He's always lording those two years over me. There's no way I can catch up, let alone pass him. And now he gets to drive. Danny comes back in line, telling Michael that his friends Jackie and Tommy Hoar, red-headed twins, are in the outside room where the guest book is. Since the Hoars only moved to the corner of our street two years ago, when they were in the eighth grade, I still think of them as the new kids, as if they, known fighters and varsity hockey players, still had to prove something. All I know is that I'm careful around redheads. They are, by my count, Michael's only two friends, unless you count Joe Marchese. Suddenly I like the attention of the mourners, this actressy feeling.

The two rooms are getting crowded. Businessmen, comfortable in their suits, hold their felt hats in their hands as they file by, gripping my father's hand and taking up more space than the parents of my classmates, who look out of place in their Sunday-funeral best. My father gives up making introductions to us because the line stretches outside the entry door. Mr. Sampson whispers to my father that this number of people might affect the air-conditioning. His face is so smooth, so round, like a pale moon.

There is no room to move. Michael's bulk is on my right, and Danny, who only comes up to my chin, is on my left. I can't sneak away now, but the crowd is so much better than the room's earlier emptiness. The lady with the rosary and the frown is lost in the well-dressed throngs. People have been coming in no order, but now it seems as if there is a plan: businessmen friends of my father's and their beauty-parlored wives, neighbors, classmates—the boys wearing clip-on ties, the girls in full skirts, circle pins, and shoes with tiny heels—the occasional parents of classmates, and now a gaggle of my mother's relatives up from Connecticut.

My grandmother, also Elizabeth McCue, stands an inch shorter than my father, who squeaks out at six feet. At sixty-eight, she has a neck so large she can't fit a piece of jewelry around it, and rolls of flesh soften her strong jaw. Gram's dark eyes are piercing, penetrating. In my grandmother's parlor where we gathered three or four times a year on Sunday afternoons, she amazed me with her magical gift for playing the piano by ear, dropping cigarette ashes on the yellowed keys. If my father had a glass of whiskey in his hand, he sang right along with her husky, tobacco-coated voice. My father's mother, Agnes Rohan O'Malley, wore white starched aprons, made apple pies, and always had unopened packages of vanilla-filled wafers in her pantry, but my mother's mother didn't care whether we ever ate.

My favorite cousin, Pat, is with my McCue aunts and uncles. Her mother, my aunt Grace, who is divorced, married a sailor during the war, and Pat has always lived with my grandmother. When I was eight, I asked my mother where my aunt Grace's husband was and why my cousin Pat didn't live with her mother, but she would never answer me, not really answer me. "Your grandmother takes care of her," was not really an answer. "That's enough, Carole." I knew a warning when I heard one. Pat is so pretty and has perfect skin and wavy hair, never tortured by the indignity of home permanents or pimples, like the one budding on my left cheek right now. I reach up and caress it, as if I could brush it away.

My grandmother bear-hugs my father, and his shoulders start jumping up and down, all a-quiver. Out of the corner of my eye, I check to see if Pat is watching them. She isn't. She's coming toward me.

"I'm so sorry, Carole, about Betty. Nana's been sitting in a rocking chair, just rocking and staring, ever since your father called." Pat calls my mother Betty, and our grandmother Nana, but we call her Gram, which I like better. When I was eight and Pat was ten, we used to pretend we were sisters. Pat runs her warm brown eyes, a shade lighter than mine, over my clothes.

"I like your blouse. With our dark coloring, we look good as gypsies." Gypsies? Do I look like a gypsy in this peasant blouse? My mother wouldn't want me to look like a gypsy at her wake and funeral—I'm pretty sure of that. Wrong, wrong, wrong—everything just feels so wrong. Right now, I wish more than anything that Pat weren't here to see us, my father sobbing and me in my "gypsy" blouse.

"My mother's coming in the car with Ruth and Bill. They should be here soon," Pat says, scanning the crowd in the entryway. Over the heads of the mourners, I spot my aunt Ruth, my mother's sister, with her navy eyes and mounds of white hair, holding the arm of her Protestant husband, Bill Wiley. Like my aunt Grace, Ruth, too, married outside the faith. My mother's family is Catholic, but not the way my father's is. Pat nudges me, saying with a touch of excitement in her voice, "Oh, there's my mother," and with smiling eyes she leaves me. Pat's mother is still alive anyway. That's something, I think, and a hard loneliness hits me. I bite down on my lower lip as if I could gnaw away at the loneliness and be safe again. Watching Pat and my aunt Grace, I feel the emptiness of wanting my mother. Maybe I'm just mean, but I'm being pricked with pins of jealousy.

There is a parting of the crowd, a shushing sound from the clucking women my father has started calling the professional wake goers, as Father Power, pastor of Our Lady of Hope Church, barrels into the crowded room. Short and squat, Father Power carries his Saint Joseph missal and his black rosary beads in his pudgy, immaculate fingers. Nodding knowingly to the left and the right to his parishioners, he seems to be keeping score, taking note, giving some vague clerical credit for attendance. When he reaches Joey, I hold my breath, afraid the pastor might lecture him, but Father Power just shakes our hands, listing our names, our report card names, Joseph, Gerald, Daniel, Carole, Michael, as he stares into our eyes, passing along the line until he reaches my father. Only then does the pastor stop and speak up. "Cleon." My father hates his real name, Cleon, an Irish name he gave up after the war, preferring to go by Joe, his middle name, or C. Joseph.

"Cleon, we cannot understand God's mysterious ways." Father Power bends to kneel on the burgundy velvet stand in front of the coffin and the crowd, now hushed, follows his lead. Michael's knee holds the hem of my skirt down, as Father Power drones on through two decades of Hail Marys, announcing the sorrowful mysteries in his chill-wind voice. His round, smooth face reminds me of a drawing of the Cheshire cat in *Alice in Wonderland*.

The background stillness in the room is getting to me. I nudge Michael with my elbow for him to move his knee. He grumbles "What?" as if it's my fault that he is on my skirt. In a minute, Gerry and Joey have stopped saying the rosary and are shoving each other. Leaning across Danny, I tell them to stop. "Father Power's here!" I say. Gerry opens his mouth in mock alarm, puts his hands together in prayer, moves his lips, and bows his head as if overcome by the Spirit of the Holy Ghost. He does make me smile, but he's such a faker.

Father Power stops, gazes at my mother in silence, shakes his balloon-head, heaves himself up, and comes over to the line of us again. This time with his missal under his arm he clasps my wet hands in his; his beady black eyes peer into mine, and I think how tonight, Father, I don't want your prayers, your useless prayers. Prayers don't work for me.

When he turns away, moving over toward the "professionals," my father leans over, whispering to Michael, Danny, and me that it's an honor to have the pastor here. Father Power doesn't come to just any wake, he says. I can't tell if my father's trying to be funny.

"Dad, I don't want the honor," I say, licking my lips. He arches his eyebrows and winces as Michael and Danny wait for him to respond. At last my dad chuckles and manages to say, "Respect, Carole, show a little respect."

When my classmates, all the eighth graders at Our Lady of Hope with six days left until our grammar school graduation, arrive, it is hard for me. I was hoping they wouldn't all know about my mother, but of course they do. My two best friends, Dianne Thinel and Anne Sullivan, are giving me the scoop on Monday's eighth-grade trip to Look Park—who flirted, who got in trouble. When Dianne lowers her voice to report how Sister Agnes Edward yelled at Francis Harrington for ducking Fern English in the deep end of the pool, I suddenly start crying, sobbing, and then gasping for breath. Suddenly I am outside of my body, blinded with my tears and lost in blackness, when I feel my aunt Madeline's dry hand on my elbow.

"Carole, come with me to the ladies' room," she orders and steers me away from my mother's coffin down a flight of stairs to the ladies' room. At the vanity, the two women dabbing on lipstick stop their chatter, snap their handbags shut, and hurry out. Although I have no idea who these middle-aged women are, their grim retreat confirms my suspicion that no one can bear being with a motherless girl in tears.

"You're going to have to pull yourself together," my aunt says, sitting me down on a velvet stool. Barely able to hear her over the noise of my wailing, I rest my head on my arms, unable to move. "It's what your mother would expect of you." My aunt's words nail the half-orphan stigma, packaging it in primary colors. How can I pull myself together? I wonder. How do I do that? My behavior, my emotional storm, has disappointed her; I have let her down. "Now, now," she soothes. A whiff of Jean Naté, my mother's perfume, escapes from her delicate wrists.

After a few minutes, even though my mother's scent is in the air, my body stops its thrashing. I have no more energy left for tears and I am still, shaken but still. I lift my head but am not ready to open my eyes. Inhaling, Aunt Madeline puts her hands on my shoulders and turns me around to look at her.

"You need to be brave for your brothers and father, Carole. You need to be strong for them, especially now. They're counting on you." Flattening a tissue, she hands it to me, and I wipe my eyes. I study the gaudy mirror with the splashes of black and gold lines spread over it, finally taking in my reflection, my red swollen eyes and my purplish shiny nose. The small room with its fake gold and phony glamour is closing in on me, trapping me. Peeking at the mirror, I wonder if I look brave. What does brave look like? Does brave have brown eyes, straight brunette hair, and a pug nose? Or does brave have curly hair and flawless skin? So maybe I'm half brave.

My aunt draws a compact from her purse and powders my nose and around my eyes. I don't wear makeup because I don't want to look cheap, but the powder does make my nose look less like a headlight.

On the way back upstairs I study how my aunt's high heels sink into the carpet threads and decide I will never again give in to crying. The Sullivan twins, Monica and Veronica, are waiting for me back at the receiving line, and I note that all of the four Sullivans in my class have come to my mother's wake. My entire eighth-grade class is here at Sampson's; the girls came first, then the boys, all shaking hands and whispering. And I bet they're all going to Friendly's later for sundaes.

4. Chocolate Cake

AFTER THE WAKE, my aunts and uncles, friends, and neighbors all crowd into our kitchen. The whiskey bottles are lined up on the counter, their caps swimming in little puddles of spill. I have tasted whiskey before, but I don't like the taste, and the smell alone can make me gag. My aunts are putting food on the table when Mrs. Metzger comes over from next door, carrying a chocolate cake with chocolate frosting. Mrs. Metzger would never buy a mix. If I stand in our driveway, I can smell her baking, how the butter and sugar fall over one another. Except for her tomato soup cake, which she makes at Christmas, my mother always uses the red and yellow Betty Crocker cake mixes advertised on television. I think Betty Crocker is smarter, but I am watching Mrs. Metzger cut the cake and put the pieces on a plate. Michael, who has been standing by himself in a corner, and Danny whose dessert antennae are just like mine, get the first pieces. Since the pieces are pretty much all the same size, I take just any one, using my hand as a plate.

"Carole, Joey is getting chocolate all over him. Find Mrs. Meade. He needs to get to bed. Gerry, too." My father points to Joey kneeling on a chair at the table. Chocolate is smushed all over his face so I reach for one of the paper napkins and hand it to him.

"You heard Dad. He wants you to get to bed," I say, hinting if it were up to me I'd let him stay up until midnight. Joey turns and sees my father talking to my uncles. "Gerry's going to bed, too." No scenes, just go. Joey assesses, negotiates.

"I'll go if I can have another piece of cake." I nod, relieved, knowing that

Mrs. Metzger's cake has handed me a cheap, painless peace. Mrs. Meade, who thinks she's a guest tonight, shows up with Gerry with her arm around his shoulder. He bolts out from her grasp and runs over to the table.

"How come no one told me we had cake? There's not even a whole piece left." He scoops up the crumbs, inhaling them. With us kids, sugar is a god.

"The little ones went to bed like angels tonight, Carole, the poor things," Mrs. Meade reports to me in her whiny voice. I wish she'd shut up. Mrs. Meade usually goes home at six o'clock when my father gets home from work, but tonight my mother's wake throws everything off. Although she's smeared lipstick on, her lips still have a purple shine. She's wearing a dress I've never seen before. "The house was so empty with all of you over at Sampson's, Stevie and Bobby just wandered around. They looked like lost little boys. Tommy went to bed without a peep. No mother, oh, my," she says, wiping tears from her eyes. I don't think she has a right to cry. Tommy's only two, still in diapers. I was eleven when Tommy was born. I think I wanted the new baby to be another boy so I'd still get to be the only girl, although I won't admit it to anyone. A boy or a girl doesn't make much difference; babies are work.

The kitchen is empty—one glass with watered-down whiskey next to the Seagram's bottle. I put the whiskey bottle up on the top shelf with the others and my father's glass in the dishwasher. My three aunts, Mad, Stella, and Lee, have cleaned the kitchen with Mad and Stella doing most of the work and Lee, who maybe dries a glass, doing all the talking. Madeline would never leave the whiskey bottle on the counter. I open the refrigerator and see the shelves stacked with all the leftovers in their plastic containers. I wish I had another piece of Mrs. Metzger's chocolate cake.

I've been to funerals before. I got to wear my first pair of nylons when my grandfather died. Maybe I was too young—ten, halfway through fifth grade—but I begged my mother, who couldn't stand it anymore and said yes. Not a happy yes, though, more like a yes and now leave me alone and take your baby brother (then Bobby) for a walk. I would have walked the baby for an hour for those nylons.

We won't be going to school until after the funeral. It feels funny on a Wednesday morning to be home when everyone else is in school. It's the second day of my mother's wake and although it's early June, it's 90 degrees outside. The sun is beating down like a mid-August day. I am putting away the cereal boxes when my father walks into the kitchen. His nose and cheeks are shiny and have that right-after-shaving glow. I can smell the piney scent of the Fitch dandruff remover shampoo my father uses. Up until about a year ago, he always wore his hair parted down the middle, the exact same haircut he'd had since high school. After we all teased him about his haircut being so old-fashioned, he came home one Saturday from Art, the barber, with a crew cut, the same crew cut my brothers all had. I remember him standing in the doorway, patting his hair and telling us, "If I'm going to grow old, I'm going to grow old gracefully."

He opens the refrigerator and pulls out the gallon of milk, checking to see how much is left.

"Out of respect for your mother, I don't want you kids running around outside today," he announces in a low tone, the milk still in his hand. The only sound in the house is the hum of the refrigerator as my father closes the door. Michael and I are the only ones in the kitchen. Michael rubs his eyebrows with the back of his arm.

"The little kids went outside right after breakfast. I thought it was all right," I explain defensively.

"Listen to them, Carole. That Joey's running around like a madman," Michael reports smugly. "Why, you can hear him yelling from in here." In a triumphant gesture he pushes aside the curtain on the back door. Hunching my shoulders, I shrink into myself. I wish that I had jailed my younger brothers in the house and shown the proper respect for my mother. But I had just about shoved them out the door. "You two are the oldest. I want you to get them back in here, Carole. For one day, they can stay inside. Michael, come with me. I'm going to pick up Mrs. Meade now. I want you to drive, get a little practice in." My father tosses over the car keys, but Michael doesn't get his hand up in time, and the keys fall to the linoleum. He kicks them over to the doorsill and stoops to pick them up.

"I made a bad toss," my father says, giving Michael an excuse as always. My father and I both know I would have caught the keys. As Michael and my father get into the station wagon, Gerry runs over and grabs my father's arm, begging to go along. My father points in the direction of the back porch. Gerry sticks his lower lip out and turns toward me. I motion him in.

"Why won't Dad take me in the car? Just because Michael is driving," he says, smacking his hand on the table. His blue eyes look around, take in the empty kitchen. "Why isn't Joey in? And Stevie? And Bobby? And Tommy? Why am I the only one here?" Gerry asks. "I'm going back out." He makes a move for the door, but I get there first.

"No, Dad wants us all to stay in today. I'm going down the street and getting everyone back in the house right now. Want to help?" My father has only given the order that we stay in the house. Other than that, he has said nothing about my mother's death to me. Maybe I made a mistake letting the kids out to play. I don't know what I should be doing.

"No, I'm not helping you." He picks up a baseball glove lying on the porch and begins punching his fist into the mounded leather, making a thwacking sound.

"Gerry, come on, help me round them up. Why do I have to do everything?" Gerry's fingers stretch the lace knot on the pocket of the glove.

"You're special." His sarcasm drips down to the linoleum floor.

"Yeah, I'm special, all right. Be special with me." I wheedle helplessly.

"You think I'd fall for that? Besides, Dad asked you, not me. Do we have to stay in tomorrow, too, the day of the funeral?" As I make a move for the door, Gerry scoots in front of me back outside. I catch him by the collar and lead him back into the house. A few minutes later, I'm running by the Ruscios' house up toward the empty lot where my brothers are playing their endless war games. I begin screaming their names, Joey, Stevie, Bobby, Tommy, yelling at them to get back into the house in a voice so loud, so filled with venom, that they stop to stare at me, fear darting in and out of their eyes. "Dad says we need to stay in the house today," I command. On our way back home, with my brothers bunched up and marching in front of me, I feel embarrassed by my shouting when Mrs. Metzger, a bag of trash in her hand, nods to me from her driveway. All we need is a flag flapping for our angry parade. But I've heard you yell even worse, Mrs. Metzger, I think.

Pushing the damp hair from my forehead, I turn to look up and see Gerry staring out from the upstairs window. I wave to him and I see him smile. Then he draws the curtains together and disappears. I wish I could still see him because, although it's only been two days since my mother died, I worry when any of my brothers goes off alone. Her death makes privacy seem dangerous.

5. Perfect Skin

EVEN BEFORE BREAKFAST, it's hot out. The outside door is open, but no air is coming in. The house this morning is quiet, except for Tommy, the baby, sitting in his wooden high chair, slapping it with his toast. Tommy has torn up his toast, smearing the grape jelly all over the high chair tray. Now he leans over in his chair and points to the toast scattered on the floor. I grab a dishrag from the sink, spin around, and see my father glancing at Tommy. My father likes to play a game with the baby where he picks him up, rubs his nose against his baby cheek, and asks Tommy who's his favorite. My brothers and I stand there hoping he will point at one of us, but Tommy always picks my father. There is no game playing today. Tommy reaches his chubby little hands, covered with soggy crumbs, to my father, calling "Da, da," with a small smile, but my father just walks over to the kitchen door on his way to pick up Mrs. Meade. He turns to look again at Tommy and tells me that I'll need to help find summer clothes for my brothers.

"Mrs. Meade still has the baby in his winter pajamas. I'll talk to her about finding the boys' summer things," my father says.

"I think I know what closet they're in," I say, babbling like June Cleaver in her shirtwaist dress. I would rather spend the afternoon crawling around dusty closet floors than let my dad suspect the hurricane impact that my mother's death has had on running our shaky household.

"Well, show her this afternoon, then," he says, opening the screen door. Tommy is wearing baby-cute pajamas with footed feet and blue and yellow cowboys bucking on horses. He waves bye-bye to my father's back, gazing at the open door, but lunges as soon as he sees the facecloth in my hand. I do a wrestler's headlock hold on him as he jerks away from me, run the facecloth across his apple cheeks, and scrape most of the crumbs off his hands. When I unbuckle the high chair's belt from his round tummy, I dab at the bread crumbs on his lower lip. Free at last, he leaps into my arms, and the snaps on his cowboy pajama top pull loose. I touch his cheek, set him on the floor, and watch him toddle off toward the back room. Throwing the facecloth on the kitchen counter, I am hit with the injustice of Tommy's velvet baby skin and wishing I weren't too old for a pair of cowboy pajamas. There is something sad about being a teenager, watching grown-ups go gaga over babies—the perfect skin.

The funeral Mass is set for ten o'clock, and we have to be back at Sampson's by nine. I am hurrying everyone into the car, in charge of what my father calls gathering the troops. Michael grumbles and tells me Gerry is inside watching television. I hear an accusation in his voice, as if I have somehow allowed this behavior. Danny is in the bathroom in front of the medicine chest mirror wetting his hair, stamping the curl out. If he brushes it one way and then the other, the curls come out, but he has already hogged the bathroom for half an hour this morning just so his hair would look good. It's so annoying for me with my stick-straight hair to listen to his anti-curl strategies. I knock on the bathroom door and tell him to forget the curls, hurry up and get in the car. I am trying to shield my father from our rushing, bickering, rounding up and ask Mrs. Meade to help me. Finally, we are all in the car. My father comes down the back steps and looks across the street. I turn to check if one of my brothers is still in the driveway and wonder what my father sees. When my father gets into the car, he usually turns to the back seat and asks the little kids if everyone is ready, as if driving to eight o'clock Sunday Mass were some kind of adventure, but he says nothing today. His eyes take in my brothers, one by one, all dressed up with their clip-on bow ties. Michael and I as the two oldest are sitting in the front seat. The radio is turned to one of my dad's stations, an Elvis-free station, but he flips it off. "We don't play the car radio driving to your mother's funeral," my father says with his fingers lingering on the radio knob. Michael frowns, a line forming over his right eyebrow, and gives me a sharp elbow in the ribs. Pushing his arm away, I glare back at him. Does he think I'm about to break the silence by belting out the lyrics to Bobby Darin's hit, "Splish Splash," a song even my dad likes?

"Dad, Joey's punching me in the arm," Gerry cries.

"Yeah, well, you're sitting on my pants," Joey says.

"You could have asked me to move over. Where am I supposed to move? There's no room," Gerry says between sniffles. The sniffles sound a little stagey to me. I turn around, tell them both to stop it. Gerry sticks his tongue out at me and Joey raises his fist. I can feel my father sitting next to me, smell his shaving cream, see the tiny dark hairs on the bridge of his nose. He grips the steering wheel tightly and looks in the car mirror. When he stops for a red light at the corner of Armory and Liberty Streets, he turns around, puts his right arm over the back of the front seat, and says, "Enough out of you, boys." Good, I'm not included. We drive by the bakery, the stone library, the A&P, the Liberty Bar, and Mastroianni's gas station. Back in seventh grade, I had a crush on Jackie Mastroianni. I am looking out my father's window. I don't want to look out Michael's window, the side of the street Sampson's is on. I know where we're going, to the funeral home, to my mother's funeral, to church, to Saint Michael's Cemetery, but I don't have to think about all that. I'd rather think about Jackie Mastroianni in his white shirt with the rolled-up collar.

My father signals a turn, and we pull into the parking lot of the T. P. Sampson Funeral Parlor. T. P. for Thomas Patrick, I bet Danny the first night of the wake. Michael harumphed at us as if he had been to funeral parlor behavior school. My father switches the engine off and turns to the back seat. "This is when we say goodbye to your mother. A lot of people will be at the church and cemetery today watching the O'Malleys. No kicking, no punching, no fighting. Do you hear me?" my father says in a mild voice, the smell of mouthwash on his breath. I keep my eyes glued to the white station dial on the car radio.

"Joey always starts it," Gerry says.

"You heard me, Joey?" my father says and pats his hand up and down on the back of the seat.

"I heard you," Joey says, his voice low.

"Look, I left Stevie, Bobby, and Tommy home with Mrs. Meade. They're too young for a funeral, but I expect you to know how to act." His eyes, the left one with its odd droop of the lid, sweep over Danny, Gerry, and Joey.

"I know how to behave, Dad. You don't have to worry about me," Danny announces, bending forward to stroke his hair in the car mirror.

"Dan the Man," my father says with a shake of his hand. Danny thinks he's cooler than I am—not just me, though, everyone. Gerry opens the back door, waits until he sees my father walking away, and slams the door before Joey can get out. I hold still for a second waiting to see if Joey's fingers were caught in the door. No crying, good. Joey may be a hitter and a fighter, but Gerry likes the sneak attack. We troop out of the car and file behind my father across the parking lot. Staring overhead at the green awning, I walk up the steps for my mom's goodbye, and I mumble a thank you when I pass in front of the sandy-haired attendant holding the door for all of us. I'm the last one in, not like me at all. I like to be the first to show up my brothers. But I'm just feeling so down and lonely.

The funeral home is hushed. The dark-suited pallbearers are standing in a group over by the side of the coffin. Congressman Eddie Boland, a bachelor and my father's boyhood friend from Mooreland Street, leaves the other men and comes over to us to pump our hands up and down. He wears thick glasses and has slicked-back black hair. He flings an arm around Michael's shoulders; his other arm he drapes over Danny's shoulder. He motions with his head for me to come closer.

"I loved your mother, you know, but she wouldn't have me. She picked your old man," he says and nods toward my father, who is kneeling at the coffin. I wonder if he's lying. Eddie Boland has told me that he's waiting for me to grow up and marry him, so I know he kids a lot. Jerry Lee Lewis married his thirteen-year-old cousin, but thirteen-year-olds in Springfield, Massachusetts, don't get married. Still, I feel a warm flush every time he says it.

"If you kids ever need my help, don't hesitate to call me. I love your father like a brother. I have seen many marriages, but your father and mother had something special going. And all you great kids." His words drop off, and he gazes at my father, who is rubbing his hands together. The congressman walks over to my father, and they hug each other. Then Eddie scans me and my brothers with his quick black eyes and turns my father away from us, guiding him over to the pallbearers. I recognize the men, these friends of my fathers, men he has chosen to carry my mother's coffin. Matty Ryan, the newly elected district attorney, who grew up on Parkside Street, is Stevie's godfather. Judge Keyes, Eddie's best friend, sits on the bench of Superior Court. Mr. Metzger, our next-door neighbor, is the election commissioner, but has not been able to come into Sampson's without crying; he runs in crying, leaves, and comes back, only to cry all over again. Bill Raleigh, our carpet man, said that he and my uncle Bill were the only pallbearers without an official government title attached to their names.

I'm embarrassed and ashamed for Mr. Metzger because of all his crying and running. I hate crying. When I lay in bed last night, right before I fell asleep, I decided not to think about my mother and that she is dead. I don't know anyone whose mother is dead, just us. Her death makes me different, makes us different, which I hate, even more than crying. I'll pretend she is only away, and I won't let myself think about her. I can do it. I don't even need to pray about it. At the wake when Di mentioned Fern English getting ducked in the pool, I had an out-and-out crying fit. It seems funny now because Fern English is fourteen, she was held back in first grade, wears thick glasses, and doesn't remind me of my mother at all.

Mr. Sampson crosses his hands in front of his chest and walks to the front of the room. He whispers in my father's ear, and my dad nods his head in agreement. Then my father bends his fingers at my aunt Madeline in a signal. On cue, like politicians in a parade, my aunts and uncles march two by two to the front of the room and stand in front of the coffin. One after another, each makes the sign of the cross and walks out, giving a slight shake of the head. The circle of pallbearers lower their voices, and Eddie Boland places his hand on my father's shoulder and leads them outside. Except for the motor of the air conditioner, everything is quiet; now, other than the funeral parlor attendants, we're all alone in the chilled room with my mother in the coffin. In the low-lit receiving room it could be night, but I know it's not yet ten a.m. A few red petals from the giant rose heart my father sent have fallen to the carpet. I study the gold letters spelling out the word "wife" on the white shiny ribbon. In the coffin next to my mother's left elbow—Mr. Sampson must have put it there this morning—is the smaller, pink rose heart with gold letters spelling "mother" in the same fancy Palmer script. These flowers, the two hearts, make me feel that my father has done the right thing. He always used Cerago's, the florist, when he sent my mother flowers after a horse at Narragansett came in. Joey sits down on one of the maroon velvet chairs reserved for family and priests and begins swinging his legs back and forth. Mr. Sampson strides over to the coffin, motions to one of his workers, and announces, "It is time for you to say goodbye. The procession is forming outside."

My father beckons us all to the coffin. "I want you all to say a quick prayer and kiss your mother goodbye." Michael goes first. I'm next. Since I don't have a prayer and I don't know of any saint who is a patron saint of dead mothers, I'll just stare at the silver crucifix dangling from the rosary beads. I picture my mother's jar of Pacquin's hand cream in the medicine chest, her red Maybelline eyebrow pencil, and remember how in the late afternoons when I was little I would watch her as she darkened her eyebrows and studied her face in the mirror. I would beg her to let me use the pencil, and I remember her telling me how I was blessed with my dad's black eyebrows. But I want your eyebrows, not Dad's, I want to scream. Kneeling now, I make the sign of the cross, just like Michael did. My tears, dreaded signs of weakness, sneak up on me as I realize this is the last time I will ever see my mom's hands, with her long slim fingers and her perfect half-moon fingernails. Suddenly my body is lurching with sobs, and I drop my head to the kneeler. When I shut my eyes, I see my mom flicking her eyebrow pencil, her honey-colored strokes. Please, let me stop, I beg, and run the back of my wrist across my face. A wad of Kleenex appears on the arm rest, and there is the slight pressure of a hand on my shoulder. Sobbing, sobbing—will I ever stop?—I bend in to kiss my mother, and leap back when I feel the cold skin of her cheek. The unexpected cold hardness terrifies me, and as I jump up, I step backward into a stand of flowers. Next, my father holds Joey up so he can reach over and kiss my mother. Unseen, I reach my hand behind me and, like a grave robber, twist off a bunch of flower petals and slip them into my skirt pocket. When my dad puts Joey back down, Joey comes over to me and holds my hand. And, at last, my father is on the kneeler, praying, sobbing, with his face in his hands. Watching my dad falling apart makes me squirm because it seems that now, with him such a red-faced crybaby wreck, there is no one to take care of me. Although I look away at the wide arch in the entryway, as if I am measuring the angle of its curve, the ragged sounds of my dad's crying make me feel as if I am disappearing, and I feel so, so helpless. Do I need to take care of *him too*? I can't lean on him, the way he is now. For me to be the "strong Carole" my aunt has asked me to be, I will imagine my mother on a cushioned chaise lounge in a backyard part of heaven that is saved for me and my family, where she is drinking a Manhattan and smoking a filter-tipped cigarette. No kids' fighting in heaven. No crying in heaven. No yelling in heaven. No Cheerios, no Franco-American spaghetti. I don't really see how my brothers and I have a prayer of getting in. Interrupting my fantasy, my father taps me on the arm and asks me to take Joey downstairs to the bathroom.

"He's big enough to go by himself, isn't he?" I ask with a whine.

My father looks at me and sighs. "All right, I'll take him myself," he says, his shoulders sagging with the effort.

"I'll take him down," I say and grab Joey, twisting his hand.

"Let go, will you? Leave me alone." Joey yanks his hand away and runs ahead of me. Some help I am, I think. I've let my dad down and tried to hurt Joey.

There is a wide steel door at the end of the hall. If Danny were here, we might open it and see where the corpses are kept. I'd like to explore, open that door. Someone in there fixed my mom's hair because it has the same crimpy waves on the sides as it does when she comes home from Paula's beauty salon. Now I know why my dad was taking the Christmas pictures of my mother from the living room, so the hairdresser for corpses could copy, get the part right. I'm glad Mr. Sampson is outside because I don't think he's seen a lot of running and jumping on the stairs at his funeral home. Funny, how it's called a home. I wonder if people live here, sleeping at night with dead bodies in the front rooms. I shiver waiting outside the door for Joey, who is taking much too long. There is the sound of water running. I hope he's not getting all wet, backing up the sink. Just as I'm about to knock, Joey walks out and wipes his wet hands on my skirt. "No towels," he says and zips in front of me. I smoosh the beads of water into my black skirt and feel a resentment boring its way into me like a blood-sucking tick on a dog's neck.

When I come back up the stairs, I slow down as soon as I see Mr. Sampson standing by the door, with his arms folded mid-chest covering his dolphin-shaped stomach. His pale, sandy hair is coated with hair creme, making it darker and holding the thin strands in perfect place. There is no expression on his bland face. I have been watching him off and on for three days and haven't yet seen him smile. I haven't even seen his teeth. He looks as if he disapproves of us, as if he's waiting for us to remove ourselves from the Sampson's Family Chapels so that a staid propriety may return. When I glance over, I see my father still on the kneeler, dabbing at his eyes with a white handkerchief. Come on, Dad, get up. Mr. Sampson floats across the room and places his big, white paw-hand on my father's shoulder, and I hold my breath watching for my father to get up. At last he puts his palms down on the kneeler and pushes himself up. Then, as if an angel of lightness is whispering in his ear, he faces us, smiles, and says with an old, familiar energy, "Let's get this show on the road." He does everything but clap his hands together.

6. Anne of Green Gables

THERE IS TALK about who gets to ride in which limousine once we're out on the sidewalk. Joey and Gerry, in a protest instigated by Gerry, are refusing to ride in the smaller limousine with Aunt Madeline and Uncle Bill. Michael, Danny, and I, the big kids, know that we will get to ride in the first limousine, right behind the funeral car. For a minute I am afraid my father might ask me to ride with the little kids, but I calm myself, knowing my aunts and uncles are there to take care of them. Well, Gerry crabs his way into our limousine. So that means Joey has to come with us too. There is plenty of room, not like our station wagon, but Gerry and Joey are playing with the buttons on the side of the door as if they were riding a spaceship. When Gerry yells, "Take off!" my father looks at him. The chauffeur has a black uniform hat on and drives so slowly I can read on the poster in the window of Liberty Bakery that a Boston cream pie costs forty-nine cents. I do wish my classmates could see me riding like a bride-to-be in the limousine. My father straightens his tie and reaches over for Gerry's arm.

"That's enough, Gerry. I don't want you playing with the buttons," Dad whispers. I jump in and tell Gerry that he better start acting like one of the big kids if he wants to ride with us. He makes a face at me and looks out the window at Bottle Park on Carew Street with the old men smoking cigarettes and sitting in the shade. He sneaks his finger back on the button when my father isn't looking.

The hearse leads the funeral procession. My mother's golden bronze coffin is covered over and surrounded with flowers from the funeral home. The hearse drives right through red lights, and the parade of cars follows. For as far as I can see behind us, there is a string of cars with Sampson's funeral flags perched on the drivers' fenders. Although it is still mid-morning, the cars all have their headlights on. Bill Kelly, the Armory Street policeman, waves the hearse on and holds the traffic up for us. In front of Our Lady of Hope Church, my class is marching up the steps, two by two, boys first, girls next, behind Sister Agnes Edward. The driver pushes a button and the window separating the front and back seats glides down with a smooth, easy sound. The driver keeps his head forward and says, "Mr. O'Malley, you and the children will be the last ones in. You'll go to the front of the church where an usher will show you to your seats. Then the pallbearers carry the casket in. No one can see in through these special windows." My father nods as if he knew exactly what was going on all along. I'm just glad someone knows what to do, because I have no idea what will happen at the cemetery. Danny lowers the window to wave to Brian Long, one of the boys in his class, until Sister Maurice Joseph steps next to Brian and cuffs his ear. "What are you doing, Danny? You fool," Michael barks, leaning forward and putting his hand on the window. Then he smirks, slinking his eyes over to my father for a sign of approval. My father stares out the window, his eyes on the group of pallbearers standing on the sidewalk, where Mr. Sampson is passing out gloves to them. Then Mr. Sampson points in the direction of the hearse and signals with a lift of his chin at the church steps. The grim-faced pallbearers slip their gloves on and gaze at the limousine.

The sidewalk outside of Our Lady of Hope is just about empty. A few stragglers hurry in, using the side doors. The driver opens the limousine door. We march up the wide stairs in a parade to the front of the church. I keep my eyes fixed on the gold crucifix hanging over the altar but catch Gerry out of the corner of my eye waving to a row of fourth-grade boys when his teacher isn't looking. When we reach the front of the church, we genuflect and make the sign of the cross.

"Sit between the little kids, Carole," my dad whispers. So we file into the first pew, Joey first, me, then Gerry, Danny, and Michael. My father sits in the aisle seat. I'm kneeling, pretending to pay attention to Father Power, who has started the requiem high Mass, the Mass for the Dead, and my palms begin to sweat when John Brody and John Burke, my classmates, enter as the altar boys. It bothers me that they're in such good viewing distance of me and my family.

Our Lady of Hope Church has oak pews and an aisle down the middle. The columns flanking the altar have elaborate carvings. Ionic, Doric, or Corinthian, I wonder, when Gerry nudges me with his elbow.

"Carole, is Mommy in there?" he asks, his eyes darting to the bronze casket, and back to me. My mother's casket is in front of the altar gates, alone in the middle of the aisle. Father Power is throwing holy water on the casket, circling it so he won't miss a spot, the drops forming small circles on the metal.

"Mom's not getting wet, is she?" Gerry asks. Joey leans forward so he can hear Gerry. I shake my head, suspecting Gerry's trying to be funny—he knows my mother's in there—but see what may be alarm in Joey's eyes. Bending down, I say, "The casket keeps her dry," when Michael sticks his turtle head out to frown at us. Danny fiddles with a brass button on his sport coat and straightens his striped tie. Twelve-year-old boys are vainer than their thirteen-year-old sisters—this much I know.

Father Power waddles over to the pulpit, folds his chubby fingers together, and clears his throat. He looks left and right, pleased with the size of the congregation, pleased with his throat clearing. He uses his hands for emphasis, pausing for dramatic effect, making us wait for his words, but when he finishes, I realize that I have sat there the whole time staring at the Greek letters, the Alpha and the Omega on his chasuble, and heard nothing. If Father Power had mentioned my mother by name in his sermon, I know I would have heard it.

My father backs out into the aisle and waits for us to file past him to receive Communion. "Go ahead, Carole," he says in the whisper we use in church. I am the first one to receive Communion. Last one in church, first for Communion. After Communion, I kneel on the foam-padded kneeler and wait for Father Power to finish giving out the hosts. But Communion is taking forever. Father Power keeps lifting his pea-sized eyes to gauge how many communicants are standing in line. Trapped with nothing to do, I put my hands together and fake that I am praying. I'm really giving up on praying because God has decided not to answer my prayers. Or maybe God has. Back in fifth grade, maybe sixth, I read the book *Anne of Green Gables,* the story of an orphan girl, and I secretly thought, wouldn't I make a wonderful orphan? Running through the meadows on Prince Edward Island, making the stern, cold Marilla Cuthbert love me. I cried reading that book, sobbed, had to hide in the backyard from my brothers. Gerry, Danny mocking me, Carole's crying over a book. A book. Now that I'm half an orphan, I wish *Anne of Green Gables* had never been written. The Green Gables Anne was an only child; she didn't have seven brothers. I have secrets now—the Anne of Green Gables orphan wish and my decision to abandon prayer. I may go back to prayer someday, I'm not becoming an atheist or anything. I'm afraid to pray. I'm afraid to think. If my dad were to die, then I'd be an orphan like Anne. I hate the very word "orphan"; it's so frightening.

When the Mass ends, the six pallbearers line up on either side of the casket and begin rolling it to the back of the church. The pallbearer parade sets off a crying signal; from behind me I hear the sounds of sniffling, sobbing women reaching into their bags for tissue. My father and Michael are in front of me, their shoulders shaking, as we walk back out of the church. When I try to breathe, my throat feels swollen, as if there were a fuzzy tennis ball lodged in my throat. Tears cloud my eyes, and then I see Aunt Madeline and remember, Brave for my brothers. Hold them together. But I lose and the tears come anyway.

Saint Michael's Cemetery is halfway across town, closer to Uncle Bill and Aunt Madeline's house. The cemetery is a maze of streets, all named after saints. I know the basic, everyday saints, and pretty much know the names of the twelve apostles—I usually forget Simon—but there are saints' names here I can't even spell. So many miracles.

We are waiting in the limousine; my brothers have pushed, touched, and lifted every button and switch within reach. The car's novelty has worn off, and there are patches of unfamiliar quiet in the limousine. It is almost noon and Gerry says he's getting hungry. The driver, a freckle-faced man with a bulbous, comic-book nose, turns around and offers us all a bag of peppermints.

"I keep a bag of mints in the glove compartment. Just hand me the wrappers when you're done. Mr. Sampson doesn't like food in the limo," he says. My father thanks him and passes the bag over to Gerry.

"One for each of you, and pass the wrappers up front." Danny sucks the peppermint, puts it between his teeth, and says, "Candy is dandy, but liquor is quicker." My father closes his eyes and puts his fingers on his eyebrows. Michael sneers at Danny. Stuffing the candy into his cheek, Danny protests, "Dad, and Uncle Bill, and Mr. Metzger, and even Mom always say it."

"This is not the time!" my father interrupts. Tapping feet. Fidgeting. Pretending. Waiting. I guess the family always goes last on the way in, first on the way out. I collect the wrappers and hand them to the driver when there's a knock on the driver's door.

"It's time," the driver says, stuffing the wrappers into the ash tray.

Another line by age order. We are standing on a bright green, fake grass carpet in front of the deep grave. I can feel the sun blazing down on my shoulders, the sweat dripping under my arms, and I'm glad the blouse is black. Father Power is standing in front of me with piles of freshly dug dirt behind him, its rich smell competing with the delicacy of the funeral home flowers heaped on top of my mother's casket. Father Power opens his black missal and begins reading in Latin. I imagine Danny and me forming a battering ram and knocking Father Power into the open grave. The priest does the holy water thing again, this time into the grave. He reaches down for a shovel and throws a handful of dirt into the grave, my mother's grave. The sun is making me dizzy. I sway slightly as stripes of heat float in front of me, and my father takes me by the elbow. I can't faint. He whispers, *it's almost over,* and in a minute the ceremony ends with Father Power bustling over to shake my father's hand. I step aside, turning, and see a wall of red eyes. The crying. The sobbing. The tears. Uncle Bill props me up in his bear arms and says, "Katsy, Katsy, Katsy." I'm comforted by this old joke of a nickname, and I hide my tears, dropping my head to the shoulder of his navy suit.

More kissing, more hugging, more crying. Then we traipse over the grass, passing the lowered casket with the "wife" and "mother" hearts tossed in a heap into the grave. The guests begin slipping away to the long row of cars and their death-free luckier lives as the ritual winds down slowly, quietly, with fallen chrysanthemum petals lying all over the grass. Soon brown. Soon dead. In the limousine, the driver has left two bags of peppermints on the seat. Opening the window partition, he says, "Go ahead, kids. I'm breaking the rules today. Finish the bags."

After the funeral lunch, my uncle Bill, as always, is the last to leave. He puts his hands on my shoulders, smiles, and says, "Carole, your old man's gonna need your help. Go easy on him."

"I will. I will. I will," I answer, but what does he mean, go easy? Fears, unnamed and shapeless, squirm through me as I cannot guess what he means. Am I supposed to tell my father what to do? Then my uncle drops the joking, pats me on the back, and says, "Kiddo, you're going to be all right." The screen door closes behind him.

All right? I am all right, I think, and scoop up the dregs of potato chips from the bottom of my mom's mixing bowl. Is there anything else that could happen to me? Licking the salt from my fingers, in the middle of a heat wave I'm bone-cold.

7. Graduation Dress

"DAD, I NEED a white dress for graduation." I pick up a milk-soaked Cheerio from the table and flick it toward the sink. My father is sitting at the kitchen table in his robe with white piping, staring at the white refrigerator door, an untouched piece of buttered toast in front of him. I think about just sneaking down to his bedroom and slipping a few bills from his wallet. His wallet is in his pants pocket hanging on the closet door. At least, he's still predictable about the wallet.

"What, Carole?" my father asks, picking up his toast.

"I need to buy a white dress for graduation, Dad. It has to be white. I graduate this Friday. The nuns are making us. Every girl has to wear a white dress." I speed through my list of arguments, afraid to slow down, afraid to let my needing show, afraid he'll fade off to his new faraway world.

"Well, all this seems a little unfair to me," he says, his brown eyes engaging mine.

"Unfair? What's unfair?" He's confusing me.

"That the boys don't get to wear white dresses." He picks up his cup of milky tea and smiles at me. I get his little jibe.

"Yeah, James Harnois is really upset." I intentionally choose a boy bigger than my father, a boy he knows. "Picture him in a white dress," I say, trying to continue the moment, but I have made a mistake. When I was back in seventh grade, Father Miller started a spiritual book group, and James Harnois's mother and my mother were both in it.

"I wish your mother were here to take you shopping," he says. He takes the teabag out of his cup and squeezes it with his fingers so hard the paper breaks. Why does he say things like that? What good does wishing do? Besides, my mother and I fought whenever we went shopping, but I say nothing about our fighting.

"Now you can read your fortune," I point to the floating bits of tea.

"Yeah, I guess I can," he answers with a half-smile. Maybe the tea leaf remark changed his mood a degree. At night now, I feel as if I need to break into a tap dance to jar him back from wherever his sadness for my mother has led him. Tap dancing works in the movies.

"Let me get the money from your wallet," I offer. He waves his hand in the direction of the bedroom, swatting me away as if I were a pesky fly.

"Just take the money," he says, emptying his tea into the sink, pushing the toast down the garbage disposal.

"How much money should I take?" I ask, needing some direction, some spending limit.

"Take whatever you want," he answers, so unlike my mother, who was careful with money. Odd, how different they are, were, I think as I am walking away when I hear the sound of Danny's outfielder's glove hitting the kitchen table, water running in the sink, a glass hitting the counter.

"Dad, how come she gets to take as much money as she wants? Why is she so special? It's just an eighth-grade graduation," Danny argues. "I want some money, too." I swear, my brothers can smell money. Danny has to horn in, always has to get his share and more. I will my father to tell him no, that he can't have any money.

"Go see your sister. She's got my wallet." Danny storms down the hall and sees me with the wallet.

"How much money are you taking?" he asks, flinging arrows of accusation at me. Michael, who has had a whiff of the word "money," appears from the back room, where he has been watching Saturday morning cartoons.

"Does Dad know you're taking money?" Michael demands. Two against one. Carole, the common criminal. I picture my mug shot, my ski jump nose, all my identifying scars. How many times have Michael, Danny, and I, aiding and abetting, lifted change from Dad's pocket?

"I need to buy a graduation dress," I snap back. "Dad told me I could take the money." My hand is sweating, and I can feel the leather of the wallet sticking to my palm.

"You just bought all those clothes at Forbes," Danny says.

"Yeah, from that fashion show you were in." Michael gets just the right note of sarcasm in on the words "fashion show," and he and Danny smirk at each other at this shared joke. Me, their sister, a model in a fashion show.

"Just a jersey and shorts set I didn't even get to wear." I'm defending myself against them when a clear image of my mother in a black square-necked sheath with white trim—for sure the prettiest mother, with her toothpaste smile—at Michael's graduation flashes into my memory. I feel a hole-like thing growing inside me where I have to sink these old thoughts of my mother. Thoughts of how my mother was at Michael's graduation, but she won't be at mine.

"I need a white dress. Sister Agnes Edward said all the girls had to wear white dresses. They did in your class, too, Michael, when you graduated." I want to get the nicest white dress, better than Marilyn Martin, who has nicer clothes than anyone else in the class and naturally wavy hair.

"Leave your sister alone," my father orders my brothers. Michael makes a grunting noise and stomps off, but Danny hangs in. "What makes her so special? Why does she have to get everything? Because she was in a stupid fashion show?" he argues, baiting my father.

"Danny, that's enough." My father can be pushed only so far, and Danny knows it. Sliding out, he throws a final shot: "I need money, too." My father rolls his eyes and hands me some bills.

"I can call your aunt, and maybe she can go with you," he says with a sigh. "Other girls will be shopping with their mothers."

"Dad, I have been clothes shopping by myself since the fifth grade.

I bought my first-day-of-school dress when I was ten. I bought it at Lerner's—it was yellow and black plaid with little clocks all over it."

"I guess you have been on your own for awhile."

"I'll just take a bus downtown." I'm ready to run out the door and down the driveway to Liberty Street before he starts talking about my mother again, before his eyes fill with tears, before I feel like yelling at him. And I can't yell at my father for crying because his wife has died. She was his wife, my mother, which I guess makes a difference. Right now with my father as some romantic hero mourning his lost love, the only way I can be brave is to escape. Maybe, if I stop mentioning my mother, he'll cry less. I'm digging a hole for my sadness with a teaspoon as my tool.

The Wilbraham Road bus drops me off on Main Street right across the street from Steiger's. In an hour and a half, I have combed through the aisles and racks at Steiger's, Lerner's, which I now think is cheap—well, ever since Marilyn Martin told me her mother won't let her shop there— Forbes and Wallace, an eight-story department store, and Peerless, and have seen every white dress in downtown Springfield. At Peerless, my last stop, the saleswomen on the first floor with their black pointed penciled eyebrows and fake white flowers pinned to their dresses make me so jumpy I run up the stairs from floor to floor, not waiting for the elevator. Even on the fourth floor, the teen floor, there is beige carpeting, long three-way mirrors on every wall, and a glass vase of yellow forsythia branches on a table. The saleswoman here is younger, smells a bit like Jean Naté, and has a big, fake magazine smile. When I spot a full-skirted white dress floating on the rack, I lift its price tag, taking in a quick breath, and let it slip back in, hoping the saleswoman isn't spying on me. I have enough money and my father wouldn't care, wouldn't even ask how much I spent, but I knew my mother would care. Then, I see myself in the mirror, see my black gypsy blouse that Mrs. Meade has ironed and its fashion show skirt; here at Peerless I look silly, as though I should have a rose between my teeth. That's what my father said when he first saw my outfit, that all I needed was a rose between my teeth—as if he even knows any gypsies.

I start all over again back at Steiger's. I am holding the bronze entrance door open for the slow-moving, white-haired lady behind me, feeling as if Sister Agnes Edward should be handing me a politeness medal, when

I spot Kathleen Cullinane and Mrs. Cullinane getting off the escalator. They fail to notice me or my door holding as they head toward the middle aisle, each of them carrying bags from Steigers and Forbes, smiling, talking. We almost bump into one another by the lipstick counter, where Mrs. Cullinane is twisting the golden tube of a coral lipstick. I see Kathleen shaking her head "No."

"Hello, Carole. Do you like this color? Kathleen hates it when I wear anything new." Mrs. Cullinane draws a thin pink lipstick stripe on the back of her hand and holds it up to examine it. Her lips are a tangerine-colored smear, and the coral would be better. Kathleen is shifting from foot to foot. Just about every boy in our class has had a crush on Kathleen, with her blonde hair, wide blue eyes, and skin so pale it colors when she sneezes. She is the class saint, may even plan on becoming a nun, if not a martyr, and has nothing to do with boys.

"My mother doesn't listen to me," Kathleen complains. Tossing a glance at her mother, Kathleen pronounces that the coral is too circusy and seems pleased with her word choice. And the tangerine isn't? I think. We spend five minutes talking about graduation, only five days away. I hadn't done a finger count, but Mrs. Cullinane had. Kathleen rolls her blue eyes when her mother says that she thinks there is no other store in all of downtown Springfield that can compare to Steiger's, far superior to Forbes. If I'm looking for a graduation dress, she adds, I should try the second floor back. Kathleen is fussing with the Steiger's bag and about to show me her dress when they spot the Carew to East Springfield bus pulling up outside. I watch them hurry out and wonder for a second whether my mother preferred Forbes or Steiger's—not that it's important . . .

"May I help you?" the saleswoman asks in a department-store voice. She has crept up behind me in the back by the evening gown section and caught me off guard. Her question makes my shoulders jump a little, my stomach tightens. I hear no kindness in her voice, no genuine offer of help, more boredom, duty, and even a little suspicion.

"Would you like to try those on?" she asks, her sharp eyes alerted to criminal activity by the four white dresses looped over my arm. Usually I make no eye contact and say I'm just looking, but right now I want to tell this tight-curled saleswoman with her own coral-circus lips that I am scrupulously honest, overscrupulous. "Scrupulous" is a word Sister Maurice Joseph taught us in seventh-grade religion class, and it is a word I love. And, besides, I have enough money to buy any of these dresses, any two of these dresses. So there. Then I remember how my mother had told me that discussing money, like boasting, was impolite. Why, I'll never know.

The saleswoman pats a tissue to the corners of her lips, crumples the tissue in her hand, sticks it in the open neck of her shapeless polka dot dress, and leads me to the dressing room. The third dress I try on fits, has a tiny lace row edging the collar and the waist, fabric bows on the cap sleeves, a pleated front, and a full skirt with a crinoline already sewn in. The stiff net fabric of the crinoline is a little scratchy and cuts into my waist, but when the saleswoman asks me through the velvet curtain if I need any help, I answer "no" right away before she can stick her head in and catch me in my underwear.

At the cash register, I slip out two ten-dollar bills from my red Lady Buxton wallet, a Christmas present, and hand her the money.

"Isn't this a lot of money for you to be carrying?" The saleswoman wipes the black hairs on her upper lip and does not wait for me to answer. As she wraps layers of tissue paper around my dress, she draws in a breath, checks me over with her steel-grey eyes, and adds, "Ever since the middle of May, every girl and her mother have been in this store looking for a white dress. Fighting with one another, arguing over the dress—the mother just wants the daughter to find a dress, any white dress, and the daughter thinks she needs to be Cinderella. Or the mother cares about every detail of the dress, every dart, every pleat, and the daughter would be just as happy wearing a pillowcase. No middle ground there, and I can tell you I don't know why they want to float like Cinderella because there aren't going to be any Prince Charmings hotfooting it down the aisle at these grammar school graduations." She interrupts herself to chuckle, looking up at me as if she expects me to fall to the floor laughing. I give her a sick smile and fiddle with the snap on my wallet while she reaches under the counter and pulls out a Steiger's box.

"You were smart to come shopping alone. Just get it done. Not too many white dresses left, nowhere near so many as last week, you waited a little too long. You don't know how lucky you were to find this dress. I hope you appreciate the detail work in this dress. Of course, I didn't see how you looked in the dress, I like a little modesty in you teenagers. I can't understand why these schools insist on putting these teenage girls in white. A waste of money, as far as I can see. I'm sure your parents authorized you to spend this much." There is a question in her voice. I think of my father's words, "spend whatever you want." But I feel as if she's caught me out, as if she knows that it will take more than a yard of lace edging and a couple of bows to turn me into Kathleen Cullinane. The saleswoman ties string around the box, secures it with a knot, and hoists the box on the counter. "Between you and me," she lowers her voice to confide, "I don't think you'll ever wear this dress again." She leans so close I can see the melted peppermint Life Saver in the middle of her tongue. I'm halfway down the escalator when I remember I forgot to say thank you and imagine my mother sighing.

Three Carew to East Springfield buses have come and gone, and still no Falls via Liberty. Waiting in the shade under the metal canopy outside Steiger's, I calculate bus injustice. The strip of sky overhead turns suddenly dark, and heavy raindrops pelt the canopy. I draw closer to the group of women hugging the entrance door, but the rain hits my legs, turning my white canvas sneakers gray around the rubber soles. The dress box is awkward, bulky against my side as I switch it to my left arm, shielding it from the rain. I run my thumbnail back and forth over the damp string until I spot the Falls via Liberty bus down the block in front of Lerner's.

I sit by the back door of the bus and prop the dress box on top of my Keds. The box has spattered, irregular dots where the rain has hit, and I wipe these off with my fingertips, drying my fingers on my skirt. The white dress I pray, like the gypsy blouse, will hide my perspiration circles, which can fan out, grow as big as softballs. I will wear my graduation dress to church every Sunday morning this summer and prove the saleswoman with the candy mint breath wrong. So Kathleen Cullinane's mother was right about the second floor back. I would have found the dress on my own, I think, and feel a hot flush mounting my face, from the neck up.

When I open the back door, my dad is at the kitchen counter opening a family-sized can of Campbell's pork and beans (99 percent beans, 1 percent pork, Danny once calculated). I drop the box on the table.

"Success, I see? Or is it an empty box?" he asks over the whir of the electric can opener, a Christmas gift from him to my mother. "Steigers, must be quite the height of fashion." He hands me a dishtowel, and I wipe the rain from my face, relieved that he hasn't mentioned my mother. I'd like to know whether my mother preferred Forbes or Steiger's but can't risk his tears, his memories that his words turn into sad, painted pictures—pictures I do and do not want.

"Do we, mere mortals, have a formal showing of this confection? My only daughter floating in her white dress? I'm sure you'll look like an angel gracing earth's sinners. Well?" He empties the beans into a saucepan on the stove and boils water for the Oscar Mayer hot dogs lying between the stove's electric burners.

"Hot dogs and beans. Good, I'm hungry." I smell the ketchupy Campbell's beans, and so do Michael and Gerry, who wander into the kitchen.

"So no fashion show tonight? Your brothers would like to see you in your dress," he says with a glance at Gerry.

"Yeah, I just left the eighth inning of the Red Sox game so I could see you in your white dress," Gerry says. "Dad, have the Red Sox ever scored eight runs in the last inning? Against the Yankees?" Gerry has an anxious look on his face. Dad laughs and tells him to pray for a miracle. It is only the middle of June, and we are already praying for the Red Sox. My father drops the hot dogs into the pan and sings, "Hot dogs and beans, down in New Orleans." Michael, Gerry, and I grew up hearing my father sing the hot-dog-and-beans-New-Orleans rhyme on Saturday nights. Gerry sneaks a smile at the familiarity of the singing, the pink hot dogs, the yellow French's mustard. Their sameness, their predictability, especially my dad's singing, relieve me too. In first grade at Glenwood School, the report cards had a grading system with the dreaded NI, needs improvement, category. Our family right now is NI, in need of improvement, so my dad's singing helps. Needs improvement—not yet a U, for unsatisfactory. Gerry is licking mustard off his finger when my father reaches into the top shelf of the cabinet for his whiskey bottle. I shake my head at Gerry, lift the box from the table, and run upstairs. I hear my dad singing, getting the ice cubes out of the freezer, "Hot dogs and beans, down in New Orleans."

8. Honor and Privilege

"CLASS, THIS IS a wonderful day for you and your families. With the Lord's help, I have prepared you for high school. With continued work and application—" she pauses, "I think you will do well." This is an extraordinary day, Sister Agnes Edward has never been so peculiar . . . kind, almost.

The eighth-grade classroom is summer-ready. The erasers have been clapped, the textbooks stored, and the desks scrubbed. Sister Agnes Edward places the fleshy part of her palm on the chalk tray and scans the classroom. When she finds nothing out of order, she leans back against the board behind her desk and runs her fingers along the black, dull rosary beads as if she is searching for the heavy crucifix. Sister's eyes are a pale gray, more cat than human, and she has tiny white whiskers on her full cheeks.

"And let me say how lovely you all look," she says with a loopy smile, "and how pleased I am to have had the honor and privilege of teaching you."

Although Sister has all but chirped this birdsong of flattery to the entire class, I know she has really meant me, just me—as if she has just noticed I am wearing my graduation dress. Up front, where Sister can "keep an eye" on the troublemakers, Francis Harrington and Donald "Toothpick" Taupier squirm in their seats. Then Mark Coffey throws a pencil on the floor, bends to pick it up, and swivels in his seat, facing the back of the class. Pointing to his chest he mouths the words "Honor and privilege. Me, an honor."

"Mark, do you have something you'd like to share with the class?" Sister asks, catching him with the "share" question for maybe the fiftieth time since eighth grade began. Mark reddens and mumbles, "No, Sister." Mark's father is my mother's Fuller Brush salesman but, unlike his son, I have never seen him smile, even when my mother bought the moth balls and a toilet bowl brush she would later regret. Jackie Fitzgerald is scuffing his shined shoes on the floor, Paula Zygarowski is examining a freckle on her forearm, and Diane Scagliarini is cleaning her glasses when Mark raises his hand.

With her fingers tightening around the crucifix, Sister calls on him. "What is it, Mark?" He stands up next to his seat, buttons his sport coat, bows from the waist, clears his throat, and says, "Sister, it has been an honor and privilege to be in your classroom this year."

Putting my hand over my mouth to hide my smile, I hear soft laughter floating in the air. Sister Agnes Edward turns her back to us, picks up a piece of chalk, and begins tossing it in the air, up and down, catching it. The kids in the front row are on the edges of their chairs, leaning forward and trying to see Sister's face. The chalk flies up and down, five, six, seven times, and then she holds it, closing her hand into a fist. When she turns to face us, Sister is laughing and wipes the tears at the corners of her eyes. "Why, thank you, Mark," she says in the same respectful tone she uses when she addresses Father Power, "I am sure I'll remember your kindness."

This just proves what I've thought all along: Sister, like most nuns, prefers the boys. If any of the girls had done that, she'd probably yank the girl right out of the graduation ceremony. I kind of wish I had thought of the "honor and privilege" thing, though, like Mark. But with my mother barely in the grave I'm not supposed to joke, I guess, for a while.

Out in the schoolyard where we are lining up for graduation in height order, I am not sure what to do. Sister motions to me and lowers her voice to say, "Now, Carole, I know you've missed all the graduation practices through no fault of your own, so I'd like you to stand next to Mary Anne Sullivan and to follow her lead. I know that you'll do just fine." Through no fault of your own? I should say not! My mother's death, wake, and funeral are excellent excuses, I say to Sister in my head. Sister, you were even there at Sampson's, an eyewitness. I have no need for lame excuses. Mine are jewels.

Sister Agnes Edward lines everyone up, checks and rechecks her pocket watch, and marches up and down the line, sniffing out gum or candy. I love my dress and ran to Baker's yesterday afternoon to buy pointed white flats with bows to wear with it. I know Baker's is cheap, Marilyn Martin would never even look in the window at Bakers, but Di Thinel got hers there and we wanted matching shoes. The truth is I forgot all about the shoes until Dianne asked me on the phone what mine were like. My friends are afraid to call, afraid they'll catch me crying or moaning, so I'm glad Di called or I'd be wearing black shoes.

Sister claps her hands and the girls at the front of the line, the short girls, turn around and shush the rest of us. When I see Anne at the end of the line, we roll our eyes.

"Class, I want you to line up with your partners, the way we practiced. Officer Kelly will hold up the traffic for us so there's no need for running. Your mothers and fathers and families will be watching you, so I expect you to act accordingly." The word "mother" bothers me, especially when I catch Marilyn Martin with her soft hazel eyes turning around from the short section to check up on me. Although Marilyn confesses that she is completely spoiled, even her brothers worship her, and she has the best clothes, Peerless, never Lerner's, she is still the nicest girl in the class. I can't figure it out, and think I'd like to be Marilyn Martin for a while. I want to be worshiped by my brothers; as it is, I'm barely tolerated. So much for bravery.

In Loco Isto Dabo Pacem. These are the Latin words carved over the entrance to Our Lady of Hope Church that I study on my way in. Usually I keep my eyes straight ahead, but today I decide to look up at the stone carving, and I catch a bolt of sky so blue it cuts me, making me think of God the way it does, the way the carving does. While Kathleen Cullinane and Marilyn Martin get aisle seats right up front near the altar, I'm stuck in the middle next to Mary Anne Sullivan. We're comparing arm hair, mine darker, thicker, but no freckles, when I hear Sister Agnes Edward from somewhere behind me clearing her throat. For a minute, I put the heels of my shoes up on the kneeler so I can admire the bows.

Although I didn't see my father outside, milling around with the other parents, or in the church, I know he's here. Maybe he's sitting with my aunts and uncles. Scanning the boys' side, I am trying to spot my father when I meet Sister's full frontal glare: eyes of cold steel, a deep, vertical frown line over her left eyebrow tilting her face a little off center. I face front. Well, she's more her old self now. An honor and privilege, yeah, sure. Father Power drones on with the same sermon as usual, pointing out sins, finding faults; I examine my jagged fingernails and pluck a word from his dull buzz every couple of minutes. I am just waiting for him to finish so I can slouch a little. Being a priest seems like a pretty cushy job to me—I wonder what they do all week between Sundays, study up on new ways of sinning? Since Father Power's brother owns a Cadillac dealership over in Worcester, Father Power drives around Springfield in a shiny blue 1959 Cadillac Seville. While my father and mother were walking out the door for the eleven o'clock Mass one Sunday, I overheard my dad tell my mother that Father Power is so short that he needs to put pillows behind his back to reach the car's gas pedal. My mother pointed to her ear and then over her shoulder to me peeling potatoes at the kitchen sink, but my dad just shrugged. The priest's vow of poverty didn't count, I guess, if there was a Cadillac dealership in the family. Even so, I wonder how many future martyrs or candidates for sainthood are out there driving around in baby blue Cadillacs.

The baskets of white lilies on either side of the altar remind me of Sister Maurice Joseph's seventh-grade English class, when we had to go through the torture of analyzing a poem for theme, symbolism, and figures of speech. If the poem was anything but "Casey at the Bat," or, maybe "Hiawatha," the boys would groan, and, in all honesty, I have to admit I am just like them because I don't get poetry. I could pick out figures of speech; Sister taught us the word "onomatopoeia," a word both my dad and mom didn't know, where the sound suggests the meaning. Similes and metaphors were pretty easy for me, but I could never find the theme and always had the symbolism wrong. Sister said that lilies were often considered a symbol of death, and all that did was ruin lilies for me. While I didn't say anything in class at the time, I am sitting here thinking who gets to decide these things? What do pansies symbolize? Geraniums? And who gets to decide that dandelions are weeds? The answer has to do with rarity. I am going to become rare, less available, learn to say no. I begged my dad not to give my mother a lily when she was back in the hospital at Easter, too afraid to tell him it was a symbol of death, but he either didn't hear me or ignored me and went with what he always does.

The hissing snake voice of Father Power, onomatopoeia, stops. Making the sign of the cross over us, he stretches the blessing out to a minute and leaves the altar with the two seventh-grade altar boys following him. A whiff of Mary Anne's underarm odor hits me when she nudges me, harder than she needs to, and whispers, "Face the aisle."

After the class picture on the church steps, everyone scatters to their families, who have gathered into groups on the sidewalk. Fathers, not mine, have taken off their sport coats, mothers are using tissues to swipe at their eyebrows. Way off to the side, I spot my dad, standing next to the curbed-off square of grass.

"Carole, your dress is just lovely," my aunt Madeline says, her eyes scanning the pleated front, making me wish I were flat-chested and less doughy. My aunts Stella and Lee chime in their lovelies, and I hear approval in their voices and think I have passed some life test. A life test is different from a school test because in school I never know exactly what's right, whether to circle a, b, or c, but this dress is the correct answer. Mad and Bill, Stella and Bunny, Don and Lee—my uncles and aunts have come in pairs to my graduation. Madeline steps back and places her hand on Bill's arm, but Bill is talking and gesturing to my father, who is studying the ground. Bill keeps talking until my father shakes his head. Then Bill turns to Mad, lowering his good ear to her, and she and Bill change places. Now, my aunt is talking to my father. The rule is my father can't be left alone for a minute.

"Hey, Miss Nibs, big day for the little lady," Uncle Bill says to me, a big smile spreading across his pale face. "You're going to head up that honor roll at Cathedral next year, just the way your aunt did. First honors for you." His eyes skip over to Aunt Madeline, then back to me. He never sees me without slipping in a "Katsy." When I was ten years old, I was shopping in the basement at Forbes and Wallace with my mother on a Saturday afternoon in October when I overheard a mother in the next aisle call her daughter "Kitty." This was it, a magical name. I longed for a name with an e sound at the end, and Kitty would be perfect. To me, Kitty had the sound of a television name. I put down the pair of boy's flannel pajamas I was holding and announced my new nickname to my mother. I waited for her enthusiastic response. Disappointed when she did not even lift her eyes from the boys' dress shirts, I pressed her on this television-name until she agreed that we could give it a try. At home, I made the big mistake of telling everyone that from now on, they were to call me Kitty. I would not answer to Carole anymore. I had given my brothers a subject for ridicule, ammunition and a loaded gun, and Kitty became the family joke. *"Here, Kitty, Kitty, Kitty." Mewing, purring sounds. "We'll have to get Kitty declawed." "Kitty, there's a bowl of milk for you by the refrigerator." "Carole, did you give any thought to 'Puppy?'"* The nickname torture lasted about two weeks. I began to hate Kitty until Uncle Bill, a man who, like my dad, loves nicknames, started calling me Katsy. So for a month or so, to retaliate, I started calling him Uncle Bulgy after a comic-strip character until my aunt asked me to stop, which made me feel ashamed. But I do like being called Miss Nibs, another nickname, and although I won't admit it, I don't even mind Katsy.

"Here's a little something," he says, shoving a card into my hand, "and don't spend any on your brothers." I don't think there's any danger of that. With my brothers, I'm pretty selfish, calculating every penny I have ever loaned Michael and Danny over and over again. Not that it does any good, because they either have no memories or are just outright thieves.

To each aunt and uncle, I murmur a thank you, lacking in grace, as if those two words get lost somewhere inside me and need a map to reach my tongue. Maybe it's just the shortness of it, the two syllables. Since my aunts sign the cards, as if my uncles have forgotten their Palmer method penmanship, my uncles do the handing, slipping me the cards. With the heat, my hands are so sweaty I can feel a dampness crawling out on the edges of the envelopes. I glance over and see Di clasping a stack of cards and wish I came from a French Canadian family with dozens of uncles and aunts. Di is having a big family picnic at Look Park this afternoon, but my family has never had picnics, even before my mother died, so for my graduation we end up doing nothing. Just another ho-hum, no-big-deal day.

9. Complete Change of Scene

THE TUESDAY MORNING after graduation, I am in the kitchen half-listening to Mrs. Meade tell me stories about her son Wally's weak heart, his being a blue baby and all, when my father walks in lugging a suitcase. A suitcase? We are a family of surprises, but the suitcase shakes me because I have no idea where he's going or what he's doing. Since it has been only two weeks since my mom died, I'm fluttery about any change.

"Your uncle and a few friends and I are going to Florida to play a little golf," my father explains. My father is not a golfer. He cannot hit a golf ball ten feet, and while his friends have joined the country club, he has not. When I learned the Springfield Country Club had a swimming pool, I begged him to join, but my mom said fees and that was it.

"Your aunt's coming to stay with you kids," he yells from the cellar stairs. He means Aunt Madeline; I have come to think of her as the reliable one, and she is my father's sister, not an aunt by marriage, like Stella and Lee. From the cellar, there is the clank of metal as he moves the broken bikes around so he can reach the golf clubs. A bike falls to the floor, and my father mutters a dammit. With the clubs clashing together like my brothers trapped inside on a rainy afternoon, he climbs back up the cellar stairs.

"Look at those cobwebs on my driver. Three or four spiders must be doing a slow waltz," he says, reaching under the kitchen sink for an old T-shirt rag.

"I've got ironing to do. I'm not staying in this kitchen, Mr. O'Malley, with spiders running around," Mrs. Meade says, hurrying off to the safety of a laundry basket full of damp clothes. My dad and I look at each other, chuckling at Mrs. Meade. Spiders don't bother me, and I am fascinated by the spindly design of their webs, although the scattering of trapped insects awaiting a sure death disturbs me.

"You're fearless," my dad says, "at least when it comes to bugs." He's wadding up the cottony spider web with his fingers.

"Have you ever seen a tarantula?" I ask. The summer I was ten, Michael and Danny tortured me with a "There's a tarantula on your neck" period before I found out how rare tarantulas are in Massachusetts. The creation of the spider torment came from too many science shows on television, and to protect myself I decided that I would leave the TV room whenever any science reference crops up. There is now no space left in me to worry about plants, insects, and animals that will never dart across Main Street in downtown Springfield.

My dad sponges off the golf bag, checking for scuffs and black marks.

"Well? The tarantula?" I ask again.

"No, I have never seen a tarantula," my dad answers and turns the bag around in the light, giving it an up and down.

"Not even in India? Or Burma?"

"Even in India," he answers. Asking about India is a trick I try to get my dad to talk about his wartime service there, but the most Danny and I have ever pried out of him on slow Sunday afternoons is that he was in counterintelligence, which means he was looking for American soldier spies. Laughing, he told us he spent too much time lurking in men's rooms. Confused, Danny and I kept badgering him with questions—did you ever catch any spies?—but he just sipped his Manhattan until my mom looked up from her magazine and said, "Carole and Danny, that is enough."

"I may be a terrible golfer, but at least no one will be able to make any remarks about the condition of my clubs," he says as he props the golf clubs along the sill of the back door and runs his fingers along the curved leather strap. "Carole, people forgive a lot," he adds, "if you've gone to the effort to look the part." I don't get the same kick out of looking the part that my dad does. In the last two weeks, I've been the grieving daughter in the black peasant blouse and then the smug Our Lady of Hope graduate in the Steiger's white dress. I'm pretty much costumed out.

"How long is Auntie Mad staying for?" I ask, trying to pin him down. At the lunch at our house after the funeral, I overheard Mrs. Blackmer whisper how good it would be if my father could get away for a few days for a complete change of scene. What about me? I wanted to say, but didn't let on I was eavesdropping. I have a gift for eavesdropping, though Michael and Danny claim it is nothing more than being nosy. Still, the funeral lunch eavesdropping keeps the Florida golf trip from being a total shock.

"Your aunt's staying for the weekend. On Monday, Mrs. Metzger's taking you kids to Kelsey Point while I'm in Florida. Grant Proper's giving us a cottage for a few days." One question about my aunt and now we're going to the beach in Connecticut for a week. A complete change of scene for me as well, thank you, Mrs. Blackmer. I'm not exactly dancing a jig because I've been to Kelsey Point before, and I have scraped and cut the bottoms of my feet on its rocky beach, so rocky it hurts even to sit on Dad's old army blanket. But my dad said Grant is "giving" us the cottage. Feasts and the loan of beach cottages follow death.

"I'm expecting you to help her," he says, looking across the tarred driveway at the Metzgers' house. A two-foot privet hedge separates the identical driveways, spelling out identical property lines.

"You know I will," I answer quickly. Did he really need to say that about my helping? "Do Michael and Danny know you're going away golfing and about the beach?" I ask, looking for an edge.

"You're the first." Some small satisfaction for me, knowing before they do, as if I were higher up on the family totem pole. "Mrs. Meade is doing the packing. Let's just hope it stays warm."

Gerry slams the screen door and checks behind him, concealing his ten-year-old body behind the door.

"I wasn't sure if Paul or Joey was behind me," he sputters, "I just escaped from enemy lines. We were playing war in the desert but I've had enough." The desert is a huge field of soft, white beach sand behind the Corlisses' house.

"World War II, the Revolution, or the Alamo?" I ask, not much caring. War is such a boring game, I gave it up the summer I turned eleven.

"You just stopped playing because we wouldn't let you be an American general all the time," he taunts, filling a jelly glass with water. True, whenever I played war with my brothers, I was always the enemy agent or a "lobsterback" at the Boston Massacre.

"I'm tired of being outside. I think I'll watch television." Gerry gulps the water down. There is a perfectly formed line of dirt in a crease in his neck safe from any washcloth. When he spots the suitcase, he studies it, takes it in for a second too long. Then he asks us in a slow quaver who's going away as he walks to the sink and puts his glass on the counter.

As soon as my dad tells him about the beach plan, Gerry runs back out, hunting my brothers down to report on the beach/golf trips, and this morning's *Price Is Right* has lost another viewer. I hope he's smart enough to tell the little kids first and Danny last, or Danny will jump right in and latch on to the trip news for his own. I don't mind Gerry's telling because twice now turning the corner from Thornfell Street, I've glanced up and seen him standing behind the plaid café curtain in the upstairs window just staring. He disappeared when I waved to him. He was looking down at Lynwood Terrace as if he were waiting for my mother to come back from the hairdresser, returning home a little taller and a little more relaxed as the afternoon sunlight caressed her wavy hair. There is a tight, cottony feeling spreading in my throat, and when I am where no one can see me I let the tears come.

10. Kelsey Point

IT HAS RAINED here for three out of four days, and although Mrs. Metzger is in no way to blame for the weather, in my head I blame her. I'm almost ready to pray for sun and apologize to God for my complaints about rocky beaches. Rocks are fine, God, I prefer sand, but rocks will do. All part of Your creation. I am sick of Gin Rummy, Crazy Eights, War, Fish, and watching the rain. At least there is basic arithmetic involved in Twenty-one or Blackjack, with Danny always pushing for the dealer's advantage. The little kids play Slapjack until one of them cries.

Gerry likes to make up a rule now and then and see if he can slip it by us. "The three of hearts is a wild card," he'll say with a straight face. Danny and I will smirk and Michael will rub his eyes, studying the three of hearts for an answer. "Everyone knows the three of hearts is a wild card. How come you didn't know that?" Danny or I will confront him until he pulls back. "You never know. I just thought I'd try it. Sometimes it works." He'll shrug, smile, and pick up the newly tamed three of hearts.

Mrs. Metzger summons me from the hallway interrupting a game of Gin Rummy in which I am just one queen away from winning. "I'll be right back," I say.

"No, Carole, I think they better finish the game without you. I'll need you for awhile," Mrs. Metzger says. Since I'm more than ready to leave the card game, I feel only curiosity and follow her into the cottage's small bathroom. Why the bathroom? Since there is no area of housekeeping Mrs. Metzger has not mastered, I wonder what holes in my domestic education she will fill on this rainy morning. Last summer she taught me to sew, and I have the dresses and skirts to prove it. Only the corduroy skirt with its nap was a disaster.

"Carole, as you know, your mother was too sick to toilet-train Tommy." Mrs. Metzger's explaining, but is she blaming too? My mind races as I wait for her to continue. "But it is time, and I'm going to help you with toilet-training your brother," she says, pointing to a potty seat. Amused, she smiles and I do, too. The thought leaps to my mind that I never saw my mother toilet-training my brothers in a formal, rule-following way and that, of all of them, only two-year-old Tommy is still in diapers. Bored with cards, I can't really say no to Mrs. Metzger, but I'm feeling ridiculous and inept. Sensing my helplessness, Mrs. Metzger zings me with, "I discussed it with your father, and we thought it would be a good idea for me to start you off with the training." Well, if my father thinks so. He's golfing in Florida and I'm about to undergo a regimen of toilet-training lessons on a rainy Connecticut beach morning.

"Isn't Tommy too short to reach the toilet?" This question of mine really means, Do we have to do this? Couldn't we wait until he's taller? Tommy turned two on March 8th —how about waiting until he's two and a half? I lean over and tear off a sheet of toilet paper and crumple it up in my hand, pleased by how easily I can alter its shape with my fist. The bathroom is small, damp, and has a smell of urine. I can see dark, puddled spots and stripes on the linoleum floor where my brothers have missed their target. How much accuracy can be needed? It's not as if the toilet is a moving target.

"Carole, this is the way I've trained Paul and Billy. Jimmy is already trained," Mrs. Metzger says. Her comparison of Jimmy, her baby, and Tommy, my brother, bothers me because I detect a "so there" hidden in her clipped words. Pointing out to her that Jimmy is at least two months older than Tommy, if not three, and that Tommy has just lost his mother will get me nowhere. Mrs. Metzger has a philosophy—growing more apparent to me—of "let's move on," and messy emotions, like sadness and loneliness and just wanting what's not there, don't fit into her high sense of order. And like an animal dropped into a new environment, I begin an adaptation process where I will not let anyone know that my mother is dead. There's something so needy and embarrassing about not having a mom. I will be above mentioning her death and spare everyone's pitying me.

"You must do this at the same time each day, particularly after meals." Well, there goes my summer. As if she has looked into my selfish heart, she adds, "You'll get Mrs. Meade to help you." I think of blue-lipped Wally and Billy and Blackie, "that boy always in trouble with the law," Mrs. Meade's three sons, and feel a reprieve coming on. Her sons may have health and criminal problems, but they are toilet-trained. Then I wonder if poor or negligent toilet training, which is about all I can aim for with Tommy, will contribute to a life of crime?

She shows me how to put the "potty seat" on, which I already know, and I keep nodding my head and making "hmm" sounds, realizing that my life is no longer a weekly spelling test where I could spend a few minutes glancing at the words and get them right. "Potty" is a word not used in our family, and I decide I will ask my father what word we do use, though he will only chuckle at the question if he even hears it.

Did my father and Mrs. Metzger really discuss the toilet-training issue or is she just saying that? Maybe I could have been part of that discussion, although what would I say? The word "potty seat" offends me, or maybe the whole, entire potty issue offends me.

There is no magic to getting the hang of the potty seat. The victim is next. Directed by Mrs. Metzger to remain in the bathroom while she gets Tommy, I look in the mirror, exploring a pimple by the side of my nose. The judges at the fashion show never would have selected me if I had this berry growth shouting on my face a month ago. Clearasil is guilty of false advertising, and I am living proof.

"Now, Tommy, Carole's here," Mrs. Metzger croons to a crying, squirming Tommy who almost succeeds in getting out of her grasp. Good, Tom, go for it, I root from a dark, hidden inside part of me. "Carole's right here," she says again, naming me clear and loud as executioner. Tommy jumps into my enemy arms and puts his head down on my shoulder, closing his long-lashed eyes to the unknown. Danny, who studies these things between card games, reported yesterday that Tommy had the longest eyelashes in the family. That's what a few rainy days at the beach will do to you.

The weight of his round body heaves against my front and my hands feel his chubby, baby legs sticking out from his seersucker shorts. He's wearing the spanking new red Ked sneakers I bought him for the beach. When I unpacked them, Danny and Gerry gave a collective hoot, insisting boys could only wear navy sneakers, as if this were a clothing commandment. Joey sneered and piped up that he'd run away from home before he'd be caught wearing red sneakers. What if Marty Sullivan caught him wearing red sneakers? I backed against the kitchen door with a sneaker in my hand, aiming it at Danny and Gerry, until my father noticed Tommy take the other sneaker from the box and put it in his mouth, a sign, my dad said, that Tommy liked the red. Maybe Joey should take over shoe selection. He's eight years old; he already knows everything.

"Whas that?" Tommy asks in baby talk, his brown eyes like mine looking at me as if I am his personal savior, as if I'd jump in front of a moving train for him. He's too young to get my "martyrdom is overrated" speech, a heresy I'm sure, and one I keep to myself. I steal a glance at the two of us in the medicine chest mirror with the light shining on our brunette, almost black, hair.

"Now, Tommy, you know what that is. That is what the big boys use to go the bathroom," Mrs. Metzger says in a voice reeking with calm.

"I don't know if he's seen that kind of toilet seat before. Ours at home is a little different." I have no idea what our toilet-training seat looks like, but I know it's different from the Metzger family seat. My fingers circle the roll of sweet toddler flesh at his ankle. Not listening to my feeble protest, Mrs. Metzger reaches for Tommy and takes him from my arms before I even sense what's happening. *Take care of my baby,* my mother's last words to me. Barely three weeks later, I betray him in this cramped, over-lit bathroom. First, the red sneakers, now this toilet seat, this toilet training. *Take care of my baby.*

"Carole, the toilet seat makes no difference," she says to me, placing my squirming, now yelling baby brother on the toilet seat. "Kneel down. Talk to him," she directs me. The calmness coats her like hairspray. OK, I kneel down, and my feet touch the wall, my shoulder scrunches under the sink.

"Michael sat on a seat just like this, Danny sat on a seat just like this."

I have his attention. The litany of brothers I recite in a rhythmical sing-song is quieting him, a comfort to hear their names in birth order. Mrs. Metzger nods her head at me, my Mother Goose performance. And I run through the names again. While I consider Tommy's peace and quiet a victory, a huge victory by my standards, my commandant, Mrs. Metzger, is disappointed, wanting more than a weak, baby-teeth smile. Tommy has not delivered. We will try again after lunch, she tells me smugly. Victory will be ours, if her will has anything to do with it.

When I walk back into the living room, Gerry looks up from some card trick and says, "Well, how'd it go? Get it?" Nudging Danny with his elbow, Gerry repeats his dig. Did he go? He's cracking up at his pathetic bathroom illusion.

"You can laugh all you want, Ger. After lunch, Mrs. Metzger said you'd be in demonstrating your bathroom ritual to Tommy."

Of course, she has said no such thing, but the words fly out of my mouth and Gerry is speechless for a good thirty seconds. I love the idea, the audiovisual effect of my brothers' lining up to whiz into the toilet. I picture them in a line, Look, Tommy, look what Michael is doing.

By late afternoon, Michael and Danny are reading Marvel action adventure comics about asparagus-colored aliens while I stick to Archie, Jughead, Betty, and Veronica for the twentieth time. I am annoyed that the heartless Veronica is dark-haired and wonder whether, if Michael wore a sleeveless black sweater vest with the initial M like Archie's A, he would give up fault finding and have even one friend from high school. Joey is in the doorway throwing rocks way past the bushes and into the empty road. Plopped down on the sofa, Gerry is staring out the window at the soft rain. He throws his head back against a sofa pillow and says, "It's raining. The beach is rocky. I wish we had never come. I wish we had just stayed home." The toilet training must have worn me down because I don't have the energy to disagree. Mrs. Metzger is in the kitchen pouring coffee. Looking up, she says nothing but gives us all a quick scan.

After dinner, Mrs. Metzger says, "I think we'll go home tomorrow morning. I'll call Donald and your father tonight. Enough is enough." I take in the news of this reprieve in disbelief because leaving the beach a day early is unheard of in our family.

When a stay at the beach turns into a failure, I wonder if there is there anything left for us.

11. The Boys at the Corner Drugstore

AT THE CORNER of Woodmont Street, there are three boys standing on the corner, and two of them are blowing smoke rings, a trick I would give anything to be able to do.

"What would you do if those boys called us maggots?" I ask Kathy. "Wouldn't you just die?"

"They will not call us maggots. The curly-haired one goes to Tech. He's a junior." The curly-haired one is the best-looking of the three, so good-looking that I can almost feel his confidence radiating across Newbury Street like space rays in a comic book. "Richie," Kathy adds. "I don't know his last name. Don't look at them." So much for the top *Seventeen* magazine how-to-be-popular tip: Smile and be friendly.

"They're crossing the street. They're coming to see us," I say in a whispered rush.

"I have eyes. I can see them." Kathy can get away with being a little mean because, after all, she is two years older, and a cheerleader at Tech besides. I picture Kathy leaping in the crisp fall air in her orange and black uniform. "Just be cool," she whispers as if I have to work harder at coolness than she does.

The three boys strut across the street, betting that any oncoming traffic will stop for them. A green Chevy pulls up and waits. As they pass in front of it, the white-haired driver leans on his horn, and Richie and another boy jump and scamper to the sidewalk. But a boy with a hair-stick crew cut just keeps on walking and waves to the driver as if they know each other. The driver yells out, "Punks!" as he drives off. The man reminds me of my grandfather, old and angry and full of hate.

"Skip, you made a friend," Richie says to Skip, who is leaning against the fender of a parked car.

"Hey, everybody loves old Skip," Skip says with a shrug, as if that is the way it is, this burden of love.

"So do you girls love old Skip?" Richie asks, his blue eyes shifting from me to Kathy.

"The gent in the car wasn't all that happy," I say quickly. When Richie smiles, the puckered frown in Kathy's forehead disappears. Kathy and Richie begin talking about Tech, football, cheerleading, and we slide into picking up one another's names. No Emily Post, no handshaking, but we all find out who the others are. The five of us walk to Dave's—the sign above the door says the Carew Street Pharmacy, but everyone calls it Dave's. I don't know Dave, the balding pharmacist and owner, the way Richie, Gordie, and Skip do. Even if I did know Dave, I would never call an adult by his first name. On the way in, Richie holds the door for Kathy and me. I could get used to this white knight chivalry (I doubt if Michael or Danny has ever held a door for a girl), but I'm hoping this gesture doesn't mean we owe him anything.

For the next two nights, Kathy and Richie and Gordie and I meet at Dave's and walk around the neighborhood. Lucky Skip has gone to the Cape with his girlfriend and her parents for the Fourth of July weekend. "You can guess what's going on there," Richie says, making himself and Kathy chuckle. I smile too, pretending to know what's funny, and imagine the Cape with its sandy, no-rock beaches, so unlike Kelsey Point. Pairing off, I end up with Gordie, who with his wavy brown hair and gray eyes is OK, though he's no Richie.

After ice cream and sodas at Dave's, the four of us are strolling up Newbury Street, with Gordie and me, the supporting players, a few steps behind Richie and Kathy when Richie reaches for Kathy's hand. Why, Kathy, why? A panic hits me in the back of my throat. Please, God, don't let Gordie try to hold my hand, not with my sweaty palms. If I wipe my hands on my shorts pockets and Gordie sees me, will he think I want him to hold my hand? I'm not ready, I'm just not ready, I'm thinking when I hear my name being called.

"Carole, Carole, is that you?" I look up, and there's Linda Sullivan out on her back porch, frantically waving both arms. Linda lives alone with her grandmother on the top floor of a mustard yellow two-family house.

"Yes, yes, I'm here," I yell up, in an unladylike manner sure to disappoint Sister Maurice Joseph—but Linda, my angel of mercy, is saving me from holding hands with Gordie, letting me breathe.

"Carole O'Malley, is that you?" Linda yells again. Although her grandmother broke down and bought her glasses this year, Linda's still half-blind. In the middle of seventh grade, she moved to Springfield from California, and she's been calling attention to herself ever since.

"My grandmother bought me a transistor radio for my birthday," Linda yells and begins shimmying to a song I can't make out. We keep yelling up and down at each other until Linda's grandmother from somewhere inside begs us to stop, to turn that radio off, and orders Linda to get in the house and try to be civilized. Civilized. What could be more civilized than Linda Sullivan's saving me from the hand-holding moment? For the whole time Linda and I are yelling, I could feel Gordie standing next to me. I half hoped he'd try to catch up with Kathy and Richie, but he's taking this couple thing about as seriously as Noah boarding penguins on the ark. When I turn around to wave goodbye, Linda leans over the railing, points at Gordie, and then she clasps her hands over her heart. I think this gesturing of hers is connected to California, but I'm just relieved Gordie didn't turn around and see her grabbing her heart.

Parting with the boys at Newbury Street, Kathy and I are walking home in the dark a half hour later.

"Richie told me that Gordie likes you." And I like Richie, I think, but I hold back from telling Kathy that I would like to be with Richie with his black curly hair and easy smile. If we were still in school, I'd sit in my math class and write Richie's initials with mine in a heart off in the margins on lined notebook paper. I am kind of pathetic the way it takes so little for me to fall in love, but it is easier if the boy does not go to school with me. There is something so unfair, so settling, about being paired with Gordie. I have to pretend for Kathy that Gordie is OK, but I am not the random loose-lipped kisser that I was back in sixth grade.

"Well?" Kathy asks me, her sky blue eyes narrowing at the corners as we pass under a streetlight. "Do you like Gordie?" Like him for what? I think. Boys are just another multiple choice test, and with seven brothers you'd think I'd have some of the answers. Stalling, I kick at a loose stone with my sneaker and watch it skitter, coming to a stop against the curb. If I answer no, I don't like Gordie, I'll stop this boy/girl game before it even begins. I still haven't answered when we get to the dirt road shortcut behind my house. "Sort of," I say. Kathy smiles her cheerleader smile as if my "sort of" is the correct answer. She leaves me at the corner of Sedgelia just as the overhead streetlight flickers and dies.

The backyard gate is open as usual. We have locks, but we never use them. The kitchen light is on, spreading a dim glow behind the house and back to the flagstone path. There are only a few red roses still left on the bushes, and fallen rose petals are scattered in the brown dirt border. Twisting the stem of a rose back and forth, I hold the soft velvet petals and breathe in so deeply I barely smell the rose and the outside layer of petals floats to the ground. As I near the house, I pass the chaise lounge where my mother used to drink beer with my father and tan herself on the sun yellow cushion on hot Sunday afternoons. My father doesn't come out here anymore. Unseen, I sprinkle a few rose petals over the chaise and jam my index finger into one of the thorns, pushing it in until a spot of blood fans out. Satisfied, I throw the broken stem into the hedge lining the driveway.

From the back steps, I see Danny at the refrigerator drinking from a milk bottle, which he passes to Gerry. There is a jar of Skippy peanut butter on the counter and my dad's whiskey bottle in its spot next to the dish drainer.

"Come on. Use a glass," I say, the big rule-following sister, easily earning their dislike. They shrug and their eyes say who are you? Danny leaves the kitchen, but not before shrugging me off as if I were a housefly in a sugar bowl. They break a rule and I point it out, as if I can't help myself; I just fall into it. Carole, the nun. I let the screen door go, letting it bang, and hear the sound of a car sputtering up Thornfell.

"The Princess is back," my dad calls out like a game show announcer. Even from the porch, I could hear Frank Sinatra crooning his sad, love-lost songs from the living room. I head for the living room, skirting by Joey on the floor spreading out baseball cards.

"They're drinking from the bottle again?" A comment really, not a question for me to answer. My dad lifts his eyes when he sees me and sips from his drink, letting the milk issue drop as well as my failure to enforce a family rule.

"Dooby, dooby, doo," I sing. "I don't see how you can say anything about Elvis, Dad. At least, there's no dooby, dooby, doo in 'Heartbreak Hotel.'"

"You have a terrible voice, just like your mother." My father smiles at me, raising his head to sip his whiskey. No reaction to my mention of Elvis tonight. In sixth grade, I was president of the Elvis Presley fan club. On Saturday afternoons, we listened to Elvis albums, talked about boys, and ate homemade brownies in Mary Ellen Lynch's basement. How I could stoop to listen to Elvis Presley music bothered my father. Those gyrations. Those antics, he'd say. At least, back then, he noticed things.

"Betty could not carry a tune for love or money, and you have a voice just like hers." A new habit of his, slipping my mother into every conversation.

"That's why Sister Rose Catherine told me to stop singing in second grade. A musical talent lost at age seven. A listener." Sprawling on the green armchair, I examine a nick in my leg where I cut it shaving. I put my finger in my mouth and wipe off the slit of dried blood.

"Carole, will you play that album again?" my father asks. His arm reaches down to put his glass on the carpet, the shrunken ice cubes swimming in the amber-colored pool. The Frank Sinatra album cover, for lovers who have lost lovers, is lying at an angle on the blonde record cabinet. How long has this album been out, I wonder, as I glance at the black cover with a picture of a whiskey glass, an ashtray full of cigarette stubs, and the fuzzy red tip of a lit cigarette. My dad's got the whiskey part down pat, but my mother was the family smoker with her oval-shaped fingertips clasping the white and gold pack of Chesterfields, handsome package, pure, regal looking. I hope he doesn't go back to talking about my mother and sliding off into some imagined Frank Sinatra world. Because of him, I've given up mentioning the word "mother" anymore. It's not really all that hard. I pretend to myself she's downtown shopping and I have no idea when she's coming home. More than anything, I want my old father back. No sofa, no Frank Sinatra, no Seagram's.

"How old do I have to be before I date?" I ask.

"Date? You mean with a boy?" He raises his bushy eyebrows and looks at me.

"Yes. With a boy."

"How old are you now anyway?" my father asks and his *Time* magazine with a picture of Vice President Nixon on the cover falls on the floor next to his empty drink. I roll my eyes. Does he really not know how old I am?

"You know how old I am—I'm thirteen."

"That would make you fourteen on your next birthday," he teases, making a tent out of his fingers and resting them in the middle of his chest on his white, starched shirt.

"Yes, Dad. Thirteen plus one. I'm quite the mathematician."

"I wish your mother were alive. She could talk to you about dating."

Why did I ever ask him? Does everything make him wish my mother were alive? Even if my mother were still alive, I could never tell either of them about Gordie and Richie. I'll have to figure dating out for myself.

"I guess you're old enough to date." This isn't the answer I want. My mind flashes to the Sullivan twins, Monica and Veronica, who have hands-down the strictest parents in eighth grade; the twins can never do anything without their father pelting them with questions. My father and mother never asked me questions and pretty much always let me do whatever I wanted. I just don't know what I want with Gordie.

"Dad, do you think my left hand might sweat more because I'm left-handed?" He drains his glass and, before he can answer, Stevie bolts into the room crying. His face scrunches up with all his sniffling and sobbing until he blurts out that Joey had ripped the new Superman comic right out of his hands.

"Carole, would you go in and see. . . ."

"I'll go in and referee," I chime in, hoping my dad picks up on the resignation in my voice. With Frank Sinatra in the background spinning his web of sadness, my dad unbuttons his cuffs, folds up his shirtsleeves, and lifts his arms behind his neck, staring blankly into space again. With his lollypop-sticky fingers clinging to the hem of my Bermuda shorts, Stevie warily follows me out of the room. "Hey, it's just a Superman comic," I say, only making him cry harder.

Dave is standing at his cash register looking at the four of us as if he's been watching too many television shows about juvenile delinquency and he's half expecting us to pull out a gun and rob him blind. With packs of cigarettes rolled up in their T-shirt sleeves and hair gunk so thick it has a whitish crust, Gordie and Richie don't look like Eagle Scouts. Kathy and I have our collars up and four-inch elastic belts around our waists. When Kathy brags about her waistline, she makes me want to lie about mine, but we both think Scarlett O'Hara in *Gone with the Wind* never had an 18-inch waist. As proof, Kathy wants me to go home tonight and measure Tommy's waist. Even if we had a tape measure, I could never find it in our junk drawer: tape measures, rulers, and Scotch tape disappear in our house as fast as an opened package of Hydrox cookies crouching in a cabinet.

The four of us are dawdling at the counter coupled off, Richie, Kathy, me, and Gordie. Our empty soda glasses with the white Coca-Cola script sit in front of us. While the script, the long-tailed initial "C" especially, is not Palmer method, there is something slick about it. As soon as Kathy reaches for a napkin and begins wiping up a drop of soda, Richie leans over, looks at Gordie, and lifts his eyebrows, a signal if I ever saw one. When Gordie puts thirty cents down for their cokes, Kathy pulls out her wallet from her straw bag while I reach into the pocket of my Bermuda shorts for the exact change. Because Gordie and Richie do not fork money up for our sodas, my neck relaxes a little. No way I want to owe them anything. Walking out, I think I can feel Dave's small eyes staring at us, worried that Richie or Gordie will lift some aftershave or a hot rod magazine.

Out on the street, a blast of hot air hits us as if the July heat had been waiting for a Friday night meltdown. As we walk up the street, Richie and Gordie talk about cars—engines, headlights, and prices. I pretend to pay attention, but I can't tell one car from another and have only just learned what a tailfin is. If they ever get around to tailfins or the Boston Red Sox and the despised why-do-they-have-to-win-everything New York Yankees, I'll say something.

In the middle of Newbury Street, while talking about the pits in chrome fenders, Gordie reaches for my hand. It's not as if he's going to lift my hand with its short fingernails to his lips and kiss it, after all this is Springfield, not Paree. But still I don't like it. No rescue by Linda Sullivan on her grandmother's upstairs porch tonight.

Since we left the drugstore, Gordie has been inching closer to me. Although Gordie will be seventeen on July 14th, Bastille Day, he seems more like twenty. He asks me in a half-joking way if I will be getting him a birthday present. He tightens his grip on my hand, and I can tell he expects something besides a birthday present from me. Up ahead of us is the entrance to Van Horn Park. It's not quite dark, but the streetlights have come on. The four of us stop at the street corner.

"Let's go for a walk in the park," Richie says, and Kathy reaches for his outstretched hand. Is she in love with Richie? I wonder. There is a warning bell in my head clanging, Don't go in the park. Richie puts his arm around Kathy's shoulder and they snuggle against each other. I imagine us as the cover of a romance comic, the one with the red heart in the corner and the blonde crying six-inch tears, Have I lost him forever? Kathy is looking at me and blinking her eyes the way cheerleaders are trained to do. She wants me to say yes—I will ruin it for everyone if I say no. Then a voice inside my head says, "You don't have a mother anymore to take care of you, Carole. You have to take care of yourself."

"I told my father I'd be home early tonight. I can't go," I lie, and Gordie drops my hand. On the way home, Kathy and I are quiet. Finally, she asks me, "Your father's not even home tonight, is he?" Then she sighs and says, "You act like you're thirteen."

After that night, we go to Dave's one more time and Gordie and Richie are not there. A few nights later, Richie calls Kathy and tells her Gordie's going out with someone seventeen, a bleached blonde. I feel relieved, as if I've stepped out of a spotlight. The next day, Kathy goes to Lake Wickabogue with her aunt for a week, and she never calls me again.

12. My Mother's Closet

"OUCH!" I YELL, as the backs of my legs touch the sun-scorched stone wall in front of Cal's Variety Store. Watching me from his carriage, Tommy's eyes fill with fear, then tears. Quickly, I hand him pieces from my Mounds to distract him. When he crams the dark chocolate in his baby mouth, his tears miraculously stop. The candy, dribbling down his chin, works its tranquilizing sugar magic, lulling Tommy into staying in his carriage instead of trying to climb over the side on this endless afternoon. I am on a mission to Cal's and have bought Hostess cupcakes for Michael, Superman comic books for Gerry, and red licorice for Danny with money they scraped together or borrowed from one another. Now, to pass the time, I'm flipping through Gerry's Superman comic book when the sky suddenly changes from gray to charcoal and the temperature drops.

"Tommy," I say, bending down, "I'm playing a new game, it's called run as fast you can, and all you have to do is to hold on to this bar. If you keep your hands right here all the way home, you win. Ready set, and what is it you say?"

"Go, Cawol, go." He's a little shaky on his *r* sounds, so I chuckle when he says Cawol. Trying to beat the rain, we run down Liberty, swerving by the rocks and holes on the side of the road. "Go, go, go faster," Tommy chants, thrilled with my beat-the-rain game. Mother Nature pelts us with gumdrop-sized raindrops that bounce back up off the corner mailbox. With no breath left and a pain throbbing in my side, I turn the corner onto Lynwood Terrace and see three cars parked in front of our house, my aunts' cars. Odd, for a Tuesday afternoon in the middle of July. What's going on now? I wonder, brushing the smeared chocolate off Tommy's little face, a face so like a Gerber baby. What now? I hold my breath.

"Your aunts want you in the bedroom," Mrs. Meade says, as she sponges down the kitchen table. Her eyes, newly red from crying, alarm me. "Look at the chocolate all over that sweet baby face. I'm gonna get you, Tommy. I'm gonna get that baby boy," she says when Tommy scurries away on his chubby legs from her aproned front. When he scoots away, I'm secretly pleased. Mrs. Meade is not our mother. She's just not.

In my parents' bedroom, my mother's clothes are spread out on the bed in orderly piles. Caught off guard by the neatly folded clothes and the half empty closet, I hide my surprise at seeing my aunt Lee sitting on the floor in front of the closet and handing my mother's wedge-soled shoes, high heels, and slippers to my aunt Stella. With her free hand, Stella, my godmother, pats me on the shoulder. Of all my aunts, she is most tolerant of my tomboy ways, ways I've pretty much given up. The clunky wedges ، remind me how I hated being seen with my mother when she wore those thick-soled beige shoes. Shoes for a nurse, but not my mother, I'd tell her. Feeling a creeping shame for my bratty remark, I look down and notice Stella is wearing identical wedged shoes but in a thunder-cloud gray color. Since Aunt Stella pretty much makes all her own clothes out of a coarse gray or beige fabric, and hems her dresses so that they cover her kneecaps in a prim way, I expect her to be wearing the wedges. Her warm brown hair is tightly curled, always the same, and I have never once seen her without her thick glasses. Her eyes, a dull brown, match her hair as if she has custom-ordered them. Yet in spite of her pilgrim look, Stella has a rich deep laugh that can raise the temperature in a room. But she has two strikes against her, she is Polish and from Maine—not Irish, and not from the neighborhood. She loves to tell us how in grade school her classmates tormented her by taunting, "Stella Gondela from down in the cella."

Aunt Madeline, my father's sister, studies me as my eyes again dart back and forth between the bed and the closet. She may be remembering when my mother bought these clothes because every Thursday night Aunt Mad and my mother had an early supper at Steiger's tea room and then shopped until the department stores closed. Without my mother, I wonder if she still shops on Thursday nights. Because I have dark eyes and hair like my father and my aunt, sometimes people think I'm Mad's daughter.

"Your father asked us to clean out your mother's things," Aunt Madeline says in a calm voice. My father—did he forget to tell me that my aunts were coming over this afternoon like a well-trained demolition squad to dismantle my mother's closet? Appraising me silently, my aunt asks in a clipped voice, "Did your father tell you we were coming?" The piles of clothes, pieces of my mother, are making me feel a tightness everywhere, a terror I must hide, a need, deep in myself, to just keep watch.

"Maybe he forgot," I start to explain and dig my cold hands into the pockets of my Bermuda shorts, pressing my fists along my hip bones.

"I guess he didn't get around to it," Mad says, a look of disappointment shadowing her face. "But he wanted us to ask you if there's anything here you want. Of course, your brothers wouldn't be interested," she adds, pointing to a stack of my mother's church and party dresses. Before the cancer made my mother so skinny, she wore a size 16 dress. She was busty like a movie star, and when she wore a fitted linen sheath dress to Sunday Mass, I could see my friends' fathers look at her. I think she knew it. And liked it.

"No, Auntie Mad, I don't want any of her clothes," I answer when my aunt runs her hand along the blue beaded dress my mother wore to the Federal Hill Club on New Year's Eve.

"We realize the clothes are too big for you," Mad says with a hint of defeat. I hold off on saying my friends aren't wearing sheath dresses, how they're not a big fashion look in the eighth grade.

"Carole, we wanted to wait until you got home from the store, but I have to be at work early tonight," Lee blurts out. Her toes, painted a brownish-red, stick through her white slit sandals and a stripe of lipstick borders the bottoms of her big teeth. Lee has a big way of talking, gesturing, and doing a lot of teeth-clicking with the new tut-tut sound of sympathy that she showers on me.

I'm relieved that Mrs. Meade is back out in the kitchen ironing and humming to herself, and not in here with us.

"Most of Betty's things will fit me," Lee says, holding up the deep-blue beaded dress. True, Madeline and Stella are small-boned, tiny, but, please, Aunt Lee, don't ever let me see you wearing my mother's clothes. My aunts Madeline and Stella trade looks as Madeline reaches for my mother's white fake-leather jewelry box.

"Carole, we're going to put aside some of your mother's jewelry that I know she would want you to have," Madeline says in a firm, yet soft voice. So she doesn't really know my mother wants me to have the coral necklace and the fake pearls? Maybe she's really saying, "Carole, we don't want your aunt Lee to get her hands on the jewelry. She can have the clothes, but there are limits." I sense greed, acquisition, material goods in Lee's wide eyes and her open glossed mouth. I try to remember if greed is one of the seven deadly sins, and then it hits me. I don't care. Let Lee have it all. Lee dresses trendy, hip, she cares and I don't. I want what I can't have—flawless skin, an in-ground swimming pool—but I don't want my mother's blue/black plaid Bermuda shorts that she wore to Matty Ryan's election party.

Madeline says, "Carole, you're young now, but someday you will feel differently." Young? What is so wrong with being young? Am I some kind of mistake because I'm thirteen?

"We'll put things aside for you. You don't need to stay. Only if you'd like," Madeline says, finally offering me a chance to escape. Before I can climb over my aunt's legs, Lee holds up my mother's mink stole.

"What about Betty's stole? She loved wearing this animal." Lee's right. My mother loved the mink stole with its beady black eyes, looked glamorous in it. During Sunday Mass I'd play with the clip on the mink's mouth, opening and closing it, over and over again, as if it were a puppet. My mother never yelled at me, never told me I would break it. Lee has appealed to Madeline, clearly the boss, to decide on the fur.

"We'll put this in the front coat closet until Carole's older," Madeline rules. I picture me on Halloween, red-lipstick mouth and my mother's mink draped around my shoulders, fueling my brothers' need to ridicule me and my Hollywood getup. Then I imagine my mother's face in a corner of the ceiling silently watching us as we divide her clothing. Her mouth opens and there is a voice like a banshee wailing of death suddenly surrounding me. The voice orders me, *Leave, Carole. Get away from this bedroom, get out of this house now.*

As if she could hear it, Madeline says with a squeeze of my hand, "You may go, Carole." Free, at last, I bolt out the back door, picking up speed, and hop on my bike. My ankle hits the chain guard and a trickle of blood drips down to my sneaker. Pedaling madly up Liberty, I realize I don't know what to do or where to go. If Kathy and I were still friends, if she weren't away with her family . . . ? Why did I even have to be there in my parents' bedroom? With all those clothes? With my mother's disappearing on me without a trace? I look down and see the blood spotting my sneaker, and my eyes are hot with tears. *Pedal. Pedal. Pedal.*

SAINT MICHAEL'S CEMETERY

SETTING: State Street, Springfield, Massachusetts. Saint George's Section Plot 583. A sunny, but cold morning in March 2006.

(*Carole parks her silver convertible under a tree and sits in the car, her hands on the steering wheel. Inhaling audibly, she reaches for her gloves, slips them on, and hesitates.*)

CAROLE: Come on, you can do this. You can do this. (*Carole places her gloved hands against her temples and lowers her head on them for a minute. Sighing, she opens the door and walks over to a white stick planted a third of the way into the section. She reads the rough-drawn number 605. Carole begins searching for her mother's gravestone, a marble rectangle planted in the grass, but the Massachusetts winter has been hard and maintenance has been poor, making the gravestones barely visible. Kicking the overgrown brown grass aside, she reads the letters and moves down the row to the next marker. Five minutes later,* she has cleared half a dozen graves well enough to read the inscriptions and hasn't yet found her mother's grave. She heads toward the car, stands still, and turns back. In a frenzy, she gets down on her knees and pushes the weeds back on three more graves until she finds her mother's grave.) OK, OK, now what? (Beat.) (Carole kneels at her mother's grave, bends down, and rips the dirt and grass away with her hands.) I'm sorry, Mom. Maybe, I'll call the office and see if I can pay a special fee for maintenance. (Hurt.) I wish you had an angel monument. You deserve more than this 10 by 13 marble rectangle. (Carole examines her knees where the wet earth is seeping through her panty hose.)

I know I've rambled on to you here before. But today the cemetery is completely empty. There's no one here, not even a grounds attendant. So I can yell if I want. Cry even. (Carole rubs away the dirt on the inscription.) I'm probably going to go all over the place today. I feel cheated, Mom. Cheated that I never got to be a daughter. Even before you died, I was your helper. I sound like I'm back at twelve years old again and whining, lashing out at you. (Childishly.) "Why don't you ask Michael or Danny to push the baby in the stroller?" I could have walked cross-country with all that baby carriage duty . . . (Jokingly.) Finally I'd get to Disneyland. I was a kid, and a bratty kid—the nuns would have called me disrespectful—and at thirteen I was way more interested in hanging out with my friends in the neighborhood than taking one of my little brothers out for a joy ride. Vicky, my youngest daughter, went on a language trip to Costa Rica and stayed with a family with six children. When the mother would ask her oldest son to help her with some task, he would always whine, ¿Por que yo? (She laughs.) God, I could have been that boy. When Vicky—I forgot, she's Victoria now—told me, I held myself back from getting a T-shirt printed up with ¿Por que yo? on it. (Carole stares at the lone cypress tree hiding the mid-morning sun. Leaning back on her heels, she buttons her shearling coat and pulls the hood up over her head.) (Revealing herself.) You see, Mom, I was always a mother, never a daughter. I was a caretaker, a caregiver, but not a care getter. When I think of you with eight kids, I feel ashamed and I tell myself I have no right to complain. No right at all, but there's another tiny voice in me whispering it's OK. Get it out there. (There is a long pause. Carole's shoulders are shaking, and she pulls her arms tight around herself.)

When you died, I thought I'd have Dad all to myself. (*Jokingly.*) I kind of liked that idea. He was the generous parent, never yelled at us. Looking back, I think that Dad, a master of manipulation, might have set you up that way so he could always be the good guy. (*Suddenly aware.*) David does that—he's Santa Claus and I'm Moses, laying down the commandments.

I'm grateful to you, Mom, because I do know that you did very well in school. Aunt Anne told me that you asked a wealthy relative—I didn't even know we had one—for money to go to college. And the relative turned you down. I have trouble asking for anything. Although you never said so, I sensed you regretted not going to college. Was it this unspoken message that made me decide to go to college? To put myself through college? I wanted to do what you would have liked to have done. Maybe I was just mind reading again. She told me that you loaned your brother money to buy their engagement ring. I floated a few loans to my brothers, too. My brothers—your sons. (*Checking her watch, Carole turns to go, puts her hand on the white marker, and squeezes the post, but returns to the grave.*)

When that witch Sister Mary Matthias called me a tramp back in sixth grade, you picked up the phone and called the convent. (*Grateful.*) She was still a witch and still hated me, but I am so glad you called. (*Realizing.*) Dad never would have tried to protect me from a nun. He told me to stick it out. I heard that Sister only lasted another year. (*Beat.*) What would it have been like for us to be adults together? I would have loved to take you to lunch at Joe Allen's and see a matinee, a straight play we could later discuss. (*She stammers.*) Loss sneaks up on me, Mom. Sometimes I'll see a mother and daughter having lunch, or walking down the street, and I'll wish I could have had that moment. Yesterday, Abby and I made a plan to meet for lunch this Saturday, and I cried when I hung up the phone. I'm flying to Chicago for Susie's midterm break, invited for mother-daughter time. I am sad at how cheated I was by your loss, never knowing your opinions on anything. Child rearing, political candidates, laundry detergent, a book, what you thought about the play. Sometimes I'd find myself in the aisles of a drugstore looking for Pacquins, your hand cream, or your red Maybelline eyebrow pencil. Just to have a piece of you, to make a connection. (*Triumphantly.*) Oh, I did buy a set of your colored Pyrex bowls at an antique store on Second Avenue. The bowls cost fifty dollars but, to me, they're a treasure. I found another set in Sag Harbor, and I bought them too. I've stopped buying them though. And I have the Webster's dictionary we had growing up. The cover's falling off, but I cling to it. (*Beat.*)

Do you get news flashes in heaven? A deep voice announcing, "Betty O'Malley, your daughter, Carole, has outgrown her defiance, but she's having a hard time letting go of her sarcasm. News flash—Carole graduated from college and returned to 21 Lynwood Terrace to live. Still taking care of those brothers." For my birthday last summer, Bobby gave me a CD of songs we blared in my Volkswagen on day trips to Misquamicut Beach. The CD's in the same league as the Pyrex bowls. News flash—Taught school. Went to work in computers for Travelers Insurance, your old employer. (*With sudden awareness.*) Mom, I never made that connection before. She married David Gaunt. Not only is he not Irish, he's one of the few WASPs left. But wasn't your mother a Tyler? From northern Ireland? (*Beat.*)

I would have loved to have you meet my husband, to be there at my wedding. By the time I got married at twenty-five, just like you, I was used to doing everything by myself. So I planned and paid for the wedding, half-convincing myself that this was normal. Your absence was like a gaping hole with everyone tiptoeing around it. (*Beat.*)

Those Hallmark card moments are so hard—that's when the sense of isolation kicks in. Hard as I tried to reel myself in, I way overdid it with my daughters on those milestone markers. It was as if I couldn't do enough—some need in me to what? To balance things out, to level those scales. (*Beat.*) No one remembers anything about that first Christmas without you. Pain kills memory. I am guessing that our aunts and uncles and your friends stepped in to rally around Dad. I suspect it was a little over the top. You know Dad.

When Abby was in college, a friend was in her dorm room reading the ad we had placed in Abby's high school yearbook. The friend turned to Abby and said, "My mother doesn't know me that well." I cry for that girl. I am that girl, too. Oh, this is so hard. Why am I doing this? I don't feel better. (*Carole begins to cry. She wipes her face and looks up at the sun.*)

While I was glad that I was able to nurture and encourage my daughters, Abby, Susan, and Victoria, the granddaughters you never

knew, I would feel these unexpected waves of resentment toward them
for what I had missed growing up. How I longed for a word of encouragement. I didn't want to hit the kids with a guilt trip from my history. I
would pray, Please, God, let me live for them. (*Beat.*)

(*She pulls up the hood of her shearling coat and buttons it.*) Before I
leave, I want to report back that I am the good girl and I did what you
asked of me. I took care of your baby—Tommy worked for David for
almost thirty years. And he was the first one of my brothers to stop
drinking. Could I have been a role model for him? When I stopped
drinking, my brothers collectively rolled their eyes at me. I apologize
to you and to me, that brave little soldier, for stuffing all that grief and
pretending that your death didn't matter. We lost so much. I lost so
much. (*Sweeping away pieces of grass, Carole stares down at the marble
gravestone. As she cries, her guttural, gasping sounds disturb the somber
quiet of the graveyard.*)

13. The Boys' Bathing Suits Are Missing

"NATURALLY, YOU WOULD remember to pack your bathing suit for
a beach vacation and forget ours," Danny says, his voice all godlike judgment.

"I packed underwear, shorts, jerseys, towels, and toothbrushes," I say
lamely.

"Just admit it. You forgot the bathing suits," Danny taunts me, waiting
for my answer. His accusation gets to me. As if I have forgotten intentionally. As if I planned to forget their bathing suits. As if I even knew where
Mrs. Meade had packed them away.

"OK, I forgot." I count the five mostly matched chairs in the kitchen
and even with Tommy's high chair, there are still not enough seats for us
all. We mostly eat in shifts anyway, the little kids first, followed by the big
kids. But, here at the beach, everything has a walking in and out feel to it.
And our meals are like that.

The open army trunk sits open on the kitchen floor, its contents heaped
on the kitchen chairs. No boys' bathing suits, making me, the packer, the

family joke. I know this failing will be carved in stone in the family memory, another beach story, when Gerry walks in with Stevie following him.

"Carole forgot to pack our bathing suits." Danny can barely wait to announce my mistake and folds his arms across his chest. Gerry looks at me, scans the tabletop, and reaches over to pick up a toothbrush.

"Toothbrushes, that's great. And you remembered the toothpaste, too, I suppose. Here I am at the beach and I can't swim, Carole, but I can brush my teeth. I'll really enjoy that," Gerry says, zinging me. I laugh and feel relieved. "Why would anyone prefer swimming on a hot August day when he could brush his teeth, I ask you. Carole, I think you and Dr. Dougherty are in cahoots." Dr. Wilson Dougherty, with an office on Main Street and old copies of *Jack and Jill* magazine in the waiting room, is the family dentist.

The kitchen feels crowded before my father walks in carrying Tommy, whose hair is flat and sweat-soaked from his nap in the station wagon. I am putting the shorts into piles by size while Danny, Gerry, and Steve all talk at once, trying to beat one another out on telling my father about the bathing suit crisis. Kissing Tommy's flushed cheek, my dad says he'll give me money to buy new bathing suits in Niantic and we'll pick up the groceries there before Aunt Mad and Uncle Bill arrive.

I can tell by Danny's sneer that he's disappointed at my reprieve. Knowing Danny, he probably pictured me tied to a stake with flames dancing around my feet as my brothers circled me in a tribal war dance. Gerry says he's going to the beach anyway and just don't get him a white bathing suit.

"You're not going to yell at her? Dad, she remembered her bathing suit." I feel a tightening at the back of my neck.

"Dan, you're going to get a new bathing suit out of it. Hop in the car, if you're coming. Where are Tommy's diapers?" my father asks me. At least I packed the diapers.

Niantic has two stores that sell bathing suits. My father hands me four twenties and drops Dan and me off. Behind a display of sand pail and shovel sets and inflatable tubes, the boys' bathing suits are lined up on display racks against the wall. I am checking for sizes and matching a suit with each brother when Danny announces, "Look at these bathing suits— I'm not buying one of these. I'm going to the other store." Danny has style, one more thing he's vain about.

"Dad said he'd meet us back here in ten minutes."

"I'll be back. Anyway, you can wait for me. I have money." Danny always has money. My father hangs his pants with his wallet inside the back pocket on the corner of his closet door, and each of us has caught the other lifting change from that pocket. I watch Danny walk out the swinging door, and I gather a pile of six boys' Jantzen bathing suits in sizes 4, 6, 8, 10, 12, and 16, skipping 14 since Danny's gone in search of coolness. My mother taught me to size things for my brothers by adding two to the age. It doesn't always work for odd numbers, but I round off. The Jantzen suits might cost a dollar more in Niantic, but I recognize the brand name from when my mother would come home from Saturday shopping and announce how she bought the Jantzens on sale in Forbes's basement. The clerk looks at me strangely when I hand her the matching red plaid bathing suits.

"There are no returns on these suits. You can't bring back any of these," she says in a stern voice. I nod my head. When she hands me the bag, she makes a clucking sound with her tongue. I look out the streaked glass window and see my father and Danny outside the door.

"Mission accomplished?" my dad asks me.

"Six bathing suits," I report. "None of them up to Danny's standards though." I want my father to reprimand him, at least to ask him how much his bathing suit cost.

"He takes after me, I guess," my father says instead. "Let's go get the groceries."

Inside the car, Danny sits up front, but even from the back seat I can see in the brown bags the beer bottles and whiskey bottles my father just bought at the package store. I can smell the whiskey on his breath, too, and wonder where he stopped. Since my mother died, I gauge my father's drinking by whether he talks or not. If he's had just one or two drinks, like now, he can be fun; his cheeks get red, he talks. But any more than that and he can cross over into one of his teary, "Remember this about your mother" moods. I hate those moods.

My aunt and uncle's car was already in the driveway when we got back to the cottage. I felt sorry for my cousins Billy and Joan because they don't have a three-seater Ford station wagon like ours and there are only two of them. Like my cousin Jimmy, Billy and Joan are adopted, which meant, according to my mom and dad, that they were specially chosen. I thought to myself that with eight kids I was not specially chosen, and neither my mom nor dad jumped in to tell me how special I was. I knew the answer to the question why my aunt and uncle and my cousins were even here. The answer: Because my mother died. Since my mother died of cancer, a word we still don't say, I sometimes need to remind myself silently that she is dead. I wonder if my brothers are pretending to themselves that she's downtown shopping at Forbes and Wallace, or up the street getting her hair done, and will be walking up the driveway soon, the way I keep doing.

My dad, Danny, and I are carrying bags of groceries up the grassy slope leading up the back stairs.

"Come on, boys, let's get out here and help," my dad yells into the house. Aunt Madeline waves and takes a bag of groceries from Danny, who begins running to the front of the house. Before I can even point out his escape route, my dad calls after him, "Danny, get back out here and help with these groceries." No sign of Danny, who's probably halfway down Beach Road, but Michael comes out, squinting at the sun.

"Did you remember to get the bathing suits in Niantic?" Michael asks me, shoving his way by me to the car, frowning so that his eyebrows meet in the middle.

"Yes." I spit back. "That's why I went—to buy bathing suits."

"You took long enough." Michael can find a problem with anything. "You're just stupid, forgetting the bathing suits like that," he grumbles.

"I didn't do it on purpose," I explain, defending myself.

When Michael turned sixteen on July 28th, he got his driver's license the next day, and he's been driving for three weeks now. I'm so jealous I can practically taste it. Back in Springfield in the mornings now, Michael drives down to Pearl Street to pick up Mrs. Meade while my dad is getting dressed and we're eating toast and cereal. When you're in a car with Mrs. Meade, she talks all the time without even pausing for a breath so I just tune her out. At least Michael is not driving down here in Connecticut. When I told my dad that in 735 days I would be turning sixteen and be eligible for my very own license, he chuckled and told me not to plan so far ahead because a lot could happen in two years. Things could change. Meaning? Meaning what? What did my dad mean by "a lot could happen"? My hands grew cold and I no longer felt safe, terrified by the prospect of change. The hairs on my forearms stood up straight.

It doesn't rain so much on this vacation, and it feels more like a vacation because my dad is here with us. First thing in the morning, we go to the beach. I push Tommy in his carriage, and we stay there until lunchtime, a baloney sandwich with mustard, and back to the beach. My dad likes to stay at the beach until the sun is almost setting. He always goes into the water with the little kids and swims out to the raft with Michael, Danny, and me. This year, he hasn't been to the raft yet. Maybe for Danny's and my birthdays next week. I wish there were more talking though. With no stereo in the cottage and no Frank Sinatra, there are lots of silences. No mom, either. Uncle Bill is a great talker, usually about World War II, when he saw action in Africa with Patton, and the horse races he and my dad hit on Fridays, but even he is quiet. At night, I see my dad sneak out to the cottage's back porch alone, and wonder if he's crying where none of us can see him. He could be watching fireflies, or counting the stars, or listening to the crickets, but he always has his whiskey glass in his hand. Because my dad was a spy during the war, I come by spying naturally.

The Friday before we leave, I'm standing in the line at the Good Humor truck with Tommy, Bobby and Stevie. White lines of skin peek out at the waists of their bathing suits, their round chests brown from the sun. "I want the toasted almond today. I don't want the popsicle again," Steve orders. He has expensive tastes.

"Not me. I want the space bar," Bobby pipes up. The freckle-faced boy in front of us has a ten-dollar bill in one hand and a Coca-Cola in the other. Rich, I think. My dad gave me just enough money for popsicles. Toasted almonds and space bars are for rich kids.

"We're getting popsicles. Popsicles or nothing." Because I'm too embarrassed to say Dad didn't give me enough money for toasted almonds, I end up sounding mean. Steve's eyes fill with tears. He's an easy crier, I want to tell the Coca-Cola boy, who now has turned around to look at us. I imagine the ten-dollar bill pasted on this boy's forehead. Patting Steve on the top of his head, the neat bristles of his haircut tickling my palm, I calculate in my head just how many toasted almonds ten dollars would buy.

"I never get what I want," Stevie sputters. Bobby has found a dead crab and is digging a hole for a burial.

"Carole, will the crab be in heaven with Mom?" Bobby asks. This is worse than the money. Mr. Freckle-face, ten-dollar bill on forehead, now knows not only that I barely have enough money for popsicles, but also that my mom is in heaven. I look at the two girls at the front of the line, who decide they must get the same ice cream and can't decide between the chocolate éclair and the strawberry shortcake. Here I am eight years of Catholic school, and I don't know the answer to crab heaven. "There's a special heaven for crabs," I say, pleased with the sound of the words "crab heaven."

"You're a crab. You'll go to crab heaven," Steve says and drags his foot through the sand.

Handing me the popsicles, the Good Humor man pushes his uniform hat back off his forehead. Michael has his driver's license—couldn't he be a Good Humor man and give us ice cream, toasted almonds, and chocolate éclairs? But then it hits me that Michael has to pick up Mrs. Meade in the mornings, the white uniform wouldn't fit him, he's grumpy anyway, and he wouldn't give me any ice cream.

"Don't run," I yell after Bob and Stevie, who are kicking up a cloud of sand as they run back to our army blanket. Tommy's crying because of the hot sand on his soft baby feet, so I pick him up, jostle him in the process, and watch his popsicle float through the air past me.

"Pop, pop," Tommy says, pointing to the sand-coated popsicle, not knowing that once a popsicle hits the beach, it's dead. I shove my popsicle at him, trying to stem his crying fit when a bee in search of a snack circles us, picking up on our orange-sugar scents. Dodging the bee, with Tommy clinging to me I zigzag on the hot sand toward the water, where I spot Michael climbing up the ladder to the raft and my father and Danny treading water. It's our last day here, and they didn't even wait for me. No popsicle, no raft, no toasted almond. I'm ready to go home.

14. An Evening of Informal Modeling

ALTHOUGH IT HAS been three months since my mother died, the house still has a peculiar, empty feel to it. After dinner, the Tuesday night after Labor Day, my dad reads aloud from a front page article in the *Springfield Daily News* that Cathedral High School is going upscale. The downtown site on Elliot Street, overcrowded, ancient, and funereal, has been tossed aside for a brand-new building in Holy Cross parish. It was good enough for him, he sighs, but not good enough for his daughter and sons. He's teasing me, I know, but all I can think of saying is, "Dad," stretching it out as if it were a sentence. Yes, mine will be the first class to spend four years in its chemistry labs, eat a hot lunch from its mechanized cafeteria (no more brown bag lunches), and study in its sacred, carpeted library. The jewel of the diocese, Bishop Weldon calls it. "No wonder you and Michael have those snazzy new uniforms," my dad says, looking up from the paper. The snazzy uniform, the new fashion look for Cathedral High School boys, consists of gray wool blazers with the school crest on the pocket, white shirts, ties, and gray pants. My deep secret is that, with the exception of the brown and white saddle shoes that have a 1920s rah-rah Model T Ford look, I love the girls' uniform. The deep green blazer with a crest identical to the boys' emblem fits me loosely enough so I don't have to worry about my breasts as a center of attraction. I always buy a size 32 bra because I'm just too embarrassed to buy anything bigger. I have no idea whether the bra fits, but I know I would never have asked my mother anyway. I'm very private about my body. Very private. The blouse is white with three-quarter roll-up sleeves, buttoned to the neck, and the pleated skirt is a green, white, and navy plaid. A choice of socks—white crew or green knee length for winter.

"Dad, I'm going to model my uniform for you."

"Now, Princess, don't get carried away." I run upstairs, two at a time, pull out the blazer, and hunt for the saddle shoes on my closet floor. With the blazer on and carrying the saddle shoes behind my back, I enter the living room with my Forbes and Wallace fashion show walk. My dad is at the stereo with his back to me. I hear the click of the record changer, and then Frank Sinatra is singing "One for my baby, and one more for the road." Although my father hates Elvis, strangely enough I like Frank Sinatra. There's a friendliness, a me-too quality about his songs so I can easily imagine Frank Sinatra knowing our family—my dad, anyway.

"Before I give you my proper attention, let me get a drink," my dad says and walks out to the kitchen. I drop into the armchair while he is slamming the ice cube tray against the sink, another piece of his nightly routine. The habit and the predictability of this nightly ritual put me on guard. From reading the newspaper or *Time* magazine, my dad moves on to the stereo, usually Frank, maybe Dean Martin, and pours himself a glass of whiskey. If he's still on his first glass, he'll be interested in hearing me talk about my uniform, might even ask me a question or two. But if he's had a few drinks, if he's stopped off somewhere on his way home from work, I can tell he's just marking time for me to finish, to quiet down, so he can be alone with the whiskey.

"I think socks would help," my dad says.

"I wasn't planning on putting the shoes on, but you were in the kitchen."

"Rising to the challenge of prying ice cubes from their tray. Those ice cubes are a lot like your brother Joey, stubborn little devils."

"We get green knee socks for the winter. No one wears brown and white saddle shoes anymore. They are so old-fashioned."

"Your mother wore saddle shoes with ankle socks. But she stopped wearing them before we got married." So my dad has just talked about my mom in a clear, strong voice as if he could mention her without tears. I let out a breath. The silence follows whenever my mom is mentioned, like a leftover reaction from Sampson's Funeral Parlor.

"Your brother's struggling with high school, but you'll probably just sail through it," he says, a hint of disappointment in his voice. He sips his whiskey, looks at me, and I sing a line from "Anchors Aweigh."

"No singing, Carole. There's only so much a man can take." From my father's tone, I can't tell why sailing through high school is a disappointment. Does he want me to struggle? I sailed through fifth grade and fractions and sentence diagramming. On the last day of class, Sister Mary Ephraim said that she had decided to give awards to the best students in the class. First she called Kathleen Cullinane, established teacher's pet since first grade, so no surprise; then Diane Scagliarini, skinny, pale, yet by fourth grade writing poems that rhymed, usually about birds, trees, rain, and flowers (nature does not thrill me); and finally Sister called my name, Carole O'Malley. I was holding my breath, wanting it, but afraid to hope. When I went to her desk, she handed me a plastic holy card of Saint Catherine of Siena in a green gown and white headpiece, holding a lily in her hands with Saint Catherine's favorite prayer on the other side. According to Sister Mary Ephraim, Saint Catherine of Siena abandoned her rich Italian family for the church, rejected all things secular, and became an adviser to the popes. God must have been doing some mind reading that Friday, knowing I am way more secular than spiritual, because I lost my holy Saint Catherine of Siena card right around Langdon Street on my way home. When I was retracing my steps back toward school, I ran into Michael and Danny at the corner of Carew and Liberty. Michael said Sister had never given me a prize and I was just looking for a way to show off, and Danny sneered that he wouldn't walk ten feet for a holy card, certainly not Saint Catherine of Siena, although he might for Saint George, the slayer of dragons. Still, I wanted the card to show to my mother and father, but I never found it. So every now and then, my father and my brothers started calling me Saint Catherine of Siena, and I would hear my mother laughing softly in the background.

With my uniform modeling over, I am draping the blazer over my arm when Stevie runs in crying, sobbing, "Joey hit me, Daddy." My father says, "Come here, little guy." He hugs Stevie, whose crying is drowning out Frank Sinatra's loneliness, and asks me to get Joey. Joey, the hitter. Now Joey is six years and four months younger than I am, and even on his tiptoes and craning his neck, he doesn't reach my shoulder, so physically I should not be afraid of him, but I am, which makes no sense. Technically Joey, as a second grader, should not be hanging around with the eighth-grade class troublemakers, like Francis Harrington and James Harnois, yet he does. Joey has a temper and is a kicker and hitter and not afraid of any nun, even Sister Superior. I stand in the doorway of the television room and yell in to Joey, who's all scrunched up in the end of the sofa, that Dad wants to see him in the living room. Wants to see him now.

"What for?" he asks with anger in his eyes and sits up.

"Stevie says you hit him," I answer as I start to back away.

"He's such a baby. I hardly touched him," Joey says, contempt lacing his voice. He shoves his shoulder into my stomach as he passes me. "Not my fault if you're standing in my way." Steve is standing in front of the bathroom sink brushing his tiny baby teeth. I wonder if it makes a difference if you're good about brushing your baby teeth since they fall out anyway. I block the doorway in case Joey decides to go in and give him another belt, although Joey could squirm around me if he wanted to. With the palm of my hand, I mess up Steve's hair as he runs by me on his way upstairs to bed. Hard to give that good night kiss if we're always running.

---

15. The Jewel of the Diocese

HOMEROOM IS ALPHABETICAL, O through P. John Ouellette sits behind me and Noreen O'Connor front of me, two new names. The homeroom nun, Sister Peter Maria, has mixed boys and girls together, so unlike grammar school where the girls sat on one side and the boys on the other. As I study my class schedule and compare it to the school map, Sister takes attendance and tells us to raise our hands and say, "Present." If the program is right, Sister Maurice Joseph has transferred from Our Lady of Hope, I'm hoping without her steel ruler, and I have her for fourth-period English and cafeteria.

"Class, please put away your class schedules and any bus forms or cafeteria forms you've yet to complete. I'd like your full attention," Sister orders in a clipped voice. All eyes on her, Sister lectures us for five minutes on how fortunate we are to be in this new school.

"Desks without a scratch, chairs without a nick," she says without a smile.

When the bell rings to end her speech, she dismisses us with an imperial wave of her hand to the hall. The good thing about a brand new school, besides the desks without scratches, is no one has any idea where he or she is going. The seniors are as lost as the lowly ninth graders. Nuns with serious expressions stand guard duty in the halls, their arms folded across their white starched fronts. Occasionally, a nun steps into the throngs of milling students to direct foot traffic or hurry them along. Miraculously, I inch my way through the mobbed corridors to room 223, my ancient history class. Sliding into a chair without a nick, I slump with relief because I realize that not only is Latin I held in this same classroom, also taught by Sister Agnes Veronica, but my English class is right next door. With nuns loving Roman numerals the way they do, I developed my own O'Malley family system for them back in sixth grade: M, D, C: Michael = 1000, Danny = 500, and Carole = 100. As Danny delighted in pointing out to me, I am the lowest quantity, and it's out of birth order, but it still works. Standing behind her desk like a drill sergeant surveying the troops, Sister Agnes Veronica nods to her ninth-grade students as they enter the classroom. With only a seat or two still empty, she rearranges us into alphabetical seating so that she can learn our names, a goal for me as well. By the end of the 42-minute class, Sister has the boys' names down and has bored us with the governments of early civilizations. Worse yet, she's assigned a chapter of reading for tonight's homework.

Crammed in the back of the school bus on the way home, I finally see Anne Sullivan and Dianne Thinel as they board and plow on back toward me. Never have I been happier to run into my old classmates from Our Lady of Hope Grammar School—Diane Scagliarini, even—than I was that first day in the newly painted halls of Cathedral High School.

November blows in, the trees now gray and bare and the threat of winter at hand. The end of the Saturday afternoon football games at Blunt Park also marks the official end of the first marking period. With seven brothers, I understand, more or less, the importance of a first down in football, but I am just like all the other girls in the bleachers who check out one another's pleated skirts and try to get a boy to say hi. I'd settle for a wave. From the stands, I watch the team of cheerleaders leap in the air and am riddled by the sin of envy, knowing that my life would be complete if I could ever be a Cathedral High School cheerleader. I would be first in line at the April tryouts. Yet if, according to my dad, sailing through high school means making the first or second honor roll, then my boat has not left the dock. There is to be no Saint Catherine of Siena holy card for me at Cathedral this first marking period. I missed the honor roll by two points.

*   *   *

"Dad, did you ever read *Great Expectations?*" I ask one night at dinner. He asks me to refresh his memory but, before I even get to the heartless Miss Havisham, he's telling Joey and Gerry that if they don't finish their pork chops they can't have any more Mott's apple sauce. I prefer the apple sauce over the pork chops myself, think it's a fancy touch. More grumbling, complaining, attacking, and supper's over with, but no talk of Charles Dickens. A little before eight, I am crossing the living room carrying Tommy upstairs to his crib when my dad puts the newspaper down and says he'll put TJ to bed. TJ for Thomas James. Nicknames are just about a hobby for my dad, although TJ isn't sticking the way Little Guy has for Steve and Myers for Gerry. In the months since my mom died, Tommy seems to be my dad's favorite. I wonder what it would be like to be the baby, but I know that Tommy will never have any memories of my mother. At least, that's one of the things I overheard the rosary-slinging biddies murmuring at the funeral parlor when they weren't asking one another if she knew about the c-a-n-c-e-r.

While I'm sitting at the kitchen table trying to do my algebra homework, Michael opens the refrigerator on a reconnaissance mission.

"Michael, do you remember anything about ninth-grade algebra?" I ask, desperate. He pulls out the gallon of milk and faces me.

"I barely passed. Mom pulled me through algebra."

"Do you think Dad knows anything?" Michael has the jug halfway to his mouth, about to skip the nicety of a glass, when my dad walks in.

"The Old Man's omniscient, a word directly from the Latin, Princess." Easy—omnis scio, all-knowing.

"Algebra?" I ask with a hope in my voice. I can spell quadratic equations, but have no prayer of solving them. My dad pulls down two glasses from the cabinet and hands one to Michael.

"Not my strong suit," he confesses, reaching into the freezer for ice. He does not mention my mother the algebra whiz and pours himself a whiskey, abandoning the shot glass. "I can't tell x from y," he continues. For a minute, I am afraid he's going to pour Michael a whiskey. "Forget the math, all this x and y. I tell you what, Punkin'head, you can't find a vocabulary word I don't know." Easy, I say to myself, unless he was studying Dickens in the intelligence in India, I'll get him.

"Sister Maurice Joseph, my English teacher, expects us to know the footnoted vocabulary words at the bottom of each page of *Great Expectations*, words I have never seen or heard, and can't begin to pronounce. I'll stump you, Dad, with one of those reading, not-for-speaking, words."

"We're on," he says.

Princess, Punkin'head, and a word game, all in one night. Whiskey when it kicks in after nine-thirty makes for a good night.

16. The Dark Horse

NO. NO. NO. If I had only said "No" to Monica, the three-minute-older twin, when she called me Tuesday night and asked me to nominate her for class office, I wouldn't be sitting here in an aisle seat in the auditorium, surrounded by seven hundred classmates, dreading my thirty-second speech in front of the entire ninth grade. Secretly I felt flattered that Monica had asked me, but in bed last night, I just kept picturing myself tripping up the stairs leading to the stage, a slice of slapstick. The twins' plan is that one would be secretary and one would be treasurer. Now I feel something tugging at me but I don't know what it is.

Father Sears, the ruddy-cheeked glee club director, strides across the stage and orders us in a booming voice to all rise for the opening prayer. After his prayer for "divine guidance," Father walks to the podium and crosses his arms over his cassock.

"Boys and girls, we have assembled here in our beautiful auditorium," he pauses, gesturing to the heavy velvet stage curtains, "to begin the process of class elections. In a spirit of democracy, we will accept nominations for class office. For president and vice president, please nominate five ninth-grade boys; the top vote-getter will serve as president with the runner-up serving as vice president. For the positions of secretary and treasurer, please nominate five girls. Again, the top vote-getter will serve as class secretary, and the runner-up will fill the role of treasurer." The perspiration is soaking through to my blazer as he carries on about how we need to give this process serious thought. After the boys' nominations, I nominate Monica, spitting my two sentences out, my voice cracking only a little, without falling, without incident. When both twins are nominated, Father Sears beams; as altos, they are matching treasures in his glee club. Ever mindful of my "listener" label, I have spared myself the humiliation of glee club tryouts and am unknown to Father Sears. When he asks if there are any more nominations, only four girls have been nominated; there is a stir in the row behind me, and I see Susan Lytle approaching the stage. There is only one word for Susan Lytle: odd. She is an Air Force kid from Westover and has stick-bird legs. With her thin fingers flying and wing-arms, she flaps herself onto the auditorium stage and nominates me. Me.

"Politics are in your veins. It comes with being Irish. Who's running against you?" my father asks. We are finishing supper when I announce my news.

"The Sullivan twins, Monica and Veronica," Michael answers. "She'll never win."

My father frowns and says, "Powerful competition."

"I even nominated Monica." Guilt over a possible betrayal has seeped into my being like water into a cellulose sponge.

"Well, kiddo, you'll have a contest on your hands. The twins might split the vote, confuse people. I still can't tell Monica from Veronica," my dad confesses. "Is Michael supporting you? A show of family support?" he asks and looks at Michael who is slathering butter on his bread.

"Only freshmen can vote," Michael says between bites. Michael wouldn't vote for me even if he could.

"So what's your campaign strategy? You were working for Matty's election when you were twelve. We had you out in Winchester Square hustling campaign literature. Have you got some friends willing to work with you? Get a committee going." I remembered back two summers ago, when my father's good friend Matty Ryan, Stevie's godfather, ran for district attorney, how hard my father worked for his election. After work and on Saturday afternoons, he went to Matty's campaign office and organized volunteers, oversaw phone banks, and set up neighborhood literature distribution centers. He made me, Michael, Danny, and Gerry hand out campaign literature on street corners all over the city. "Vote for Matty Ryan," we would chant, and we would stick flyers into the hands of people walking by us. I loved it, working in Ward Eight and dragging Dianne along with me. My father charged Di and me with getting her French Canadian family, all her aunts and uncles, and none particularly interested in politics, to vote for Matty. We worked at convincing her dad, who finally promised us his vote. Then, at Di's family picnics in Look Park, as we passed ketchup and mustard, we begged her uncles and aunts for votes.

"We're doing some posters at Dianne's house on Saturday. Anne Sullivan's helping."

"She's working for you and not the twins?" he asks.

"They have the same name, but they're not cousins or anything."

"So she's backing you?" my father asks me. I can hear the calculation in his voice, speculating on my chances of winning. Creases line his brow, but he slowly smiles. "It's in your blood. You know how campaigns work. Hungry Hill and Our Lady of Hope parish are well represented with you and the twins. Father Power will be pleased."

"Yeah, he'll be smiling from the window of his blue Cadillac," I say.

"Carole, Father Power's brother owns a Cadillac dealership in Worcester."

"Yes, the vow of poverty doesn't matter if your brother owns a car dealership." Before my dad can answer me, Tommy almost lurches out of his high chair, pointing to Bobby's chocolate chip cookies. He makes an unh, unhing sound until my father hands him one from the package. Abandoning campaign strategy, my dad lifts Tommy from his high chair, wiping food from his baby mouth with his finger. Holding a shrieking two-year-old high in the air over his head, he teases Tommy with his favorite game, "OK, TJ, who's your favorite?" There are gray scuff marks on Tommy's white lace-up baby shoes. As he looks around at all of us, he hugs my dad around the neck. We all start protesting that my father has an unfair advantage because he's holding him, and we huddle around Tommy, saying you love me best, don't you? I toilet trained him, and he still loves my father best.

"Well, it is unfair. You are his father," I point out, and notice how sometimes I sound like Sister Agnes Veronica.

"Accept it, kids, you're all sore losers, Thomas James O'Malley loves his old man best. I am number one," my father boasts. A piece of me gets scared whenever he calls himself "old man."

17. Campaign

WHEN I PULL my Latin book from my green book bag and check the kitchen clock, I see that it is ten past ten. I love our kitchen clock, a black wrought-iron circle with wavy squiggles surrounding it and a brown and red rooster in the middle, a painted rooster I think of as the O'Malley family pet. Memorizing the vocabulary list for a Latin test, third-declension nouns and the pluperfect "era-had" tense, I cover the words with my hand, first from Latin to English, then English to Latin, my surefire method, when my dad walks into the kitchen, heads for the cabinet, and pulls down a bottle of whiskey. "A little nightcap," he says to me as he pours the whiskey into a glass. The word "nightcap" has a comfy feel, like "bedtime story."

He drinks, to the sound of the ice cubes nudging one another, and says in a joking tone, "Nothing like a little belt before bedtime." Is this what Sister Maurice Joseph would say is an example of irony? Hard to know with my dad.

"I wish your mother were here to see you running for class office, although she never did have much appreciation for politics. Said it was just another excuse to drink. Your mother could cut through things." Dad, if this is supposed to make me feel better, it isn't, I think. I put my hand over the words I already know by heart: rex, regis, bibo, bibere. Rex bibit. The king drinks.

"Mother, Suzanne is spilling the sugar. It's going everywhere." Dianne sighs and sweeps her palm over the sugar on the counter. She is reading the recipe on the box and measuring the sugar. Suzanne, Di's older sister, wears thick black glasses and is retarded. Her mouth is always half-open as if she has a stuffy nose. She's in the kitchen, helping us make fudge. Suzanne is unwrapping bars of cooking chocolate when Mrs. Thinel walks into the kitchen holding up Suzanne's red winter jacket. Like Di, she sighs, but does not yell at either of them the way my mother would have.

"Come with me, Suzanne, we're going to the park," Mrs. Thinel says and hands Suzanne her jacket.

"I want to make fudge," Suzanne says with a slight pause between each word. Even from the counter, I can hear Suzanne breathing.

"We will make fudge together when we get back," Mrs. Thinel says with an annoyed voice. With her mother holding the jacket open, Suzanne struggles to get her thick arms into the sleeves, and they walk out the back door.

I have never made fudge before. I stir the chocolate bar with a wooden spoon making spiral designs as I watch it melt. Di is rewrapping the chocolate bars. Anne, six feet and nicknamed "Sky High" by my brothers, easily puts the vanilla bottle back on a high shelf. I would have needed to pull over a chair. We let the fudge sit in the aluminum pan, clean the kitchen up, and pull out the poster board. After Kathleen Cullinane (she would be good at art, too), Anne was the best artist in our eighth grade so she brought over all the art supplies, poster paper, and markers from home. I'd be lucky to find an unbroken crayon in our house.

Since none of us is in the same set of classes, we gossip about the nuns, boys, the snooty Holy Name kids, and the priests. We come up with a slogan, "Rally for O'Malley," and Anne draws banners, flags, and megaphones on posters. Even though we're not sure whether it's allowed, Dianne and I make smaller flags with "Rally for O'Malley" to wear on our blazer lapels. We strategize about where we can put signs. Anne suggests outside the library and first-floor study halls. Dianne's father walks into the kitchen, carrying the newspaper under his arm, and stops to study the posters.

"These look great," he says to me.

"Anne's the official campaign artist," I answer.

"Dianne thought of the slogan," Anne says.

"Rally for O'Malley? Catchy, Di." Mr. Thinel squeezes her shoulder as Dianne smiles and smoothes out the lapel badges.

"So you're running for office, Carole? Good luck," Mr. Thinel says. "Please thank your father again for me for all he did. After the heart attack, I didn't think I'd find another job." If I were Dianne, I'd be embarrassed, but she keeps cutting badges out of construction paper. Mr. Thinel had been a milkman for Hood's Dairy and lost his job when he had his heart attack and couldn't climb stairs carrying heavy milk bottles anymore. While I don't even remember telling my father about him, the next thing I knew my dad had made a call to one of his politician friends, and Dianne's dad now worked as a toll taker for the Massachusetts Turnpike. The hours were odd, but he was making more money, and loved this new job. Now he pours himself a cup of coffee, sniffs the fudge, ruffles Dianne's curly brown hair, and leaves. Mr. Thinel drinks coffee instead of whiskey, and I guess that only white-shirted businessmen drink whiskey.

By the time we've finished the posters and the lapel badges, the fudge is ready. Dianne cuts it and hands each of us a neat, even piece. She takes a piece into the other room for her dad and comes back.

"My dad said for you to tell your father that he's expecting the settlement check next week and to thank him." Since neither of us knows what this means, we all shrug our shoulders. Four neat squares of fudge are in front of me.

"It even looks like fudge," I say.

"Let me take the posters home with me," Anne offers. "I know we've got tape at home." Dianne and I split up the lapel badges, agree we'll talk on the bus ride to school on Monday, and Anne and I leave. Halfway up the block, we bump into Mrs. Thinel and Suzanne, just coming back from a walk in the park. Mrs. Thinel has pink cheeks, but Suzanne is still sallow. A poster falls out of Anne's hands, and as we bend to pick it up, we see Mrs. Thinel and Suzanne turning into their driveway.

"Did you notice Suzanne's taller than her mother now?" Anne asks me.

"A good three inches. She must have grown." Suzanne will be sixteen in May, two years older than Dianne, but will always be mentally seven years old. If my brothers knew Suzanne, I wonder what nickname they'd give her. They're good at torture.

The campaign was fun, seeing the posters in the halls and asking my classmates, girls, mostly, to vote for me. My speech was horrible; even I was bored. When I won, I thought I should thank Susan Lytle, sit with her at lunch, but I didn't. Her intensity scared me. Monica came in second, so she's treasurer. At home, no one seemed to care. Gerry asked whether I got paid and when I said no, he walked away. Michael muttered that it meant nothing because the nuns ran everything anyway. Since my dad was back out on what he called the "dating circuit," he barely noticed.

⌐

18. The Dating Scene

MY DAD HAS started dating, not that he bothers to tell any of us, but Danny, a ladies' man himself, has guessed, and we all know the woman he's dating. Her name is Mary Ford. When my grandfather died, she came up for his funeral and shared my bedroom. I remembered watching her unpack a big jar of Pond's cold cream from a corner of her suitcase and how she used the tips of her fingers to pat the cream all over her thin face. The transformation scared me. What had been a bright shiny pink lipstick face became the face of a ghost in the cemetery. It's bad enough that my mother is dead, but I don't even want to think about my father going on a "date." After all, I'm in high school; shouldn't I be the one dating? There's only so much embarrassment I can stand.

One Friday night after a basketball game, I climb the back stairs slowly and make a decision not to ask my dad about his night out because I feel safer not knowing. Maybe I like the dad who lay on the living room couch staring into space and listening to Frank Sinatra croon better than the dating dad. But I'm weak and curious, so that resolve lasts about as long as my New Year's resolutions to give up fighting with my brothers. Two minutes.

"So how's your girlfriend?" I ask with a bite in my voice. After my father reaches for the whiskey, pulling the bottle down off the shelf, he turns and looks at me.

"Mary is fine. Thank you for asking." His voice sounds like mine. "Mary's staying at the Hilton."

I hate her name. I hate hearing this information.

"She took the five-thirty train in from Hartford."

"The train? Doesn't she know how to drive?" Not driving, to me, is on a par with the cold cream. Uncool and unacceptable.

"She doesn't have a car, so she took the train." He pours the whiskey into his glass and adds a little water. "What else would you like to know?"

I dig my thumbnails into the fleshy pads of my index fingers. I don't know what I want to know. I want to know everything and nothing.

"She wants to get to know you kids." Alarms and sirens start blaring in my head.

"Mary is forty, lives in Hartford with her eighty-seven-year-old mother, and works for Travelers Insurance Company. She's never married."

"Why was she mom's Maid of Honor?"

"It had something to do with the war. Your mother might have been try-ing to play matchmaker."

"Mary couldn't get her own date?"

"Carole, Carole, Carole." He sounds weary, frustrated with me. I do like the idea though of my mother as matchmaker.

Why are you going out with her? If you marry her, I'll have a stepmother, just like Cinderella. Worse yet, a stepmother without a car.

"One of these weekends we'll all have dinner at the Fort," he says as I start to leave. Michael stomps into the kitchen and opens the refrigerator. "I like the food at the Fort," Michael says. Does he not get it?

"Oh, good, I can't wait," I grumble from the hallway, unable to stop my-self.

"I heard that, Carole," my father says. On my way upstairs, I wonder if I'm breaking the fourth commandment: Honor thy father and mother. I guess I only have to honor my father now. Nowhere in the Baltimore catechism does it say to honor thy father and stepmother. So.

After my mom died, I gave up on God a little. When the random nun asks us if we remember our nighttime prayers, I rip at the tiny threads on a textbook cover. Tonight I get down on my knees. "Please, God, help me," and I throw in an Our Father for extra points. With the bedspread over my head, I remember the short story Sister Maurice Joseph assigned to us in English class, "The Lady Who Was Always Right" by Paul Claudel, or maybe it was Guy de Maupassant—some French author anyway, who writes about a woman who always did the right thing in her life, always behaved perfectly, and still did not make it into heaven. How did Sister ex-plain it? Was it something about the woman's spirit? Her intention? I just know that heaven is beginning to seem far away to me right now. Mom, are you there? I just remember you yelling at me, you being angry with me. Death is such a big cheat.

It is late March but winter lingers on. Grainy patches of dirty-edged snow are scattered throughout the yard. From the living room window, I spot Gerry and Billy Metzger sledding on Thornfell Street. Then Gerry begins running toward home, dragging his sled after him. Alone, Billy is at the bottom of Thornfell Street, yelling after Gerry. The kitchen door slams, and I am in the archway between the kitchen and living room. Steve, Bobby, and Tommy run in from the TV room.

"Carole, Billy just told me Dad has a girlfriend. Is he making up a story?" Gerry asks breathlessly. "I ran all the way down from Thornfell Street. Does he?" He pulls the jars of Skippy and Welch's grape jam from the shelf. The little kids are surrounding him.

"Dad is dating a woman named Mary."

"How do you know her?"

"She came up for Gramp's funeral and stayed in my room. Do you remember her?" I leave out the cold cream ghost.

"I don't remember her. So Billy was right?"

"Afraid so."

"How come I didn't know and Billy did?" Gerry flattens the peanut butter on a slice of bread and dabs on jam.

"Maybe Dad thought one of us would tell you, or maybe he just forgot."

"You know I'm in the fifth grade. I'm not a little kid anymore. Just because I'm not in high school, no one ever tells me anything. I'm not going back out until Billy's back in his house." Gerry walks to the window and pulls back the kitchen curtain, peeking through a crack. Stevie is listening, his eyes darting back and forth between us. Tommy sucks his two middle fingers.

"That's where he went this morning," Gerry asks, "to see his girlfriend?"

"I don't know. Dad didn't tell me either. I thought he was going to the cemetery." I sense an ally in ten-year-old Gerry. Then Michael skulks into the room and grabs the jar of peanut butter with a quick gesture. He tosses the silverware, hunting for a knife in the drawer. The spoons, knives, and forks attack one another with his searching.

"Shut up, will you?" Michael orders us. "Why do you care whether or not

Dad has a girlfriend? It's none of your business." In spite of his gruffness, I ignore the "shut up," which in our house can pass for a good morning, and ask him, "Dad could marry this woman. Did you think of that?"

"He's not marrying her. He takes her out for dinner," Michael says, heaping on peanut butter and slapping the slices together as if the Wonder bread has done something to offend him. I watch his jowls and jutting chin as he chews and hope that he's right about the dinner dates. Michael eats a plain Skippy peanut butter sandwich every day while the rest of us eat peanut butter and jelly. I put the lid back on the jelly jar watching the jelly spill over the top. Gerry and Michael are sitting at the table facing each other.

"You're just jealous," Michael says to me between bites, "that you don't have a boyfriend." His arrow hits the bull's-eye, so I do shut up as he bites down on his sandwich. With Michael anyway, my father's dating is a closed issue.

I'm rescued by Tommy's call for help from the bathroom. As I stand in the bathroom doorway, I shoot back, "You're no Don Juan yourself. The tea dance at Ursuline with Judy Blackmer back in tenth grade was your one and only date. So let's not talk about my boyfriends." He gets me so mad. Pulling up Tommy's thick training pants, I wonder if my dad said anything to Michael about his "girlfriend" or if Michael is just guessing. Fastening Tommy's corduroy overalls, I remember how my dad only told Michael about my mom's cancer. Maybe he told Michael he wasn't getting married, but Michael's been wrong before. Often.

19. Cheerleading and Candy Striping

IN EARLY APRIL, the sign is posted, the announcement is made: cheerleading tryouts, the day I have been waiting for. I'm clutching a white square with the number 112 on it. Already the sweat from my hands is curling the edges. Milling outside the girls' gym in an endless line of ninth-grade girls, I am waiting for my number to be called and joking with Di and Anne, pretending that the tryout is no big thing. For moral support, I have begged them both to come with me to try out, but when Di and Anne take in the size of the line snaking around the hall, they roll their eyes and suggest we forget cheerleading and just take the bus home. As if it were any other Monday afternoon.

"But this is our one and only chance to try out. The cheerleaders stay the same for all four years," I argue. "In Archie comics, cheerleaders have a better chance of dating varsity athletes."

"You're stretching. Face it, Carole. You have a better chance of being named a successor to the pope than getting a spot on the cheerleading squad," Dianne says with a soft kick to her book bag.

"As pope, I will make an official proclamation: It does look as if more than half of the girls in the ninth grade had nothing better to do today," I answer.

"Nothing better than to leap and jump for Miss Curran and the cheerleaders," Anne says, a trace of sarcasm in her voice. "That was more of a papal observation than a proclamation, I'd say."

"I'll do better."

"The line's moving quickly, though," Anne adds. "We're already here. Let's practice." Furtively, I glance around and see girls practicing jumps, splits, and arm twists until Miss Curran bustles into the hall and orders us to stop.

"Save your performances for inside the gym, young ladies," she directs, and turns her wide back on us.

As soon as the gym doors close behind her, Kathy Moynihan with her hands on her hips waddles into an open spot and launches into a perfect imitation of Miss Curran, making us laugh out loud. I half-expect Miss Curran to fling open the doors and lecture us. When numbers 100 through 120 are called in for auditions, I am still copying other girls flipping their wrists and hoping I get the hang of it.

At least Anne got by the first cut day—her brother Timmy's on the basketball team, and on her jumps she can almost touch the light fixtures—but both Dianne and I are cut. The truth is I'll never get that hand-wrist-twist-flip thing with my arms.

On Friday afternoon with five minutes of my seventh-period algebra class left, Father Sears announces over the intercom the three lucky ninth graders selected for next year's cheerleading team: Barbara Poirier, a petite blonde from Holy Name, and Monica and Veronica Sullivan, Our Lady of Hope's very own twins. I picture the twins in purple and white sweaters with "Cathedral" emblazoned across the front and in their short purple and white pleated skirts, cheering at every game. Like a twisted leafless vine, the gray-brown jealousy clings to me, tendrils threading through my hair. Guilty of one of the seven deadly sins—will my envy disappear one day? I suppose I'll live, but then remember that Tech, our rival, has a tiger mascot. Could I convince Miss Curran that Cathedral needs a panther mascot?

Anne's mother tells her things that neither Dianne nor I know. Mrs. Sullivan told Anne that Mercy Hospital was looking for high school girls to volunteer, so now, on a balmy Tuesday afternoon right before Easter, Anne, Di, and I show up at Mercy and sign up for the volunteer program.

Six high school girls sit in a pale green room, whispering in hospital voices when a frizzy-haired woman rushes in, introduces herself as Mrs. Dillon, the volunteer coordinator, and begins showing us how to make a bag out of newspapers.

"Young ladies, we are taking the time to train you this afternoon. We expect you to show up every Tuesday afternoon and to honor your commitment to the hospital." Mercy is a Catholic hospital, and the thin-voiced volunteer coordinator sounds like a nun. The candy striper uniform will be given to us at next week's meeting, she explains. Without a red and white striped pinafore, this hospital volunteer thing is beginning to feel like a mistake.

"All right. Put away the newspapers. You must stay with the aide or nurse assigned to you. Remember, if you have any kind of a problem, find me. I will be on the floor. Just check on the patients. And smile." If there's anything I hate, it's being told to smile. The coordinator splits up Dianne, Anne, and me and assigns me to the geriatric wing.

On the geriatric floor, the statue of Saint Teresa wearing a brown head covering and matching robes reassures me in a muddy kind of way. The two girls from Commerce High School, both seniors, are making their rounds—very Cherry Amesish, the word "rounds"—and I see them smiling, ignoring me. According to Mrs. Dillon, I'm supposed to be some kind of cheerleader for these old women, smiling, chirpy, helpful, but I realize that I hate this visiting the sick, cheerleader or not. Mercy reminds me of my mother; she did die here.

The patient yelling in room 306 terrifies me, and I hope the aide will suddenly appear. Inhaling, I enter the room where a white-haired woman in the bed by the window motions me over.

"Get my bedpan. I need my bedpan," she demands loudly.

"Excuse me. Could you tell me where the bedpan is?" The woman points her bony finger to the beside table. Relieved, I open the cabinet door and reach in for the only pan I see.

"Now put it under me," she orders in a stern voice. Oh, my God. I can do this simple thing, can't I?

"Lift my nightgown." Although I am afraid to touch this frail old woman with her brown age spots and thin watery eyes, I want to help her.

"I neeeed the pan," the woman pleads. So I scrunch up my eyes and stick the metal pan up against her bony bottom. There is a second of peace, and then she moans, "It's not right. It's not right." I move the pan into a better position.

"Is there anyone who can tell me what I'm doing wrong?" I yell loudly, praying someone in the hall will hear me. Silence. No answer. A few minutes, an eternity later, the aide sticks her head in, hurries to the bed, looks at the pan, stares at me, and says, "You've given her the wash basin." I'm sorry. I'm sorry. I'm sorry.

Rushing down the stairs to the meeting room, I grab my coat and book bag and leave a note on Anne's blazer. "The Cherry Ames thing did not work out for me. There is no future for me at Mercy as a candy striper, now or ever. I took the bus home. Carole."

Outside, in the mild, moist air, I inhale deeply, free of the medicine-sick-science lab smell. At the bus stop, I think how life in books and life in life are so different. How everything is just so neat in books and how things work out perfectly. No one ever gives a sick, moany woman a wash basin. I'm not meant to be a Cherry Ames.

20. Clip-on Tie

EVER SINCE PALM Sunday, Danny and I have been making the kids look out the window for the Easter Bunny. By vaguely threatening that the Easter Bunny may withhold baskets, I can pretty much head off any *intra frates* fighting all week. Joey, I can tell, is faking belief in the Easter Bunny, but Gerry with his usual flair is carrying on about the rabbit's white fur, the straw hat, the size of the basket, and the time we can expect him on Lynwood Terrace, and throwing in off-key snippets of "Here Comes Peter Cottontail." A conniver and a worrier, Gerry suspects that if he lets on that he no longer believes in the Easter Bunny, he might not get a basket—a risk he's unwilling to take, however much he wants to associate himself with the big kids. Like the rest of us, Gerry would never pass up a chance at a jelly bean.

On the Saturday before Easter, I'm putting away a box of Frosted Flakes when I hear the station wagon pull up in the driveway. The car doors slam, and Stevie is the first one in the house, carrying a bag from the meat market. There has been a steady pelting rain all morning, and raindrops have splotched his plaid shirt.

"We stopped at Balboni's for a lily for Mom's grave," Steve says, sounding shaky. He's upset, and at first I think maybe it's the trip to the cemetery. But then, tugging at the zipper on his jacket, he asks, "Do you know what Mrs. Balboni did? You know how Bobby's always been her favorite?" Bending down to help, I see the tears in his eyes. "She gave each of us jelly beans and she gave Bobby a chocolate rabbit." A tear falls from the corner of his eye and travels down his perfect little boy nose. To go with his big blue eyes and blonde curly hair, Bobby has an endearing manner that always softens the already warm-hearted Mrs. Balboni.

"Stevie, I bet the Easter Bunny brings you a chocolate rabbit even bigger than the one Mrs. Balboni gave Bobby." Twenty-four hours seem like forever to a six-year-old, but Stevie stops crying in a few minutes, and he lets me try on a clip-on tie on his jersey. When I hold him up in front of the bathroom mirror, he smiles his toothless smile and says, "Now I look just like Daddy." The clip-on tie will never measure up to the standards of my fashion-conscious father, but the "daddy" tie helps Stevie get over Mrs. Balboni's favoritism. I reach for a towel and dry his face and neck.

As I empty the grocery bags, putting the piles of butcher-wrapped meat packages in the refrigerator, my father stands in the kitchen doorway with a giant lily plant in his hands. Lily plants and chocolate rabbits—the commerce of Easter. Grabbing a dish towel, he wipes his face, his hair, and the leaves of the lily plant.

"Biggest lily Mrs. Balboni had," he announces, pride filling his voice. To me, it's just a lily—all right, a big lily.

"You know how Mom loved chocolate? Maybe you could bring her a chocolate rabbit." I'm half-joking. My dad is fumbling, trying to straighten the plant's wood supports in the dirt.

"A chocolate rabbit at the grave? No, Princess, I think the lily's enough. Your brothers would leap on the rabbit and tear it apart," he says, dismissing what might have been a cute idea. "We need a certain dignity in the cemetery." He's half-joking now.

Checking to see that the little kids are out of earshot, I rub my fingers together in a money sign and say, "Dad, this Easter, I want to get the kids the biggest Easter baskets I can find. The bigger, the better. Yellow, pink, blue, orchid, a different color for each boy." Easter Sunday will be different, if I can help it, because this past Christmas was a day I'd like to forget. Anything but merry. Without my mother's shopping list, my dad gave little thought to the process, more or less randomly selecting toys and gifts, so the Christmas tree somehow seemed sad with just a smattering of bikes and baseball gloves around it. And, besides the O'Malley Christmas greed, part of the fun of Christmas is showing off your loot to one another. Always, as we ripped apart the wrappings, my mother would ooh and ah with us over Santa's offerings, but Christmas without her was just plain quiet and over in a flash. My father reaches into his wallet and says with a smile, "Candy is dandy, but liquor is quicker, as they say." When he hands me a stack of bills, I answer, "Even though Tommy's finally out of diapers, I think he's a little young for a bottle of Seagrams."

"Just a moment of levity, kiddo. Have Michael give you a ride to the Plaza. It's pouring out. You know what they say? April showers bring May flowers."

"May flowers," I join in, pleased at how our words meld together, like a father-daughter duet.

"Tomorrow morning, this table will be a vision of colored baskets wrapped in cellophane, surrounded by rows and rows of jelly beans and troops of yellow peeps chicks filled with marshmallow."

"Peeps?" he asks.

"Those chicks with the black eyes. Only yellow. Every one of us hates those pink peeps chicks."

"A prejudice against pink peeps? In this family?" he asks, raising his eyebrows. My dad has a funny way of phrasing things. "And I thought I was bringing you up to be open-minded."

"*Daaad*, candy, it's just candy, but if you want to call it prejudice, go ahead. I think it's just your gift for alliteration." His back is to me as he places the lily in the corner, a spot safe from foot traffic.

"Look at that rain come down, kid. Look at that rain come down," he chants. "Let me hunt up Michael for you." Kissing me on the forehead, he leaves.

In Woolworth's, the Easter candy aisles are practically bare, hardly anything left. More experienced shoppers, mothers, I guess, must pounce on Holy Thursday. Under the bags of fake green grass, I find a chocolate rabbit for Stevie, rejected by pickier shoppers because of a few dents in the package. Where is Michael? Impatient, I prop the bags of Easter baskets and candy against my legs. Ten minutes later, the station wagon pulls up. With Michael at the wheel, even the car seems to grumble.

"Did you get the candy?" he asks in a voice brimming with accusation.

"You see the three bags, don't you?" I respond in kind.

"Could be an Easter bonnet for you," he says, cackling. Typical of Michael, only he gets the joke.

Back home, I open the door a crack, check to see if the coast is clear, and sneak the candy into the house, stuffing the bags under my mom and dad's bed. There is a spooky, half-empty feeling in their bedroom with my mother gone. And her clothes and jewelry and blue nightgown gone. Shivering with sadness, I bolt out of the room, breathless, afraid and alone.

*   *   *

As the "little kids," Tommy, Bob, and Steve still take their Saturday night baths together. With the Easter Bunny coming in the morning, and only to bathed children, they sprint to the bathtub after our Saturday night dinner of hot dogs and beans. The order is always the same: Stevie, as oldest, sits as engineer in front of the faucet controls, Tom, the baby, is sandwiched between him and Bobby, who hangs back in caboose position. With drops of water clinging to their black eyelashes and water-darkened hair, they are boy-angels in the Ivory soap suds. Grabbing mismatched towels from the linen closet, I notice the trap door in the floor. The hatch door to the cellar laundry makes me think of my mother, but I hurry back into the bathroom since the little kids are all yelling for towels. My dad sticks his head in the door as they skivvy into their matching cowboy pajamas.

"That Easter Bunny will be dropping baskets off at 21 Lynwood Terrace. Look how clean you little guys are," my dad says. "Let me see your finger-nails." They hold out their pruned and white-rimmed fingernails, smelling of soap. Their eyelashes are still wet, sticking together.

"You little guys pass inspection. A little television and bed. How about an Easter hug for your old dad?"

"What's an Easter hug?" Bobby asks as Steve grabs my dad around the waist. My dad picks up Tommy and nuzzles his face into his neck.

"An Easter hug is just a regular hug," I answer, "but you think of red and orange jelly beans as you hug."

"I can do that. And yellow chicks, too. I'll think of chicks," Bobby says.

After I wipe up the puddles of bath water, I am scooping up the lumped towels when the little kids, with Stevie in the lead, run back into the bath-room. "It's a commercial—it's a commercial. We want to brush our teeth," Stevie says, racing in front of me.

"When the show's over, bedtime," I say. Back at the linen closet, I lift the hatch, throw down the heap of towels into a slatted wooden cage, and watch them scatter on a mass of boy's underwear. I remember the Satur-day when my dad had Mr. Vecchiarelli build the laundry chute. When he had finished, my dad insisted that we all traipse down to the cellar and admire the handiwork and my dad's invention. Gerry, Danny, and I were fiddling with the lock.

"You'd look good in there, Carole," Gerry said.

"Like a monkey at Forest Park," Danny added.

"I don't want you kids climbing in there. If I catch you in there, I'll have to find my Army belt." Turning to Mr. Vecchiarelli, my father said, "Ben Franklin may have done electricity, but I'll take a laundry hamper any day." He opened and closed the door, checking the chute for sturdiness. "Guy, you know I am a dangerous man around tools. Nothing is safe, if I have a hammer in my hand." He clapped Mr. Vecchiarelli on the back. "Gaetano, you have created a masterpiece here worthy of Saint Joseph, the Carpenter. Come upstairs and join me and Betty for a Manhattan." My dad slipped some bills into his vest pocket, and I craned my neck, trying to see how much money there was.

"No, no, no. I just have wine on holidays. You've been generous enough," Mr. Vecchiarelli said and headed for his tool chest in the corner.

In the kitchen, my mother sipped her Manhattan and smiled. We have the same thin upper lips that elongate into a tiny line when we smile.

"I'm sorry we don't have any wine. You know how the Irish like their whiskey," my dad explained, reaching for the bottle on the top shelf. On the day of the laundry chute installation, I learned that Italians drink wine on holidays while the Irish drink whiskey.

As a family, we were sugared out. Too much sweet stuff, but still Easter without my mother was better than Thanksgiving or Christmas. I wonder if my dad noticed how I overdid it on the candy. If I learned anything, it's that next Easter I need to buy the baskets and jelly beans on Holy Thursday.

21. Auxilium Latinum

"WE WILL BE reviewing verb tenses and conjugations for two days," Sister Agnes Veronica announces at the beginning of Monday's Latin class, "to prepare you for the Auxilium Latinum test." Sister Agnes Veronica just keeps pushing us along in Latin, so reviewing will be a break for us. "This is a national test and given to Latin students all over the country." Sister never smiles and has a way of sounding like a talking test booklet. "Prizes are awarded to students who achieve a certain score." Prizes? My ears prick up because I love prizes, starting with the cellophane-wrapped trinket at the bottom of the Cracker Jacks box, which I prefer to the sticky caramel-coated corn.

"I expect you to do well. This is a class that understands Latin and with a little application, we might even have a prize winner in classroom 223." Sister's words sound both expectant and friendly, and the hint of a compliment catches me by surprise. Her intense green eyes are directed at the first row of boys. It's a stretch to expect them to do well, I think, since David Keogh will never get the uses of the ablative case. Impatient as I am, I admire him and his questions because I am way too embarrassed to ask Sister to repeat anything. In seventh-period algebra, I wish I could ask Sister Mary Amabilis, which means lovable, to repeat each and every class so that I might understand math better as she twitters around the classroom. How do nuns choose their names anyway? One tired afternoon in algebra class, as Sister stood on tiptoe to reach the top of the blackboard, she tottered backwards and fell into the wastebasket. As Joe Carestia gallantly rushed up to help her out, her false teeth jumped out of her mouth and skittered across the floor. In shock, we watched as Joe bent down to retrieve Sister's teeth. A torrent of fake coughing filled the classroom when Sister put her tiny, wrinkled hand on Joe's arm, her teeth and dignity in place if not restored. "Why, thank you, Mr. Carestia," Sister said calmly and moved the wastebasket to the corner of the room. "Such a gentleman," she said, her praise lost in our uncontrollable laughter. Bowing to the class with his back to the damsel in distress, Joe the Gentleman rolled his eyes and rubbed his hands together. That afternoon, they were both lovable.

When the bell rings, Sister Agnes Veronica urges us to do a little reviewing that evening and to get a good night's sleep. When I pass her on my way out, she says, "Good luck tomorrow, class," and I wonder whether she's talking to me or to Pamela Gardner, who is standing right in front of me. At the door I study the back of Pam's head, perfectly curled, no stray honey blonde hairs on her green blazer. My blazer has rows of wrinkles at the elbow crick, but not Pam's. Broomstick straight. A rumor from a Holy Name grammar school classmate of hers surfaced that Pam's father is dead, but she and I will never talk about our dead parent, our scarlet letter.

His death, anyway, has not affected her neatness, and Noreen O'Connor has started another rumor, a rumor I like better, that Pam Gardner is so neat that she starches her shoelaces. Since Noreen sits behind Pam in both history and Latin, she has time to study Pam's tidiness, her grooming habits, as the nuns say. Pam could teach the nuns grooming; they, I think, have never given a thought to starching shoelaces. Although I will never do it, I'm happy if there are no knots in my gray, torn shoelaces, I love the idea of this tidy perfection.

The test went well. The vocabulary and the verb tenses were a snap. Hot dogs for lunch. Another good sign. I feel an unfamiliar confidence about the test, a confidence I never feel after a math test. In Latin I feel comforted because the dead language makes such perfect sense and order to me.

"Seven Cathedral High School students have been awarded gold medals for top performance in the annual Auxilium Latinum contest sponsored by the Association for the Promotion of the Study of Latin."
I read the article in the *Springfield Daily News* reporting my name as one of the seven gold medal winners. Right before supper, my dad calls to say he is having dinner with Mary down in Hartford. Excited, I ask him if he has seen the Latin article with my name in it in the newspaper and tell him about winning the award. With Mary waiting for him, he says he's in a hurry and the newspaper article will still be there when he gets home from dinner. As if my dad's reaction is not enough, I cut out the newspaper article and show it to my brothers, who accuse me of showing off again. Defending myself, I teach them what Sister Agnes Veronica taught me on the first day of class:

Latin's as dead as Latin can be,
It killed the Romans, and it's killing me.

I just knew they'd like the killing part.

With no more taunts, but no fanfare, either, I start studying for a religion test, hearing Father Manning in my head droning on about the differences between apostasy and heresy. An apostate rejects all, *a* and *a*, my memory trick, is in my mind when the phone rings. Uncle Bill and Aunt Madeline each congratulate me, and my aunt finishes the call with a tremor in her voice, saying how proud my mother would have been. Would have been. Conditional tense. When I tell her my dad is in Hartford, I hear a silence on the phone so deep I could sink in it. "I know how proud your dad is, too," she says finally. Like me, I think Aunt Mad may keep a scorecard.

22. A Buyer of Sofas

I PLACE MY report card on the coffee table on top of the picture of Senator Kennedy and his dark-haired wife in the *Springfield Daily News,* a couple far more glamorous to me than Hollywood's Liz Taylor and Eddie Fisher.

"Dad, I made the first honor roll again. Do you want to see my report card?" I ask my dad on a chilly June night. He's lying on the couch with his hands behind his head, staring at the plaster swirls in the ceiling.

"What? I'm sorry. School's over already?" Between Easter and Mother's Day, my dad had started dating Mary on both Friday and Saturday nights, sometimes even on Wednesdays.

"Just tell me—did you get any grade lower than an A?" he asks me. The report card is sitting there, but it's a pretty good bet he's not going to pick it up.

"Dad, at Cathedral, there are no As and Bs."

"I guess it's changed since my day. Eighties and nineties, is that the grading system? Your brother gets seventies. No seventies on this report card?"

"No, Dad, but you could look." He ignores me and closes his eyes.

"A B+ is an eighty-five to an eighty-nine," he says, surprising me. "I am expecting all As from you." I think he's joking, but it's hard to tell with his eyes closed.

"Sure, Dad. When I was in seventh grade, I heard you and Mom tell Michael that if he made the honor roll, even the second honor roll, you'd get him a car."

"Your brother's a boy."

"Yeah, so what does . . . ?"

"Good grades," he interrupts me, "mean more to his future." Michael's future is different from mine. More is expected.

"Why do I have to get As if they don't mean anything anyway?" With my dad, I can never tell if he's kidding me, trying to get me to argue with him.

"Well, Carole, you are not getting a car." He picks up the newspaper and folds it in half, dismissing me for a current event or political commentary.

"Even if I get all As?" I say, and his dark eyes flash me a look warning that the father-daughter academic talk is over.

"If you can forget the Ford falcon you will not be getting for a minute, I need you to do a little shopping for me."

"At Balise Chevrolet?" I ask, but he shakes his head.

"Drop it, Princess. Before your mother died, she wanted to get a new sofa for the living room," my dad says. "This sofa's falling apart. The springs are falling out."

"It looks all right to me. I don't see any holes. Of course, I don't lie on it very much."

"Got me there, kiddo. Anyway I want you to go to Forbes and Wallace and get a new sofa."

Suddenly I feel special. Me, a buyer of sofas.

"I look at this couch and it reminds me of your mother." How does furniture remind you of someone? Then I remember how Michael, Danny, and I would sneak downstairs and peek into the living room to watch *I Love Lucy* while my mom and dad were lying on the couch, chuckling.

"Well, I can do it. I'll just go to the furniture department."

"Carole, I wouldn't trust Michael with buying a sofa. Go on Saturday. I saw in the morning paper there's a summer furniture sale," my dad says, pointing to the newspaper on the floor. I study the gray couch, the splotches of hefty red flowers and green-yellow tropical leaves. It has a gentle curved back and if there are holes or loose springs, I can't see them.

The Forbes and Wallace charge-a-plate has raised letters on the metal back, Mrs. C. Joseph O'Malley. Although the card is still in my mother's name, my dad is sure I will be able to use it.

"Especially if you're buying a sofa. If there's a problem, the store can call me at home. Or your aunt," my dad says when he drops me off on Main Street. My brothers begin jumping from the back seat to the front seat, kicking one another in the head as they jockey for my seat, before I manage to close the car door.

Last night, when I called Di, she told me to just get the biggest sofa in the whole store since there are eight kids. "Of course, I never see anyone in your family sitting down." Now, I'm beginning to wonder if Di watches my family the same way I watch her small family. "And, with your brothers," she sneered, "you can skip any sofa that's white or tan."

In the furniture department, men with slicked-back hair, suits, and skinny ties mill around talking to one another in low voices under dimmed lights. There are no signs plugging a giant furniture sale, so I hope my dad is right. With sofas and chairs everywhere, the men remain standing as if the furniture is only for gazing. I march up and down the crowded aisles, searching in vain for a couch covered with green and red flowers, like my mom's. There is one navy couch, set apart like an orphan cousin at a family reunion beckoning to me. When I get closer to it, little flecks of orange threads, not quite a tweed, pop up. The navy sofa costs $289; it's not the lowest priced, but not the highest, either.

One of the salesmen with three stripes of comb-over hair stops talking about the Red Sox and turns to look at me. Caught under his eye, for the first time I wish Di had not gone to Look Park for a family picnic.

"May I help you?" he asks, knitting his Santa-like eyebrows, and I smell the mouthwash on his breath.

"I'd like to buy this sofa," I say, my words all muffled.

"You would?" he asks, as if he hadn't heard me. "Would you like to sit on the sofa? Go ahead. Sit down. Most customers like to have a sit-down." The salesman pats his hand on the sofa back as I sit down. "You're not buying furniture, are you?" He coughs a smoker's cough and I see the pack of Chesterfields in his breast pocket, my mother's brand. The back of my neck feels cold and my palms are wet, and I have stopped pretending this is a new "doll house" game. Holding up the charge-a-plate, I think how old I look when I stand up, how I could pass for sixteen, eighteen maybe.

"Do you have any questions?"

"My father said there's a sale. Is it on sale?" I ask, folding my hands into fists so tight I can feel my fingernails. My mother taught me about sales and how to do the math, the fractions. The navy sofa costs so much more than my eighth-grade graduation dress, yet I make the decision to buy it in such a flash, I worry I'm overlooking some critical factor. Please, let me get this done.

"Charge it, please." Powerful words, magic words, but who really cares about a living room couch anyway? And *sit-down*—what kind of a word is that?

MOTHER'S DAY 1993

(*Carole's apartment again. There is a white ceramic pitcher filled with peonies and Mother's Day cards standing up on the black coffee table. Joe O'Malley smiles when he reads one of the Mother's Day cards, his expression then turning somber. He wipes a tear from his eye and drops the card on the table when Carole enters carrying a small dish of Fig Newtons and Vienna Fingers.*)

JOE: I loved Susie's note—on your Mother's Day card. Quite the tribute.

CAROLE: For a twelve-year-old, she sometimes has the insight of an adult.

JOE: Like her mother at that age.

CAROLE: (*Laughing.*) I hope not.

(*Joe slaps the sofa and picks out a white feather from a pillow. He strokes the feather between his fingers.*)

JOE: Carole, did you pick out this sofa?

CAROLE: No, I sent Abby to the furniture department at Blooming-dale's. She's fourteen.

JOE: (*Playfully.*) You're with the old man for two minutes and already you're slipping back to your old sarcasm.

CAROLE: I just slide right into it, I don't mean to. It's easier for me to be sarcastic than to bring up the purchase of the living room sofa.

JOE: (*With resignation.*) Not that again.

CAROLE: (*In disbelief.*) Again? I've never even mentioned it before. (*With shock.*) Who, Dad, sends a thirteen-year-old out to buy a sofa?

JOE: (*He is in the past.*) Every time I looked at the flowers on that old sofa, I thought of your mother, snuggling with her. And I needed a new sofa for me to move on. Was it mourning?

CAROLE: I never knew whether you were sad and that made you drink or you drank and that made you sad. Hard to say. But why didn't you pull yourself together to go to Forbes and buy the sofa yourself? You were supposed to be the adult in the family.

JOE: (*Smoothly.*) Hey, you got a kick out of it.

CAROLE: I may have felt special traipsing around Forbes with the charge card in my sweaty palm. But I was a kid. As if I had any idea of what I was doing.

JOE: I didn't know anything about sofas, either.

CAROLE: It wasn't like I was buying a gallon of milk. A sofa is a major expenditure. A sofa selected for its length alone.

JOE: That was as good a criterion as any.

CAROLE: The furniture department had a good laugh. It was funny later. Ridiculous at the time.

JOE: They probably started treating teenagers with a little respect.

CAROLE: (*Her sarcasm surfaces.*) I'm sure. So I was part of a cause. That's good to know.

JOE: You got through it.

CAROLE: I guess. (*She passes the cookies to her father.*) Dad, this is the same sofa I've had since we were first married.

JOE: Well, that David's a lucky man. And, Carole, you did get it done.

CAROLE: But look what happened to it. Apparently the sofa did not measure up. Or maybe I didn't. Either way, it had a brief life at 21 Lynwood Terrace before it was tossed.

JOE: That came later.

CAROLE: (*Ruefully.*) If I had only known then what was coming later. (*She reaches for a cookie.*) Maybe I should write a how-to book for fathers.

JOE: The past is the past.

CAROLE: Is it? I know, I know—put it behind me.

23. The Doctor's Revelation

WITH SEVEN WISE-MOUTH brothers (though in fairness, I probably shouldn't count Tommy), you would think I could stand just about any humiliation, but not my dad's dating. I just wish things would slow down for him in the romance department and speed up for me. Tonight, he's back on the sofa, tired, listening to Nat King Cole and talking to Michael as I pass through the living room, carrying Tommy upstairs to his crib.

"How about a kiss from TJ?" my dad asks. I carry Thomas James over and lower him down for a kiss.

"Worn out from all the back-to-back dating? Who was it last night—Mary or, is her name Anne?" I ask.

"You do keep tabs on the old man. Now get the baby up to bed."

Climbing the stairs, I feel the weight of Tommy's arm around my neck and I breathe in the toddler scent clinging to him. When I kiss his peach-skin cheek good night, I think how I went through the entire ninth grade without a date or even a phone call from a boy. In spite of religiously following every rule listed in *Seventeen* magazine—smile, be friendly, say "Hello," remember names—I had no date. When I jump the bottom stairs back into the living room, my dad asks me when I'm seeing Lew. Our family doctor, Lewis Blackmer, smokes so much the tips of his fingernails are yellow, and he hums the music from Dodge car commercials as he examines me and my brothers. After a visit, we crack one another up imitating him.

"What is it that you need to see Lew for? A booster shot for school?" my dad asks.

"I think it's another polio shot." Lew took care of my mother when she was sick. "Just sewed her back up. The cancer was everywhere." In those exact words, I've since heard him explain my mother's lymphatic cancer. Not when she was sick. Then Dr. Blackmer said she had mononucleosis, the "kissing disease," which I thought sounded like fun, like a disease I'd like to have.

"I hate shots. I know Dr. Blackmer's your friend, but his shots really hurt."

"You'll be fine."

"Easy for you to say. I'm getting the shot." My dad chuckles, and I think how I love to make him laugh. "Whenever he took my stitches out, he'd rip the bandages off. There'd be this tearing sound."

"The price of being a tomboy." He dips his fingers into his shirt pocket for his glasses and picks up the newspaper from the floor.

Later that night, I'm staring at the wooden pegs poking out of the ceiling light, wondering if it's supposed to be a ship's wheel. I'm wide awake, fretting about tomorrow's visit to the doctor. Dr. Blackmer couldn't save my mother, a fact I share with no one, but, even at fourteen, I know there's more to being a doctor than humming car jingles. Because my dad never pays much attention to a routine doctor's checkup, I sense that there's something he isn't saying, something he's holding back from me. Maybe I'm growing suspicious.

Dr. Blackmer's waiting room is empty, but I hear muffled voices from inside his office. There are two years' worth of *National Geographic*s piled on the table, but nothing I feel like reading. Fjords. I wish he had better magazines. Dr. Blackmer opens the door, and a mother rushes out, cradling a crying baby in her arms. She coos, "There, there," and kisses the infant's cheek. Folding his arms over his starched white shirt, Dr. Blackmer watches them go, looks at me, and smiles.

"Think you'll cry like that?" he asks, beckoning me into his office.

"Maybe I will," I say with a challenge as I pass in front of him. "Excuse me," I add, sure to please the Sisters of Saint Joseph.

"Sit down. Sit down." The chair is still warm from the mother and child. Reaching over, I hand him the form, which he drops in the sea of papers lapping over his desk.

"So you're going into tenth grade?" he asks, fully knowing the answer. Yes, I'm still two years younger than Judy, your daughter, I want to say. "And I see you're doing well at Cathedral." Well. I hadn't been expecting a chat, hadn't wanted a chat. I feel myself flush, wondering if my father has talked about me to Dr. Blackmer.

"Marian and I saw the newspaper article on the Latin award." My father hadn't said anything to them about that, had not bragged. I feel the perspiration circles welling under my arms because Dr. Blackmer is talking to me, not asking me questions about my health.

"I made the honor roll." I don't know what else to say, and school seems safe.

"I'd expect that from you," he says, knowing more than I think he should. Why would he expect that? Placing the pads of his fingers together, he makes a triangle and studies the air caught between his fingers as if it were a crystal ball.

"And how are your brothers?" he asks and loses his set smile.

"They're good. They fight a lot, but they seem all right." He shrugs as if he expected the fighting, giving it a normalcy, a blessing. After a minute of staring, he picks up a pen and begins filling out the form.

"Wait," I say. "You checked normal for everything. At least put me above average in intelligence. So much for the honor roll. First honor roll, too." He ignores my remark, my smirk.

"Carole, you seem very anxious."

"Well, I'm about to get a shot." I say defensively, gripping the chair arms tightly.

"No, it's more than that." He stares at me intently.

"I'm fine. I am." The telephone rings and I jump a little. He lets it ring and then picks it up and orders a prescription, running his index finger along the corners of his lip. During his phone call, he looks at me as if he has made a decision.

"I'd like to put you on tranquilizers."

"Tranquilizers?" I repeat, unsure of what they are. "But I'm only fourteen." What is he saying? The idea of my taking pills shocks me, setting off sharp needles of a numbing fear in my body. I'm afraid to take a breath. A few seconds pass, and from somewhere deep inside me, a voice with surprising energy and strength bellows "No!"

"You're very anxious."

"I'll be all right. I'm just nervous here, in your office. I don't need tranquilizers." No fourteen-year-olds I know are on tranquilizers. Isn't it enough that my mother is dead? I don't need one more thing to make me different. Let me be like everyone else. Please. He pushes his thick black glasses up on his nose.

"All right. Have it your way, but I want you to think about it," he says and leaves the tranquilizer subject floating in the air. Just let me have the shot and get out of here, I think.

"But there is one more thing we need to talk about," he says, "before the shot." It seems as if he is checking off the Carole O'Malley agenda items. What could it be, besides tranquilizers? What's next? I cross my arms and dig my fingers into the flesh of my upper arms.

"I drove by the house a couple of weeks ago in the middle of the afternoon and saw Tommy lying asleep at the end of the driveway." His words hit me in the stomach. I easily imagine three-year-old Tommy napping on the black tarred driveway and try to stamp the picture out of my head. There is nothing I can say. This failure to care for him is so complete and total. Tommy has been so let down, so shortchanged that I just can't let myself think about it.

"I'll say something to Mrs. Meade," I answer lamely, knowing she is not enough, I am not enough.

"Carole, you're fourteen." He remembers now, adding, "You are far too young to be taking care of your brothers." I'll go straight home from here, I think, and not stop by Dianne's house.

"Maybe if I get . . ." Before I could say Michael or Danny to help out more, he interrupts me.

"You kids need a mother." He pushes his big hands against the edge of his desk and it moves an inch. Another stomach punch making me want to run my arm over his desk and sweep the piles of papers to the floor. I had a mother, I think, I don't need another, and I feel not loss, but bitterness.

"You need to think of your younger brothers." Dr. Blackmer plays his ace. Must I? Always? Think of them? Me? Where am I in all this mess?

"Your father asked me to talk to you because he's planning on getting married in the fall." My dad has handpicked our family doctor to drop this bomb on me.

"Why couldn't he tell me?" Am I more important than my brothers, is that why Dr. Blackmer and I are having this conference, this conversation?

"He thought it would be better if you heard it from me. As the only girl, you've been acting in your mother's place."

"I can do better," I say, trying to sound hopeful, but knowing when I'm defeated.

"Carole, this is the right choice and what needs to be done. You don't want Bobby and Tommy sleeping in the driveway." That image again. Stop it, Doctor. A shudder passes through my body.

"Is it the harridan from Hartford?" I know I'm being fresh. My sarcasm is sitting on the linoleum floor, but Dr. Blackmer skirts around it, lowering his glasses to peer at me.

"Mary is a complicated woman."

"Is it Mary? Do I know the bride?" I don't want him to answer me. I want things to be the way they were when my mother was alive.

"For that, you'll have to ask your father." As he skims the health form, I stand in silence. When he hands me the paper, he says, "Good luck, Carole."

Just like an eight-year-old free at recess, I run all the way up the block without stopping until I reach Penacook Street. I imagine that little Dutch Boy with his finger in the dike holding back the sea water and saving his city. I am in a flood of change and I can't tell where the waters are coming from. I'm not ready. Ten minutes later, when I take the shortcut through the backyard, I pick up a rock and fling it at the trash barrel. The rock falls to the ground two feet in front of the barrel. Just as Danny says, I have no aim. I can't hit anything.

24. Casanova at the Beach

LIFE AT THE beach has a different set of rules. On Thursday nights, there's an outdoor movie on the beach, and tonight it's *Old Yeller*. But my dad, Mr. Romance, will be skipping the double feature because he left right before dinner to pick up his "date" in Old Lyme, his new date. When he left the cottage, Uncle Bill sang, "Some Enchanted Evening." All I know is she's not the cold cream lady.

Cathy Lamoureux, my best friend at Point o'Woods, and I are lying on an old Army blanket on the beach gazing up at the stars waiting for the second feature to start up again. Although we never talk about it, Cathy and I share the dead parent special bond. Her father, a doctor, was dead for three years before I knew her. Cathy's mother, a nurse, owns the nursing home they ran together, The Elms, in New Britain, Connecticut. I'm scrunching my bare toes in the cool night sand and half-listening to Cathy when Aunt Madeline and the little kids wave goodbye to me as they straggle their way back to the cottage. No matter what movie is playing, the little kids only get to stay for the first feature.

"It's just not the same at the beach this year. Rene's not here. She's working at the nursing home and engaged to a doctor. Pat's in nursing school." Cathy drips the beach sand from her toes. "Gerry has a girlfriend in Wethersfield and is always with her." Cathy recites the family's whereabouts, finally getting to her brother Teddy. Being cool, I feign that I have no interest in Teddy. Is Teddy here? "Teddy's here, but complains about how bored he is," Cathy says, answering my unspoken question. I have a fleeting thought. If my dad married Cathy's mother, between them they'd have fifteen children. Teddy would be what? My stepbrother. I know it won't ever happen. My dad dates only single women. Skinny women, at that.

"Teddy didn't even come to the beach tonight. He and Pat went into Niantic for a Rock Hudson Doris Day movie. Everyone's already seen *Old Yeller*."

"But that's half the fun." Around us, couples are pairing off, the soft red flame of their cigarettes dotting the dark night. Cathy's right about the beach being different this year. Is it because we're fourteen?

When "The End" lights up the screen, I feel sad. I want to freeze the night, the beach, the movie, the stars. I want to hold the moment in my hand, to clench my fists around it. Instead, Cathy and I scramble to our feet and brush the sand between our toes and from the creases of our pedal pushers. Barefoot, we walk up the street among the straggling moviegoers, the parents carrying their young children, safe, sleepy, and nestled on the necks of their fathers and mothers. There is an unwritten law that summer teenagers, the lucky ones whose parents or grandparents own cottages, do not hang out with teenagers whose families rent, and Cathy and I are but lowly renters. We can't cross that invisible property barrier separating us.

"All right, I talked to my mother, and what we'll do is you'll take the train to New Britain at the end of September, and I'll come to visit you in Springfield on Columbus Day weekend," Cathy says, announcing her plan but with a question in her voice. I answer yes, fine, great, and feel fake because I am not excited like Cathy, although I don't know why because I'd love to see where Teddy lives. Both Cathy and I have figured out the travel arrangements and checked out this exchange. My father said, he'd think about it, which I went ahead and decided meant yes.

"You'll come to New Britain on September 25th."

"Yes, the 25th. Stevie's birthday is the 23rd, so I'll remember."

"I'll miss your birthday this year, though. It's Saturday, right?"

"Right. Danny's birthday is on Sunday." At the fork, we say our goodbyes, hugging each other.

"Happy Birthday," Cathy yells after me. "Have a piece of cake for me."

Walking alone up the street, I wish Cathy were staying another week and not leaving for home tomorrow. Twenty feet ahead of me, Danny's ducking behind bushes with one of the Cunninghams, summer kids, and smokers. I check and he's not smoking, but they slink off to the Cunninghams' back yard and I'm glad Cathy's not here to see him. The Cunninghams are slick, even the girls, but, I suppose, so is Danny. When I get back to the cottage, my dad is not back from his date.

The next morning, as I'm buttering my toast at the kitchen table, I over-hear my dad talking to my aunt in the hallway. Whatever he has said, she replies, "It might be a good idea. It's worth a try." Then he tells my aunt he has not broken up with Mary, he's just trawling the waters.

"Trawling can get you into trouble," my aunt answers. I'm brushing the dry toast crumbs from the corners of my mouth when my dad comes into the kitchen. Like me, he's a tea drinker, and he fills the kettle with water.

"Tonight I'm taking you, Michael, and Danny to the movies and out for a burger." There's more coming, I can tell. "I'd like you to spend some time with Ann, get to know her, let her get to know you."

"Ann is the woman from last night?" I drop a teaspoon of sugar into my tea.

"Yes, she's over at White Sands. Her family has a cottage there." An owner, I think. Rich. A car?

"Ann will meet us at the movie theater. Have you seen your brothers?"

"I'd start with the upstairs bedrooms."

"You're probably right. Do you ever get tired of being right?" My father smiles and smoothes down the hairs on his right eyebrow.

"It's a burden." I stir my tea, watching how the milk changes its color from whiskey to beige. I sip it and feel its warmth in my throat.

From the bottom of the stairs, my dad yells up to Danny to get a move on it. Danny comes racing down the stairs patting his hair.

"Hey, you said you wanted us to look good," Danny says, grabbing a look in the hall mirror.

"It takes you longer than most," I say.

"Well, at least with me, I have curls. You don't," Danny shoots back.

In the station wagon, I wave at the security guard at the trestle and think how if this were downtown Springfield, instead of Old Lyme, Connecticut, Michael, Danny, and I would never be joining the lovebirds for a night at the movies. Danny in the shotgun seat pulls down the rear mirror, straightening his hair again, while Michael and I sit in the back.

As we get out of the car at the movie theater, my dad puts his arm on the back of the front seat, looks at the three of us and asks, "Do you think for one night you could try to be civil to one another?"

"If they don't start anything," I say, and my dad interrupts me.

"Stop it, Carole. Just stop it." Michael and Danny turn to smirk at me.

The 19th Hole is a dark wood-paneled restaurant with bowls of stale orange cheese popcorn on the table. My father lifts a bowl from a nearby table and places it in front of Ann, his date. Brown bottles and beer-filled glasses sit on the bar in front of the men and women joking with the bartender. The smell of onions crinkling on the griddle makes me feel hungry. Over platters of cheeseburgers and French fries, we say little about the movie, Ocean's 11, although during the movie I heard Ann laughing out loud a couple of times. It wasn't really a laugh—a cross between a snort and a guffaw. She shocks me when she tells us how she is dreading going back to school. As a high school English teacher, Ann has to "tolerate" hundreds of teenage students, which may be the reason why she doesn't complain or find fault the same way Mary does. I imagine Mary taking a moral high road with the movie, a few "how dare theys" laced with a couple of "what is this world coming to?" About a week after the Fourth of July, my dad hauled Michael, Danny, and me to dinner at the Fort for a rendezvous with Mary. He used the word "rendezvous," as if she were a foreign mission. We had barely sat down when Mary was ready to storm out of the restaurant because *scrod* wasn't on the menu, and "what kind of a restaurant doesn't serve *scrod?*" My brothers and I looked at one another; none of us even knew what scrod was. When my dad squeezed her knobby fingers, she calmed right down, but by then I was holding my breath, hoping no one would think she was related to me. While I was scraping up the crumbs of my chocolate cake, Mary with her pink Singapore Sling held high was flirting with the waiter, batting her eyes and telling him how "attentive" he was to her needs. Later that night after we dropped her at her hotel, we nicknamed her "the scrod lady," and my dad just smiled. One small relief is that Ann adores my father less than Mary, who has a way of pausing after every sentence my father utters as if he were Saint Thomas Aquinas.

"Have another Collins, Ann," my father urges her. Ann has a Tom Collins in a tall frosted glass, her summer drink. I like that a drink could be named after a person besides Shirley Temple and wonder what I would have to do to have a drink named after me, if that could ever happen.

"I like to stick to one. I seem to behave better that way."

"That's what I'm afraid of, good behavior," my dad says. She raises her thick eyebrows and looks at Michael, Danny, and then me, ignoring my dad.

"What did you think of the movie?" Ann asks us, and we all start talking at once. She sparkles when she talks, making her almost pretty. She has that English teachery way of keeping a discussion going, pointing out a character's strengths and weakness. She can even repeat a few of the jokes. If my father has to date someone, I'd vote for Ann.

Late Saturday afternoon, my fifteenth birthday, my dad pulls up in front of the cottage with Ann. He's carrying a wooden basket from the seafood shack in Old Saybrook filled with lobsters for the grown-ups, and she's bringing in a bag of groceries with ears of corn peeping over the top.

Michael comes out to the car, taking the bag from her, and I wonder if my father might have paid him to do it. Normally, Michael is so shy he skulks away instead of coming forward. With my dad dating not one but two women, there is no normal anymore.

Since the cottage we rent, "the Honeysuckle," is at the end of a dead-end street, we use the dirt road as a playing field. I'm really too old for games but as a favor to the "lovebirds," I'm outside after supper keeping the little kids busy with a game of hide and seek. My eyes are open a slit, cheating, I suppose, counting to a hundred by fives. In the window of the cottage, my uncle passes by, carrying bottles of beer to the dining room table. Bored with hunting down my brothers one more time, I pretend not to see Tommy and Bobby, whose whole bodies are visibly sticking out from behind a parked car.

"Car coming," I yell. "Everybody come out from hiding to the tree." The setting sun blinds me, and I squint, spotting a woman driving an old gray Chevy swerving down the street, as if she can't stay in a straight line. The car pulls up closer, and I shield the kids behind me, keeping them well on the grass. Mary is driving. I feel myself stop breathing. When she stops the car, she jerks forward, hitting the top of her head on the visor. She opens the car door and flounces her hair. This is going to be good, I think. My dad in the house with Ann.

"Hi, I just thought I'd surprise you and come down for your birthday and Danny's birthday. It's today, isn't it?" she asks. I manage a small nod of my head.

"Is it a lot to expect for you to answer me?" Mary asks. I quickly answer yes, but not before she says, "There's no need for you to protect those children. Really, Carole, I may not have a car, but I'm a good driver." With a shrug, she dances her way up the front stairs. I couldn't watch.

Ten minutes later, Mary and my dad come out of the house. She is in tears, and he has his arm around her shoulders. Even I forgive her weeping, although that mean little shell inside of me is jumping up and down, clapping almost. My dad leans over through the driver's window and holds her hand.

"Oh, go in, Joe to your 'friend.' I've driven all this way for nothing. In a borrowed car." She shoos him away with her hand, then puts her forehead on the steering wheel. From the top step, he turns to look at her, pauses,

HUNGRY HILL

and goes into the cottage. I bend over to tie Bobby's sneaker, stealing a look at her. Adjusting the car mirror, she swings it down and applies lipstick and powders her nose. Bobby runs to the backyard, yelling for Stevie. Reaching into the back seat, Mary lugs out two shopping bags just as Danny comes walking down the street with Johnny Cunningham.

"Why don't you tell your brother what happened? My humiliation," Mary hisses at me. "Your father's behavior. I'll show him." She has left the car and is in the middle of the street with the two shopping bags.

"For you. Happy Birthday, Dan," she says, handing Danny one of the bags. Danny murmurs a thank you and unwraps a football, then runs into the house to show everyone, leaving me and Mary alone.

"This is for you. Happy Birthday. I thought this was going to be such a wonderful surprise." She glances at the house and back at me.

"Open it," she orders. I dread opening the white box and am relieved when Danny walks out of the house with the football cradled under his arm. I undo the ribbon.

"What's taking you so long?" she demands. My fingers become sticks with her watching me.

"Here, let me open it." She grabs the gift from me and rips open the package. A pair of purple velvet pants falls to the ground. I reach down and pick them up, brushing off some pebbles. Overhead, the football is flying straight up in the air.

"You don't like them, do you? Do you know how expensive those pants were?"

"It's just . . . the velvet. And purple. Kids my age don't wear . . ." Mary throws the bag and box on the ground with force, lifts her right hand, and slaps me across the face. I put my hand to my cheek and hold it there. Danny is chasing after the football.

"You ingrate. You don't appreciate anything I do for you. Everything I do is wrong. What kind of girl are you? I'm glad your mother's not alive to see your behavior." Hate takes over me, like a presence. *My mother not alive to see my behavior? What about your behavior, Witch-woman?* "You've never liked me, have you, Carole?" She is reading my mind, bubbling with black hate, and yet I desperately try to reassure her.

"No, that's not true. I don't understand why . . ." Before I could finish my lie, she hits me again. If I run to the house like a baby, she'll win so I stand there on the street, making a vow not to cry. My eyes fill with hurt, shame, hate, confusion. She's making me feel as if I've done something wrong. All this over a pair of purple velvet pants.

"Go in and tell your father what you did. How you added to my humiliation. Tell him. Afraid to interrupt his lobster dinner?" I begin walking to the house, feeling the sting on my cheek, hoping it is red, that there are visible marks. Behind me the car door slams. She turns the car around and guns it down the street. I'm glad Johnny Cunningham had already gone home.

"Did she hit you?" Danny asks.

"Yeah. Twice. Is my face red?"

"I don't see anything. What did you do?" Danny passes the football from one hand to the other.

"I didn't like the purple velvet pants. You're lucky you got a football."

"You'd be a joke if you wore those pants." Danny considers himself a fashion judge. "Who wears purple velvet pants?" he asks, laughing and pointing at them.

"Mary. What a witch," I'm opening the screen door when Danny takes my arm.

"Wait. Don't tell Dad until after Ann's gone home."

"You'd think Dad could keep better track of his dates," I answer. "I'm half hoping she gets in a car accident in her 'borrowed' car. Who'd lend her a car anyway? The way she drives." But Danny has already gone in for the night, leaving me alone with my evil wishes. Leaning against the porch column, I listen to the night air, half-expecting, half-hoping to hear the sound of metal crushing—her car hitting a telephone pole. Now, that would be a birthday present.

Later, when my father leaves to drive Ann back to White Sands, I look out from my open window at the black night sky, so wanting to believe that my mother is a star with the power to protect me. In Disney movies and television and books, miracles happen like clockwork between the car commercials and in chapter endings, but on that birthday night no star shot across the sky for me, no spider spun a silken web for Carole O'Malley. At eleven-thirty when my dad still isn't back, I fall into bed. My fifteenth birthday shot, destroyed. I wonder if any birthday will ever be this bad again. If I could only be sure I'd never see Mary again, that might help.

Danny's fourteen today. Uncle Bill, who tracks the beach weather on the radio, reports at breakfast that the temperature is expected to reach the low nineties by mid-morning. "A hot one, a real scorcher, for your combined birthday," he says. Just one of the risks of a late August birthday. Instead of going to the beach for a swim, I'm sitting on the porch steps waiting for my father, who has gone to town for milk and bread. Smudge-edged puffball clouds scatter across the blue sky, and I decide one of the clouds looks like a tiered birthday cake. Although I'm partial to chocolate, the white fluff cloud has the look of white frosting. Just as I'm about to give up my post, I spot the station wagon turning the corner.

"Danny saw the second slap. He was there. I have a witness," I say. Complaining in our family, I know, only sets me up for ridicule, but Mary did slap me across the face.

"Yesterday was not a good day for Mary," my father says, putting a carton of beer in the refrigerator. Walking into the other room, my aunt has a faraway look in her eyes.

"I'll say. She slapped me across the face, Dad. Ask Danny. Once wasn't enough. She may look like a bird but she's strong."

"Mary was upset. She didn't expect to find Ann here."

"Well, that's not my fault. Maybe she should have slapped you." My dad raises his eyebrows at me.

"I'm afraid Mary can be a very nervous woman," he says, closing the refrigerator door with his back to me. "I'm sorry it happened, Carole. You're a tough cookie. You'll forget about it. Let's not waste this beach day and head on down to that water." Why am I a tough cookie and the scrod lady is forgiven everything because she's "nervous"? Maybe I should be "nervous." If it were raining out and not a "beach day," would the face slaps matter more?

None of my dad's girlfriends shows up after dinner for our birthday cake. I was slicing the petals of the pink icing flower with my fork and watching my dad drink a beer. Uncle Bill had started calling him Casanova, making everyone laugh, and I wondered if my dad had other girlfriends, girlfriends I did not know about, girlfriends who were not the nervous type.

I will never, never wear the purple velvet pants.

25. Stage Left, Stage Right, Entrances and Exits

WITH A GOOD two hours before the Saturday afternoon football game, Cathy Lamoureux is in my room, fingering the piles of clothing in her open suitcase.

"Rene's hand-me-down. They'll never fit," Cathy says with a laugh. "Is your dad driving us to the football game?"

"I think Michael will."

"You could have gone to the cemetery with your dad this morning. I could have found something to do."

"If he was only going to the cemetery, but he was going to the butcher's too. And I went last week." I wonder if Mrs. Lamoureux goes to the cemetery every Saturday the way my dad does. Cathy's dad has been dead longer, but I can't make myself ask her. Talking has a way of making things more true, more real, so I keep quiet.

"Tell me the truth. Do these pants look good?" Cathy is wearing camel wool pants, size 14, a size she hates.

"Yes, they look good, better than the plaid." Cathy has brought five pairs of pants with her.

"I'm big, like my mother."

"The pants look fine," I say, looking at the pants spread all over the unmade bed.

"Teddy calls me 'blimp' if my mother or sisters aren't around."

"Just zing them back. You can never let brothers know they're getting to you."

"I know. I was hoping when I got my period I'd slim down the way Rene did, but no. When did you get your period?"

"I had just turned ten."

"Ten?"

"I know, a freak of nature and so unfair." I don't like talking about my period either. Maybe it's different with sisters. "I thought I was dying. My mother hadn't said anything to me, so I thought I had leukemia, which I knew was a blood disease."

After the game, we hang around and meet Michael in the parking lot.

"About time they won something. Get in the car," Michael orders us in a stern voice. Cathy looks at me, and we hop in the back seat.

"What about Danny?" I ask.

"Oh, he's getting a ride with some hotshot friends. You know, Carole, he thinks he'll play. He'll never play. That coach will never play him."

"He plays JV." I don't know why I defend Danny, but I do.

"He's too small. He can drink all that canned nutrition he wants. It won't make him grow." Stalled in traffic, Cathy and I sit in the back seat under a shower of Michael's blackness.

The scent of my dad's Old Spice enters the kitchen before he does. Cathy and I are sitting at the kitchen table pulling Vienna Fingers apart to lick the filling.

"You two staying in tonight?" My dad is wearing his camel cashmere sport coat, a coat so expensive he had kept it hidden in the trunk of the car so my mother wouldn't see it. After she died, he bought a cashmere winter top coat, which he's carrying on his arm.

"We are," I say. Sixty out and he's wearing a top coat. I'm guessing he's taking Mary out for dinner. Like my father, Mary likes beautiful clothing, the purple velvet pants aside.

"How's your mother? She's quite a woman," he says to Cathy. The smell of whiskey on his breath means that he and Mary spent the crisp fall afternoon drinking in a hotel bar. "No party this week?" he asks.

"There may be, but I'm not invited," I answer with my "I don't care" shrug.

"How can anyone have a party and not invite you?" My dad loves parties, and in some way I sense I've disappointed him.

"Don't be late, Dad." As he's about to close the door, he smiles his handsome smile and waves at us.

"Your dad's really good-looking," Cathy says as if she's reading my mind.

"Yeah, it's a big deal for him that he can still get in his Army uniform." My formless prayers are answered when Cathy doesn't ask me where he's going. Later that night, before bed, I show her the purple velvet pants.

"I didn't see anyone wearing these at the game today."

"Neither did I. And they are the school color."

We pile back into the house after eight o'clock Mass, anticipating our fresh, warm Liberty Bakery doughnuts, our Sunday morning treat. The bag feels warm against my sweater. My dad had asked Michael to drive us to early Mass while he stayed home. Gerry is running for the bathroom but stops outside the locked door. From the bathroom, we all clearly hear the guttural sounds of my father getting sick. Gerry looks up at me, and I gesture for him to go to the back bathroom. My father has never been this sick before.

"Why don't you go upstairs, Cathy, and finish packing and I'll get out the doughnuts." With an understanding she manages to hide, Cathy disappears. With Cathy out of earshot, I huddle the little kids together in a corner of the kitchen.

"Dad's sick, but he'll be OK. Grab a doughnut, you can take it outside, and maybe go play in the leaves. Let's see how many red and yellow leaves you can find. You can sprinkle sugar on the leaves." Shooing them outside, I try to spare the little kids, who are frozen with fear, from listening to my dad. They quiet down, obey me without question, and run for the backyard. I watch them for a second at the window, knowing Cathy has been an unwilling witness to the aftermath of his drinking. Should I make excuses for him to her? It's too hard for me to talk with this shame spreading through me. I bite the tip of my tongue. Five minutes later, while I'm sponging confectionery sugar off the counter, my dad walks slowly into the kitchen, a bottle of Listerine in his hand. He is so pale and shaky I have to look away.

"Look, I'll take an Alka-Seltzer and I'll be fine." I so want to believe him, the way Michael and Danny do. Ignoring him, I wipe up the leaked jelly doughnut droppings as he gulps the foamy mixture and swipes at the white mustache on his upper lip. With my back to him, I throw the sponge against the sink and say angrily, "In front of my friend."

"Hey, it was a rough night. Cathy'll be fine," he answers weakly.

"Yeah, she's not throwing up her guts. Your eyes are all red."

"I'm paying the piper."

"You scared us all." The tips of my ears feel hot, like a blush losing its way.

"Princess, your old man's a rock."

"Well, I'm no geologist but I've never heard of a rock with a stomach flu," I answer back sarcastically. And then, seeking some reassurance to ease the confusion festering inside me, "What do I tell Cathy?"

"There's a stomach flu going around?" he answers with a soft grin.

My hand on the upstairs banister, I hesitate, thinking how it's been a rough morning for me, Dad. Sitting primly on my made-up bed, Cathy complains of a headache and asks if Michael and I could drive her to the station for the next train. She can barely wait to get out of here.

The performance of *Silas Marner* is scheduled for third-period assembly on a Thursday and Friday in late October. My classmates have seen fit to cast me in the role of Molly, the opium-addicted mother who, clutching her toddler daughter to her breast, drains her last dregs of the "familiar demon" and dies in the middle of a snowstorm. I can really ham up the death scene, have had no lines to memorize, and only had to attend two rehearsals. I did create a bit of a faked scene in English class when Sister announced the parts. I raised my hand and waited for Sister to call on me.

"Sister, I am wondering if this typecasting of me as the drug-addicted mother is in any way a reflection on me."

"I can assure you, Carole, that this is not the way your classmates see you." She looked around the class, spreading her hands.

"I think it is," Ernie Croughwell snickered from the back of the class. Sister just laughed and said she knew I could undergo a miraculous dramatic transformation to play the part of Molly. The truth, then, was I didn't really care, but we were about to start reading *Julius Caesar* in class and I was stalling it.

Backstage, Jeanne Ledoux is putting baby powder in my hair.

"I hate to do this to your hair," she says with her wide smile.

"Oh, it's probably an improvement. How do I hold the shawl?" We wrap Sister's heavy black shawl around my shoulders.

"Maybe you could stoop more," Jeanne suggests, adjusting the shawl around my neck.

"First time anyone's said that to me. 'Straighten your shoulders, Carole. Military posture, Carole.'"

"Are your mother and father coming?" she asks innocently. Does she know about my mother? Had she not seen my mother's death notice in the school newspaper last year? Has she forgotten?

"No, no one's coming. It's not my finest moment." I hold back the truth about my mother. My father never goes to Danny's football games so I didn't think he would come to see me in a play for my sixty seconds on stage. I hadn't even asked him.

My stage props in hand, I adjust the worn shawl and shove the brown prescription bottle of my "drug" into my pocket. On cue, I skulk on stage into the spotlight, pull out my "drug," hold it lovingly to my lips, stagger, and fall dead as the lights fade out.

Two nights after my *Silas Marner* performance, my dad gathers Michael, Danny, and me and tells us to wait for him in the living room.

"Did you tell dad about your big performance?" Michael asks, tapping the sofa arm with his left palm.

"You mean where she falls onstage and dies? I heard about it at football practice." Danny looks toward the kitchen.

"I'm being nominated for an Academy Award." I only have French homework, devoirs, left to do.

"All the sophomores were laughing during football drills," he adds.

"Why does Dad want to see the three of us?" Michael asks. I hear the clink of the ice cubes before I see my dad standing in the doorway. He walks across the living room and stands over in front of the window.

"Look, I want the three of you to know that Mary and I are getting married on Armistice Day."

No, no, no. I calculate I've got about a month to get him to change his mind.

"The younger kids need a mother," he plows on. "I want the three of you older kids to help her." I exchange looks with Michael and Danny for support.

"I'm seventeen. It won't affect me," Michael says, standing up to leave the room.

"Well, what about her job?" I ask.

"She's agreed to quit her job to take care of the kids." He grips his hands around his glass, just holding it, not drinking it. "I know you and she have had a hard time."

"Oh, you mean, the face slapping."

"Carole, I'll be here so that won't happen again." She gets her own security guard to keep her from belting me.

"What about Ann, the English teacher?" I ask, grasping for hope.

"I'm marrying Mary."

"What if Mrs. Meade and I tried to do a better job? I could quit the Latin Club." I'd do anything.

"You can't take care of your brothers. You're fifteen. I had Dr. Blackmer talk to you this summer." Why does he have to say this in front of Michael and Danny? That I'm not capable? I don't want them to know about Tommy sleeping in the driveway as if that would hide my shame. There is a tightness forming in my arms, as if they were turning to steel rods, and I feel a hardness spreading to the back of my neck.

"I have to do this, and I don't want you to make it any more difficult than it already is." My dad puts his glass down on the newspaper.

"Isn't there anyone else you could marry?" I ask as if I had a TV star in mind.

"Why do you always have to make things hard?" Michael asks me. "Mary will be all right. You're not marrying her."

"Is there a party?" Danny asks, finally speaking.

"Yes, and you all get new clothes." My dad answers, satisfying Danny, buying him off with a new sport coat.

"Oh, good, I'll wear the purple velvet." My father rubs his hands together.

"This is not a time for sarcasm. I'm doing this to make things easier for you."

"Still, I don't want a new dress. I don't need things to be easier."

That night, lying in bed, I map out a history: In June of eighth grade, my mother dies; Armistice Day of tenth grade, my dad gets married again. Enter Stepmother.

For a Saturday morning, the house is quiet. My dad packed the little kids into the car for a grocery trip and his routine stop at the cemetery. I am pulling down a jar of peanut butter for sandwiches when Gerry comes running into the house, shaking and crying so hard I can barely understand him. Checking him out for dripping blood, I am relieved to see no gaping holes.

"What's the matter? Are you hurt?" He still can't answer me. His face is smeared where he has rubbed under his eyes with his dirty hands. "You look OK. What happened?" He slumps into the kitchen chair.

"We were playing explorer in the woods and . . ." He starts crying again, sobbing the words out.

"And you didn't get to be Columbus?"

"Billy Metzger said that Dad's getting married and I'll have a stepmother. Is that true?" Gerry asks me, his tears tracking through the dirt. After I tell him about the wedding, he looks up at me and asks, "Well, how come Billy knew before I did?"

While I lay out eight slices of bread and start spreading the peanut butter, Gerry stands next to me watching, his shoulders no longer heaving.

"It smells good, doesn't it?" I search for an explanation to calm Gerry down, true or false, to protect my father, shift the blame.

"Maybe you were out in the woods playing when Dad told us," I suggest. I dip a teaspoon in the peanut butter and hand it to him. Gerry licks the spoon and drops it in the sink.

"She won't be my mother. I don't have to call her Mom?"

"No. Dad said we could call her Mary." I'm thinking of names like cold cream face, scrod lady, face slapper.

"When is Armistice Day?"

"November 11th, right after Halloween. We're all invited to the wedding and Billy's not," I explain with a "So there" in my voice.

"Good." Gerry slams the door after him, ready to taunt the uninvited Billy. As I get the grape jelly out of the refrigerator, I'm wondering what it means for my life to get easier. I hope my dad's right on this one. Let my dad be right, and like a little kid I cross my fingers and squeeze my eyes shut. From out of nowhere, those three witches cackling at the steaming cauldron in *Macbeth*—eye of newt, toe of frog, a hell-broth—pop into my mind.

ARMISTICE DAY 1994

SETTING: The Fort Restaurant in Springfield, Massachusetts. It is lunchtime.

(The waitress places a drink in front of Joe as Joe and Carole hand her their menus.)

JOE: Thank you, Gretchen.
(Carole smiles at the waitress.)
CAROLE: You're a fixture here, dad.
JOE: I have a certain loyalty.
CAROLE: I picked that up from you. I'm loyal. Too loyal, I think, sometimes.
JOE: There's no such thing as too much loyalty. *(Joe picks up an old-fashioned glass of whiskey and sips.)* Ah, the nectar of the gods.
CAROLE: How sweet it is. *(Carole holds up a glass of water.)*
JOE: Remember that food basket Rupert sent over to the house when your mother died? He's a generous man.
CAROLE: I'd take Leo's candy over the Fort's sausage any day.
JOE: The O'Malley sweet tooth.
CAROLE: Dad, you and Mary married thirty-four years ago today.
JOE: And fifteen years with your mother. I guess that makes me an old man.
CAROLE: Old and gray and only in the way. Your line. We had it backwards. Armistice Day represented the end of World War I, and with us it was Pearl Harbor. Let the wars begin.
JOE: You were a very stubborn, hard-headed teenager.
CAROLE: *(Spitefully.)* And did that mean you never needed to protect me? I'm not letting you pin it all on me.

(*Joe offers the bread basket to Carole.*)

JOE: Try a piece of the black bread. Rupert claims it's an old Bavarian standby.

CAROLE: (*Sighing.*) Dad, you can't put me off with a slice of Rupert's black bread.

JOE: You're not thirteen anymore.

CAROLE: Do you know you didn't even tell Gerry you were getting married?

JOE: (*Hopelessly.*) There were eight of you.

CAROLE: I'm sorry, Dad. I'm torn between letting the past go and learning from it.

JOE: The danger of having an analytical daughter.

CAROLE: Lifelong learner.

JOE: That's what David calls you. (*Joe signals to the waitress and points to his empty glass.*) Gerry said you're out there proselytizing Adult Children of Alcoholics meetings now, trying to rope your brothers in.

CAROLE: (*She taunts him.*) As you order your second whiskey before the food even arrives. A gift for timing, Dad. So what, Gerry felt as if he had to warn you?

JOE: We men like to stick together.

CAROLE: That's a surprise. I had given up sarcasm, too.

JOE: Sarcasm? What is this? Lent?

CAROLE: So Gerry's out there beating the family drums, letting everyone know what's going on?

JOE: You do realize that those meetings are an insult to me. (*Self-deprecatingly.*) What new failings of mine have you discovered in your Adult Children of Alcoholics meetings?

CAROLE: You sound threatened. Nothing like an ACOA meeting to take the blinders off.

JOE: Like that crack about my not protecting you? You're tough, kiddo.

CAROLE: (*In frustration.*) Because you say I am, is that it? All right. For the first six months of meetings, I went on Wednesday nights, your old Elks night, and I kept a scorecard on what kind of parent I was. I couldn't make myself look back at 21 Lynwood Terrace.

JOE: (*He is unsure.*) I don't know how much good looking back at the past ever does.

CAROLE: You're saying that to a history major? (*Carole picks up a slice of the black bread and butters it.*) Dad, do you remember when I was in that high school play, *Silas Marner*?

JOE: I can barely remember what I did yesterday. (*Carole smiles.*) I suppose it's another event I never attended. Is that the way this is going to go?

CAROLE: I didn't even ask you to come to the play. Sad, the way I let you off the hook.

JOE: Didn't you write a play called *Off the Hook*?

CAROLE: I changed the name of it somewhere along the way. Maybe I rationalized you were too busy, too sophisticated for a high school play.

JOE: Sophisticated, I'll accept.

CAROLE: You were so handsome in your Yale-Genton suits. I forgave you so much, Dad, because of your dark, Irish looks.

JOE: Another legacy of mine, these black eyes, I've handed down to you.

CAROLE: In *Silas Marner*, I played the part of a down-and-out mother addicted to opium. I stumbled across the stage, a doll in my arms, emptied a vial of drugs, and died on stage.

JOE: I don't suppose you'd care to reenact it here today at the Fort?

CAROLE: You're good. You're still funny. A pin in my balloon.

(*Gretchen arrives and places plates of schnitzel in front of them.*)

CAROLE AND JOE: Thank you.

CAROLE: Joking, making light of everything, is a defense mechanism. (*Joe, exasperated, places his fork on the plate and looks at Carole.*) I know. I know. Before therapy I used to be funny.

JOE: Now that is funny.

CAROLE: Maybe it will come back.

JOE: Let's hope so.

CAROLE: But, back to *Silas Marner* . . .

JOE: (*Interrupting.*) We're back there again.

CAROLE: The mother left the daughter, it was a daughter, left alone. Do you see the connection?

JOE: Is this your way of telling me you're on drugs?

CAROLE: (*Smiling at him.*) There you go again. You're a master. No, the child was abandoned by her parent's addiction. (*Stammering.*) I just want it to be different for my daughters.

JOE: What are you saying?

CAROLE: Death, Dad, is the ultimate abandonment. It's beyond neglect.

JOE: Are you talking about your mother?

CAROLE: Mom did not choose to die. The terror of being all alone.

JOE: Hey, I told you I'd always be there for you kids.

CAROLE: You said a lot of things.

JOE: Ye of little faith.

CAROLE: It's the family cycle of drink that terrifies me. I feel spooked that I was selected to play that role, the child of an addict. Those nuns could be Cassandras. But I wanted the merry-go-round of booze to stop.

JOE: Irish Medicine.

CAROLE: That was the name of my play, Dad.

(*They eat in silence, not looking at each other. The silence is meant to be painful.*)

JOE: Shall we indulge ourselves with the apple crisp à la mode?

CAROLE: Let's do it. Dad, I was talking to Michael about your honeymoon years with Mary, trying to remember that golden time.

JOE: You're tough on the old man. I'm bracing myself.

CAROLE: You know how Michael described that time? Not a sober minute.

JOE: Not a sober minute? It has a certain ring to it.

CAROLE: (*After a minute.*) Excuse me, Dad.

(*Carole exits. Joe is alone at the table, nodding to acquaintances. Carole sits at a chair at a vanity in the powder room. She puts her head on her arms, then lifts her head, and looks in the mirror.*)

CAROLE: A certain ring to it? What was I thinking? Irish Medicine?

26. Party Time

"LOOK AT JFK in the limousine. Eddie Boland's sitting right next to Senator Kennedy." I point to the full-page spread in the *Daily News* with half a dozen pictures of Senator Kennedy at a rally in Court Square the day before the presidential election.

"Is that a Cadillac limousine?" Danny asks. "How many people are there?"

"Over 40,000 people, the paper says. I didn't even know he was coming. Did you?"

"No, but that's why Mary Eugene was threatening expulsion to any Cathedral student who left school for any reason. The principal was afraid we'd storm the rally."

"From the picture in the paper, Dan, it looks as if every other student in Springfield skipped school to see JFK."

"Do you think Kennedy will win today?"

"Dad thinks it will be close."

The next day, November 8, 1960, when John Fitzgerald Kennedy defeated shifty-eyed "Tricky Dick" Nixon in the presidential race, Massachusetts entered a state of high-pitched euphoria, but at 21 Lynwood Terrace the mood with the approaching wedding just three days away was anything but euphoric.

My dad pats the flecks of gray in his black hair as he primps for his stag party at the Elks Club. I would take the piney smell of my dad's Fitch dandruff shampoo over his mouthwash any day. Too, his green Clorets gum has a nice scent, like candy, but has nowhere near the sugary taste of my favorite bright yellow Juicy Fruit gum. In their new wool sport coats and white button-down shirts, Danny, hair decurled, and Michael pace the kitchen, waiting, looking up at the clock.

"Dad, you better hurry," Michael says, shifting his feet. "Mr. Metzger left five minutes ago."

"But Dad's the groom-to-be," Danny answers with a snicker.

"Old and gray and only in the way," my dad chants with energy and a soft chuckle. He turns his head and runs the palm of his hand over the bristles of his crew cut. "No more part in the middle for the old man."

"Do you miss your barbershop quartet look?" I ask.

"You know what I say . . ."

"If you're going to grow old, you're going to grow old gracefully," I interrupt.

"Ah, daughter of mine. Look at this military posture on your old man. Your mother and I could never get you to stand up straight." He pulls his shoulders back, straightens his wool plaid sport coat, and heads for the kitchen door.

"I don't get to go to your stag party because I have slumped shoulders, is that it?"

"Hey, you're in charge here at the home front." I am watching them back out of the driveway when Gerry comes charging into the kitchen, all dressed up and his hair slicked back.

"They just left. Dad didn't say you were going."

"He told me I'm too young. I just thought if I got all dressed up, I could get him to change his mind." He's chewing on the inside of his cheek. "They just drink whiskey anyway."

"I'm not going either. You look good, though. It might have worked. Is that your wedding outfit?"

"How do you like my tie? It's not a clip-on." He unknots his striped tie and slips out of his jacket.

"Put the jacket away before somebody spills milk on it," I bark to his back. When I finish my biology reading, I grab his jacket off the chair. When I open the door to the living room closet, Gerry is standing there in the dark, holding a photograph of my mother. Neither of us says anything. Halfway up the stairs, I hear him say to himself, "So pretty."

Her pink lipstick bothers me. I know I shouldn't have thoughts like this in church during a wedding, my father's wedding, but I am. Mary describes her lace dress as "champagne-colored," and I have to admit it's beautiful, but I'm wary of the toothy smile glued on her talcum powder face. With Mary and my dad at the altar, I think of how we all sang, "I'm getting married in the morning," in the car ride down to Hartford, and I have to smile. Crossing over the Connecticut line, right around Bradley airport, we started belting out, "Get me to the church on time," loud, off-key, and yelling.

The priest (with bright red hair; is that a good sign or a bad sign for a wedding?) faces the church and asks if anyone knows of any reason to stop this wedding. How about the bride's a face slapper, a ranter and raver, and then she in a complete turnaround will collapse into tears? Please, God, don't let this wedding happen. Behind me, people are coughing and scuffling their feet, but no one protests. My shoulders scrunch up when the priest pronounces them man and wife, and I picture myself on a ship taking on water. Mary smiles enough for both of them, and my father, ever the joker, has a serious, tight look. Is he thinking of my mother? His wartime wedding? At the altar, my uncle Bill, best man, clears his throat. I love sitting in the front row on the groom's side where I feel that I am part of the main attraction, but everyone behind us now can witness Tommy crawling along the pew. I grab Tommy's suspenders as he crawls by and fix his crooked clip-on bow tie.

Ave Maria . . . A high-pitched soprano sings and I try to translate the *Ave* in my head, but prayers are too hard to translate with that hortative mode. The petticoat attached to my dress digs into my waist as we follow Mary, my dad, my aunt and uncle from the church. Ahead of me, Michael escorts Mary's tiny white-haired mother, holding her arm. Twice as many guests are on my dad's side, maybe even more, people I think of as friends of my mom and dad, men with suits and ties, made-up women with fur stoles around their shoulders, while Mary's side is scanty. Good.

Outside, Mary is picking dots of confetti from her hair as Tommy, Bob, and Steve run around picking up the pieces off the church steps and throwing them up in the air all over again. We watch from the sidewalk as Mary and my dad get into a black limousine with soft gray velvet seats. My dad turns to wave at us.

"Carole, we have our own table right near the front," Gerry says in a whisper out of the corner of his mouth as if this seating might be a mistake. Gawking at the fancy, carved columns, we peer through the tall picture windows overlooking the park with the gold-domed capitol building behind the trees. My uncle and the congressman are standing next to our table.

"So, Eddie, here's Joe on his second wedding, and you're still an old bachelor living with Tip O'Neill down in DC. When are you getting married?" my uncle asks the congressman, who drapes his arm around my shoulders.

"Well, Bill, if you must know, I'm waiting for Carole to grow up. What year of high school are you in now? When she finishes college might be a good time." While we all laugh at the teasing, I'm a shade disappointed since I recognize it as a line he's used before.

"Eddie, you are quite the politician," my uncle says. "So what happened in Ohio? Our man Kennedy lost there, Eddie, with you heading up the campaign."

"Now, Bill, I was just a poll watcher. Matty Ryan did a good job with New Jersey."

"But Ohio, Eddie. What happened?" my uncle asks pointedly.

"Are you ever going to let me forget it? Jack won, didn't he?" he says smoothly.

"I thought you two could pull it off, if anyone could," my uncle needles.

"We gave it our best shot, but the good people of Ohio made the wrong choice at the voting booths. It happens. Now, you kids will be voting Democratic when the time comes?" We nod our heads and murmur a group yes, unaccustomed to being treated as near adults. His eyes drift off to Mary, now legally my stepmother, waltzing in my father's arms.

"Let me find my godson. Carole, will you take me over to Tom." The congressman orders me, rather than asks, and I lead him through the crowd to Tommy, who's standing over by the windows. When I turn to leave, Eddie stops me and says, "Carole, I want you to know how wonderful your mother was, I would have married her if your father hadn't beat me to it, and how hard all this has been for your father. If I can be of help to you or your brothers in any way, I hope you'll call me. Anytime. I mean it." His hands hold mine. After a pause, he adds, "I love your father like a brother. He helped me get elected in my first campaign. We go way back on Hungry Hill. Oh, you know all that." Then he slips off with a wave of his hand while a flush crawls into my cheeks. With my hand, I touch the heavy drapery and finger the wide cord holding back the folds of fabric as I stare out at the capitol building. The onion-shaped dome suggesting some majestic foreign country looks out of place against the bare leafless trees bordering the park. A crumpled brown paper bag dances across the sidewalk. When charcoal clouds cover the sickly afternoon sun, the air has a sudden dark feel.

From across the room, my father motions to me.

"Carole, I've asked the band to play a song especially for us. So you must do me the honor of dancing with your old man. No matter what, Princess, you will always be my little girl, my star on the tree." My dad croons the words, Frank Sinatra style. The sweat gathers in circles under my arms, but I dance as he leads me to "Daddy's Little Girl," a song my brothers think is the sappiest in the English language.

"Help your aunt and uncle out when Mary and I are in Miami. We're only going for five days." My dad spends the rest of the dance telling me how I'll soon see how everything will get better, so convincingly that I barely listen to the song. Twirling, I manage the waltz without stepping on his feet. Although he sounds so sure, I wonder if he's only making excuses. Party or not, my dad all to myself, I want this day to end.

"I picked your mother, didn't I?" he asks me. And all I can think of is how my mother was always yelling at me to take Tommy or Bobby out for a walk in his stroller. I would yell back that it was Michael or Danny's turn, not mine. They hadn't walked the baby in three days, I'd argue. Summer screaming matches and now she was dead, about to be replaced by an overeager understudy.

Out on the hotel sidewalk, my dad helps Mary into the limousine, her soft pink "going away" suit lifting way up above her knobby knees. Handing her new white Samsonite suitcase to the driver, my dad gets in and waves at all of us for the fourth time as the car pulls away from the curb. Up ahead of me, Uncle Bill is walking arm in arm with Aunt Mad, leaning his good ear down to her. Whatever she is saying, his face has a somber, worried look. For a few minutes, a quiet takes him over, and my uncle's big-chested heartiness is gone. When Michael drives the station wagon up I-91, we sprawl out on the seats, quiet, vying for space, a hit, a slap, a pinch, a push, but I don't feel like refereeing. Let them fight. Michael yells at us, "Shut up, will you?" And we do shut up, until Enfield anyway.

"It rained every day. No sun in Florida for the newlyweds," my dad said, dropping ice cubes into his drink as he hands my uncle the bottle of whiskey.

"Tom, Bobby, and Stevie missed you. They really didn't have much idea of what was going on," my aunt reports.

"Thank you, Mad and Bill. I know Mary joins me in thanking you for letting us have this honeymoon. Who else but you two would take care of these eight banshees?" The three grownups study the floor. Carrying on about a splitting headache, Mary has fled into the bedroom and closed the door.

"It's a new start," my dad continues, "I'm sorry Mary has such a headache right now." Glancing in my direction, my aunt stops, puts down her suitcase, and hugs me tightly.

"Katsy, Katsy," my uncle chants. Only Uncle Bill still calls me by my failed nickname, Katsy, maybe three or four times a year. He throws his arm around my shoulder and bellows, "Hey, kid. Take it easy. We'll see you at Thanksgiving."

"Kitty, come over here, and give the old man a hug," my dad says when they leave. I am still trying to figure out what "take it easy" means when there is a clacking of high heels in the hallway. My father turns to the cabinet, reaching up to pull down another glass for Mary.

"Have they gone, Joe? I thought they'd never leave. I don't know what I ever did to offend your sister. The way that Madeline treats me." Mary's words and tone confuse me, make me want to defend Aunt Madeline, so I leave the lovebirds, a word my uncle has used, drinking in the kitchen. What could my aunt have done to Mary to make her so upset? I hadn't seen anything and, as Dr. Blackmer said to me at the wedding, not much gets by me. Didn't my aunt and uncle just come over and stay with us for five days? From the quiet of the living room, I could make out my father's soft murmurs when Mary's next words made me halt.

"I know she's invited us for Thanksgiving and this is something you started doing after Betty died, but I want to have Thanksgiving here, away from that woman." Her anger has a new rocklike force that makes me cringe. What has my aunt done to her to earn the title "that woman"? How will Mary condemn me? Careful. Careful. I need to be careful around her to protect myself.

Suddenly the house is immaculate, no more banana peels or apple cores under the den couch. Mary banishes dust, dirt, and creates a spotless environment. My brothers' school uniform shirts and pants hang downstairs in size order on a heating pipe. If cleanliness is really next to godliness, as the nuns love to say, I would not be sitting in the same room with God, but

Mary would be seated at the head table. The order of the house appeals to me, but I live in fear that one of my brothers might leave a spoon in the kitchen sink. My father is keeping her temper tantrums in line with whiskey and sweet nothings. Two, three, or four nights a week they go out to restaurants or parties or bars. When Mary is out for the evening, the house has a relaxed air, as if we could breathe easily again, as if there were dirty socks under the sofa again.

About a month after the wedding, Mary replaced my navy orange-flecked sofa with a smaller white one with a green-leaf design. I shrugged it off and said nothing, too afraid to ask what had happened to it.

27. Joey, the Bird

DO ALL NEWLYWEDS celebrate a two-week anniversary? Winking at me, my dad says he and Mary are off for the afternoon to the Sheraton to celebrate two weeks of marriage with a few glasses of "the bubbly." Closing the door behind them, and with Mary safely gone, I decide to celebrate my few hours of freedom from her eavesdropping on my telephone conversations.

"No, of course I'm not going to the EDT dance, Carole. I wouldn't know anyone there. Even if we were here Thanksgiving night, what boy would I ask? And which lucky fellow did you end up asking?"

"I asked Tommy Waldron because remember when he asked me to dance once back in ninth grade?" Before Dianne answers, Danny strolls into the kitchen and begins chuckling, acting as if he knew something about my date that I didn't. When he opens the refrigerator, preoccupied with its contents, I listen to Di again.

"Your stepmother's not there, is she?" Her question surprises me.

"No, she and my dad went out."

"I can tell by the way your voice sounds." Back in the TV room, Gerry, Joey, and Stevie have been bickering over the merits of last season's Yankee–Red Sox pitching roster. Suddenly Joey, the sole Yankee fan, bolts out of the den into the kitchen with Gerry and Stevie chasing him.

"Di, I've got to hang up." Blood is pouring from Gerry's lips.

"Yeah, I hear all the noise." *"Look, look,"* *"Do you see what he did?"* *"I was just sitting there."* *"He didn't do anything when Joey belted him."* *"I saw the whole thing."* Shouts of accusation spill over one another as if these blame-sharpened tongues of ours could lick away the blood, repair Gerry's lip. With the four of us outnumbering Joey, crowding him in, his body tenses against the gray tiles lining the kitchen walls.

"Don't any of you come near me," Joey orders, trapped in the corner, his head even with the Currier and Ives November cornucopia.

"But Gerry's bleeding," Stevie blurts out.

"You see what he did to me? Look at the blood." The blood from his mouth has streaked Gerry's fingers, and he holds his hands away from him, splaying his fingers.

"Stevie, go to the linen closet and get a washcloth for Gerry." Half-expecting him to refuse, I take a quick breath when Danny orders Stevie to go. With one final look at Joey, Steve hurries out of the room, afraid of missing anything.

"Joey, do you see what you did?" I ask, only worsening the moment.

"Don't any of you come near me," Joey yells, but Danny has already taken a step forward. Joey crouches under the kitchen table, then ducks into the living room, and runs up the stairs, yelling back at us, "I'm getting out of here!" His parting shot may be no more than a threat, but he has tried running away before, right after my mother died. Panic swirling around us, we spring after Joey.

The afternoon light behind him, Joey stands in front of the half-open upstairs window, facing us all.

"If you take one more step near me, I'll jump." With arms that won the Little League batting championship, Joey opens the bedroom window all the way up. We stand in a semi-circle as his eyes dart down to the driveway and cement stairs below. Paralyzed, we watch, and after a second Joey jumps out on the porch roof.

"Joey, you'll hurt yourself if you fall," Danny says.

"I don't care if I hurt myself." Joey bends down on the shingles and uses the gutter to support his feet.

"Look, Joey, no one will hit you, if you crawl back in here," I say.

"We won't touch you," Gerry and Stevie plea in one voice. "My lip's already stopped bleeding," Gerry adds with his index finger covering the cut. Then Michael comes barreling up the stairs.

"Are you trying to get him in?" Michael asks me and Danny. "You can't let him stay out there like that."

"We've been trying, Michael. He won't come in," Danny answers.

"He's got to get back in before Mary and Dad get home," I say, my mind jumping ahead to envision that scene. "Have you got any ideas on how to get him in?"

"It's too late now. Mrs. Metzger is peering out of her kitchen window. We have to tell Dad and Mary."

"We know that, Michael." Below, on the deserted street, Tommy and Jimmy Metzger are pedaling their tricycles, stopping when they spy Joey. Jimmy points up and Tommy's expression changes when he sees Joey hanging off the roof. Tommy yells, "Joey, don't jump." Joey gets a better footing, moves a little closer to the window. A sense of life spinning out of control hits me. It's all so fast, fast, fast moving—crisis time.

"It's too risky for me to grab him," Danny whispers under his breath.

"You're right," I whisper back, grasping that there is nothing I can do.

"Joey, Joey, Joey . . ." Tommy's voice trails off from the Metzger driveway when crying overtakes him. Then, just as quickly as he flew out on the roof, Joey jumps back through the window into the bedroom. In an instant, Danny pushes the window down and stands in front of it, blocking another escape.

"Joey, why did you do that?"

"Just leave me alone and let me watch my television show," Joey screams, red-faced, and disappears down the stairs. We stand there, relieved; yet we are somehow changed, more aware of a family streak that mocks safety and embraces danger. Gerry and I sit on the plaid bedspread, our hands underneath our legs.

"Was it Tommy's crying?" "Who cares what got him off the roof? At least, he's back in the house." "Why did Mrs. Metzger have to see it?" "What's Dad going to say? He could have killed himself." "What is wrong with him? Do you think he'll run away after this?" Talking all at once, we glance out of the window as Danny turns its lock.

* * *

After the roof incident, two things happened: my dad announced we were going to have Thanksgiving dinner at my aunt and uncle's house, as planned, and Joey got the nickname "The Bird." Or just "Bird."

28. Fledgling Journalist and Mad Scientist

THE 5 Ws and the H pretty much sum up Sister Edward Agnes's journalism class. Who, what, when, where, why, and, sometimes, how.

Who takes this alphabetic elective? Mostly sophomores and a few juniors, all of whom have bulls-eyed the honor roll from time to time.

What? To learn the basics of journalism, or just the facts, ma'am.

When? Sixth period.

Where? Room 208, across from Sister Agnes Veronica's room.

Why? The job of our journalism class is to learn how to put out the school paper, *The Cathedral Chronicle,* and to take over the tasks of graduating seniors.

How? As usual, Sister Edward Agnes runs things, but, unlike many of our teachers, she is always willing to listen to our suggestions for news and feature articles.

So now, thanks to C. Joseph O'Malley, Cleon Joseph, my dad, six journalism students are sitting in District Attorney Matty Ryan's reception area, waiting to talk to him about his role in the Kennedy presidential campaign. Since Matty is my dad's childhood friend and my brother Stevie's godfather, my dad suggested our journalism class interview him. I am both pleased and embarrassed that he set this up and more embarrassed that my hair is so oily today that I am wearing an olive green wool knit hat with mirrory spangles on it. Besides having prepared no questions, I cannot believe we are on a field trip. Over by the heavy mahogany door, Sister Edward Agnes is whispering with Walter Kusek, junior class president, who is holding three notebook pages of questions, more than enough for our class to come off halfway intelligent when Matty jets out of his office on the dot of four.

"Come in, come in," he says by way of a welcome, and shakes hands with Sister first and then goes all around, nodding at me. As we follow him into his office, without a Kusek question asked, Matty gives us a rapid-fire summary of the campaign. Distracted by the shelves of law books creeping up the walls, I'm barely listening. Before Walter, Sister's designated representative, can start with his questions, a photographer from the *Springfield Daily News* shows up to take our picture. Surprised into a group silence, including Sister Edward Agnes, we gather around Matty as directed by the photographer. Fiddling with the lapels of his suit, Matty insists I come and sit next to him. If I had known this picture would be in the paper, I would not be wearing this hat that Danny has dubbed my "Christmas Tree" hat, and I wonder if my father has arranged this publicity event as well. The grandstanding has my dad's touch to it, although I wish he had told me. Two nights ago while tweezing my eyebrows in front of the bathroom medicine cabinet, I had overheard Mary say that she thought it was ridiculous to expect that Matty had the time to spend with high school students in a journalism class. She spit the word journalism out as if it were a pornographic film. When my dad answered, all I caught was the phrase "Good politics."

"You're just giving Carole another way to show off. That's the last thing that girl needs, a way to show how smart she is." I picked up a few stray hairs in the sink and thought about showing her one of my geometry tests, a subject in which I could show off the one fact I knew: The sides of an isosceles triangle are equal.

When we put our jackets on to leave, Sister, her face all smiles, buttons her cape and shakes my hand, telling me to be sure to thank my father for giving our class this special opportunity. When the bus drops me off, I trudge up the street, shifting my book bag from arm to arm, wishing I had worn mittens. I walk quickly, unsure of what to say about this afternoon, weighing what phrases would not incite Mary's temper. Already at the door with her white dress coat on, she barks at me that she can never count on me to get home on time, dinner's on the table, she's meeting my father at a party and see to it that everyone eats. She slams the car door and speeds off. I feel like a prisoner with a stay of execution.

The group photograph at the district attorney's office is in the newspaper the next night. My brothers tease that the glitter hat looks ridiculous, and they pray that none of their friends know it's their sister. My dad points at the picture, smiles, and passes it to Mary, but she doesn't say a word.

While I am good at headlines, I cannot get the hang of page layout. Every Thursday, we turn in a writing assignment on a topic Sister has selected. One week she had us write a humor column, and she ran mine in the paper. I could see kids reading it in study hall, and out of the corner of my eye I checked to see if they were smiling. Our English teacher submitted our classwork for a creative writing section to the *Chronicle,* and Sister featured a story of mine about an orphan freezing in the cold. I shrank down in my seat, wanting to hide, while I read it in a corner of the library. On my way out, I saw the librarian reading it and watched her brush tears from her cheeks. Although I left the article in the living room right on top of *Time* magazine, I don't think my dad ever read the *Chronicle.* If he did, he never said anything.

One Friday night after a basketball game, the twins' father, Mr. Sullivan, is driving us home. From the front seat, when the car is quiet, he says, "Carole, I enjoy reading your articles in the *Chronicle.* Keep it up. You're quite good." Neither Monica nor Veronica writes for the paper, so it seems odd that he takes the time to read it. Still I feel my cheeks flush and am glad when Monica starts complaining about the Tech tiger mascots bouncing all over the floor during halftime.

It is twelve-thirty, and my father and Mary are not home yet. As I lie in bed listening for our car, I compare Mr. Sullivan, reading my articles in the *Chronicle* and picking us up after Friday night basketball games, to my dad, who jokingly describes himself as "a man about town." Di's father and Anne's father, too, all seem, well, dull next to my dad in his Yale-Genton suits with his "so many friends and so many parties." I feel almost sorry for the twins, and Di, and Anne that their fathers are not "men about town," well liked the way my dad is. But I fall asleep. I never do know what time my father and Mary get home that night.

The science laboratories are one of the showpieces of the new Cathedral High School; that's how the newspaper describes them. I am sitting in my biology class on a Tuesday and analyzing what makes this space a showpiece when I should be listening to Sister Mary Arthur. There are big worktables, instead of desks, with microscopes to share, but it's still a classroom. Holding up a gadget, Sister explains how we will prick our fingers to determine our blood types. She has passed out this razor/needle thing we are supposed to be using to cut our fingers for a blood sample. Since I have already had forty-one stitches, a family record, I think it might be useful to know my blood type. When we were little kids, maybe seven and eight, Danny and I used to have a contest to see who could have the most stitches, a contest I was winning too, ahead of him by six stitches. After a Sunday roast beef dinner when Danny and I were adding up our stitches, I remember my mother telling the two of us that a stitch contest sounded like nothing but trouble to her, and my dad laughing.

"Carole O'Malley, are you having a problem with this activity?" Sister asks, as I am trying to get my lab partner to help me.

"Sister, I can't get it to work. I've tried. Maybe I'm doing it wrong."

"It really doesn't hurt, does it, class?" Sister asks, looking around at the laboratory slides of my more successful classmates. From her desk at the front of the room, she watches me and then sighs. "Carole, come up here. I'll do it." Her voice has a weary tone. I walk slowly to her desk.

"Let me have your hand." Sister stuns it with the device and draws blood, placing my index finger over a slide. "There now, that wasn't so bad, was it, Carole?"

"For you," I say, hoping she'll laugh. She does laugh and, as if they were waiting for her cue, the rest of the class laughs.

The next day, I go to my locker before biology class and find a scarf. I fold it up on my way to class and shape it into a sling, tying it around my neck. It's hard for me to sit in biology class with the sling on my arm, but I listen patiently during Sister Mary Arthur's explanation of how blood circulates through the body. Arteries away, I'm filing in my head when Sister looks up and notices my scarf sling. I'm afraid of her reaction until she laughs so hard she crosses her arms in front of her habit. Sister can't talk and motions me to come to the front of the class. The laugh starts slowly in the class and builds.

"That's it for me. No more student demonstrations," Sister says as I pull the scarf off my arm. My risk has worked, but I'm embarrassed now and slink to my seat. What if Sister had not laughed and sent me to the principal's office instead?

On the bus ride home, Danny stops next to my seat and says, "I heard about your stunt. Mary Arthur only let you get away with it because you're a girl."

"You're just mad because you didn't think of it," I answer back.

"I don't need to pull stunts. I am who I am." He flings the words at me and struts to the back of the bus with the other football players, off their thrones now that their season is over. I wish there were a football for girls.

29. Under the Knife

RIGHT AFTER THANKSGIVING, Mary checks into the hospital in Hartford for an operation on a "hiatal hernia." At breakfast, when I tell my dad that the index to the biology text does not list a hiatal hernia, he suggests I abandon my medical research. With Mary recovering in the hospital for three whole days, a calmness creeps into the house. I no longer need to be on twenty-four-hour guard, waiting for her to find fault with me, my brothers, my friends, my aunt and uncle, the world at large. The house falls right back to being a mess, rolled-up socks cuddling under the table and dishes gossiping on the counter. Since Mary is in the hospital, my dad hires Mrs. Meade for a few days to help out.

"I miss you children so much. I think of you all the time," Mrs. Meade says with tears swimming in her eyes. Her crying makes me cringe.

"I wish I could come back. That little Joey, he's the apple of my eye." She pats Joey on the head as he stands at the refrigerator. Joey pushes her veined hand away and escapes from the kitchen.

"I'm going to get you. You little devil," Mrs. Meade teases, chasing him with a sponge in her hand. "Your father has been so wonderful to me with my boys when they got in trouble," she says a minute later, standing at the sink and peeling potatoes. "Always there to help me with his lawyer friends. They're grown up now. I can't help them anymore." With a deep sigh, she reaches for the salt shaker and throws salt over her shoulder. My brothers and I would challenge each other to see if we could name Mrs. Meade's children and which ones had been in trouble with "the law." Wally, her youngest, is a "blue baby," which means he has had a heart problem since birth so he isn't healthy enough to run around the streets and get in trouble. "A silver lining to my blue baby," Mrs. Meade would say. When I first saw Wally at my mother's wake, I was disappointed that he did not look at all blue.

"Your father's new wife, Mrs. O'Malley, will take care of you children. But there was no one like your mother." I slip away, leaving Mrs. Meade to cry alone at the sink.

Tonight after work my dad drove down to Hartford with my aunt and uncle to visit Mary at Saint Francis Hospital, and last night he dragged Michael with him. In school today, I kept drifting away because my dad wants me to go with him to Hartford tomorrow to pick Mary up from the hospital and I need to figure out a way to get out of it.

"Michael and Danny, she's coming home tomorrow. We've got to clean up the house." I'm picking up jackets off the floor and from the backs of the kitchen chairs.

"I went to see her in the hospital last night, listening to her phony moaning. Carole, she was ringing for the nurse before we had even left the room. I feel sorry for those nurses. Visiting her was enough. I don't have to do anything else."

"Come on, she'll have a fit if she sees those boots all over the place. Throw them down cellar, Joey."

"Let her yell. I don't care," Joey answers back and skims his way through the obstacle course of boots. Grabbing the boots up, I throw them down the cellar stairs, hurling them against the wall as if they were baseballs, and scream after him, "Joey, get back here! Go downstairs and line them up neatly." Joey puts his hand to his ear as if he's deaf.

"Gerry, go line up the boots."

"I'm only doing it because it's a commercial. I'm not doing anything else. Joey's not, why should I?" Gerry yells, halfway down the stairs.

"Let Mrs. Meade clean up tomorrow," Danny says with a shrug, taking the milk out of the refrigerator.

"What if she doesn't have time? Use a glass."

"I don't care if the woman yells. I'm going to work out at the Y and won't be here when Mary gets back." Danny says, guzzling the milk. "Why don't you just do your homework and shut up?"

"There's something wrong with doing homework?" I ask defensively. Chip, chip, chip. Danny's words chip away at me as I stare at the empty milk bottle. He gets me. Really gets me.

It is one-thirty, and my dad and Mary still aren't back from Hartford. Because Mary hasn't been able to find an "understanding" doctor in Springfield yet, she drives the thirty miles to Hartford for her doctor appointments. Unlike me, Mary relishes going to doctors. Gerry pushes aside the kitchen curtain, whispers, "They're back," and disappears. On cue, Michael storms into the kitchen.

"There's nothing wrong with her, you know that, don't you?" he says. Although he saw Mary at the hospital, I'm still not trusting his medical diagnosis. "You should have seen her at the hospital, the way she complained to the nurses." I open the door for Mary, who has her house key out. When I see her, I can't help wondering if they have hairdressers in the hospital.

"I am a sick woman. Not that I could expect any sympathy or concern from either of you," Mary lashes out, still standing on the doormat. Opening the tailgate, my dad lifts her "honeymoon" suitcase from the back of the car.

"Mary, I was going to ask how you were feeling," I answer, "but you just got home."

"No, you weren't. You don't care about me," she accuses in a remarkably strong voice. "You probably enjoyed it with me in the hospital." Actually, she's reading my mind, but now I have to deny it, to lie.

"Mary, we missed you. Tommy walked around saying, 'Mawee, Mawee.' " My words do not convince me.

"Tommy. He's the only one of you children who cares whether I live or die." In spite of her "fragile" condition, she grabs a dishrag and washes crumbs off the counter. "I see you didn't clean up while I was gone. Is that too much to expect?" Mary asks me, and I feel as if I've circled all the wrong answers on a test I didn't even know I was taking. There is a blackness growing inside my head. When my father opens the door, Michael takes the suitcase from him and walks off.

"She looks pretty good for a woman who just had an operation, doesn't she?" my father asks me.

"Yes, yes, she does," I answer a smidge too enthusiastically. Mary's body relaxes with his praise.

"Oh, Joe, I haven't even had my hair done," she teases him, flirting. Her lipstick is pink perfect. Her eyebrows are pencil arched and her cheeks are a pale blush pink. My father asks me to bring Mary a glass of water and ushers her into the living room.

I hand him the water when he comes back.

"A drink will fix her right up." He pours himself a whiskey.

"Kiss of the hops," I answer.

"Beer. The kiss of the hops is beer," he says with a half-smile, his eyebrows lifted, correcting me.

Christmas came and went. She may have had her fits of rage, but I have to say when it came to this Christmas, Mary was a really big spender. I was given the perfect "in-crowd" outfit. In my John Meyer of Norwich mint green cardigan sweater, matching A-line skirt, and a McMullen round-collared blouse, I could have stepped right out of the pages of *Seventeen* magazine. The cardigan had a border of grosgrain ribbon a shade darker than the sweater, and the skirt had microscopic threads of blue and yellow and orange that disappeared into the mint green. My mother would never have spent that much money on me, a truth I kept hidden. Since Mary and my dad had done the Christmas shopping, I just bought my usual seven pairs of pajamas for my brothers. While Gerry bought one children's book for the seven of us to share, he said he had saved me the "honor" of reading it to my brothers. We taunted him for his basic cheapness. Proud of his purchase and the way he could get to us, Gerry strutted around the house for the next few days until we mutinied and threatened to throw away the book.

30. Dress-up Day

AFTER OUR JANUARY exams, Sister Mary Eugene awards the students "a dress-up day for all our hard work." Since my John Meyer outfit cried out for the perfect shoes, I copied Maria Scibelli and Ellen Seymour's choice of Bass Weejun loafers, shoes not carried at the low-end Baker's. In Springfield, a girl with money shops at Casual Corner and Peerless, shunning the look-alikes at Lerner's and the even lower King's and J. M. Fields. Last night, while I struggled to jam pennies into the loafers' leather openings, my dad had chuckled, asking me, "If you're doing all that work, why not go all out and put in dimes?"

On "dress-up" day, the cooler nuns, those who have not lost touch with the outside world, prowl the halls eyeballing the girls' outfits, ready to pounce on anyone bold enough to wear a culotte skirt or, far worse, a pullover sweater. While cardigans, roomy cardigans at that, are allowed, pullover sweaters, particularly those tight enough to reveal a girl's breasts, violate God's fashion commandments, though if a girl wears a blouse underneath her sweater, she may get away with a crew neck. The nuns make no distinction in the size of a girl's breasts: girls with just the hint of a ripple in their sweaters as well as well-endowed girls fail the standards set out by the Sisters of Saint Joseph and march to the auditorium, hunching their shoulders to conceal their breasts, a shame-coated lesson I had mastered back in grammar school. After upbraiding their victims, index fingers pointed between the culprits' eyes, Sister James Martin and Sister Marie de Lourdes sentence the apprehended wearers to sit in the auditorium for the entire day. "All work will be made up on your own time," they bark out as their stern reprimands echo off the walls.

By third period, the boys are outdoing themselves, contriving subtle misbehavior that will land them in the auditorium for the rest of the day, but just this side of the sort of sin that will land them in the principal's office. Of course, the "trollop team" catch on to their tricks in less time than it takes a girl to roll down the waistband of her skirt.

The sad truth is that if there were an honor roll for fashion, Carole

O'Malley's name would not be on it. How was I to know that Maria and Ellen had abandoned their Weejuns, may, in fact, have never owned a pair, and had worn matching round-toed Paradise Kitten black flats with a side buckle? I can't keep up.

With my round-collared blouse and circle pin, I was trying to look exactly like the Holy Name girls in their Casual Corner outfits, but the garden of pimples blossoming on my forehead, cheeks, and the tip of my nose, creating a Rudolph the Red-Nosed Reindeer effect—an effect not lost on my looks-conscious father—betrays me. If only a woman's even temper and kindness mattered as much to my dad as her fair complexion and her good wool suit, I might worry less about the future, even never knowing what my next scuffle with Mary might bring.

"I talked to Lew and he's recommended Dr. Hollander. He's a dermatologist and is in the medical office building on Maple Street. Mary's made an appointment for you, so you'll go after school tomorrow." This is good, my father and Mary conspiring together over my "acne." Mary's white, flawless skin makes me think that she never had a pimple.

"The Clearasil and Stridex aren't working. They work on television but not on me," I say lamely, hating my skin and the feeling that I have disappointed my father. I have read every article on acne I can find. *Seventeen* magazine reports that if you have oily skin as a teenager, your skin will be less likely to wrinkle and will age well. Well, that's just perfect: When I'm fifty I'll look good.

Checking both sides before crossing Maple Street this afternoon for me has nothing to do with safety issues and everything to do with being seen by anyone I know on my way to a dermatologist. Please, don't let anyone see me going into the Medical Center for an appointment with a dermatologist for my SKIN.

The reception area is the same gray as the color of the underarms of my uniform blouses, a gray Pam Gardner's blouses have never seen. Between my acne, a word so like acme, and my ever-spreading pools of perspiration, I am a mess. A square formica wall of fake maple surrounds the receptionist, who looks up from the get-well card she is addressing. "Get Well" from acne, is there such a card, I wonder? Her face is a perfect advertisement for Dr. Hollander's work, or she has been blessed by the goddess Venus with flawless skin. Should I tell her that there is a likelihood she will not age well?

"I have an appointment at four-thirty," I mumble, afraid to look directly at her, afraid she will judge my skin and what? Turn me away? A case too hopeless for Dr. Hollander. She checks her book and asks me my name.

"Carole O'Malley."

"You don't have anyone with you?" she asks the empty reception room. I want to say my dad's hiding under a chair, and then it hits me she's not concerned about my personal welfare but about money.

"No, but I have a check." Because my dad doesn't know Dr. Hollander the way he knows Lew Blackmer, he's given me a check.

"Good, because the doctor doesn't accept Blue Cross. Fill out this form."

Forms. Parents. Mother's name. Elizabeth or deceased? The form asks for my mother's name, not whether she's still alive. Debating with myself whether to note that my mother is dead, I push the pencil eraser against my thumb and slide it back and forth in my fist. Before I can decide whether to put Mary's name down and cross out *mother* and then write in *stepmother*, the receptionist asks me if I am having a problem filling out the form. A form scrupulously filled out by me with everything spelled out perfectly. I take everything too literally, my father says and, right now, I cannot explain to this stranger, or bring myself to say the words, "My mother is dead." A wave of heat rushes to my face when she asks if she can help me. The dread of anyone's feeling sorry for me feels like a hump on my back—unwanted and deformed, yet its ugliness is part of me. Shaking my head no, I scribble in Elizabeth and hand her the form, wondering if Dr. Hollander can do what Clearasil cannot.

Dr. Hollander has skin so paper white I look closely to see if he shaves. He interrogates me about my skin care and leads me into a side room. Neither friendly nor unfriendly, he instructs me to lie on his examining table. Unlike Dr. Blackmer, he does not have a signature song that he hums when he picks and probes my sea of blemishes with his hooked metal knife. My blackheads displease him and cause him to make a clicking sound with his tongue. If it will improve my skin, I will endure any kind of skin-piercing torture. Dr. Hollander's voice rises slightly when he explains to me about the benefits of ultraviolet light, a treatment he routinely uses with "some" success for my "condition." Now I've graduated from mere acne to a condition. A nurse enters, which seems to be a signal for him to disappear while she wipes away the trickles of blood and turns on the ultraviolet light, putting dark plastic glasses on my eyes and telling me to stay absolutely still until the timer goes off. The heat begins to build, and I hope the rays have the same magical power as the bracelet bands Wonder Woman wears. I lie here thinking of my zits getting zapped. With my mind racing, I wonder why kids don't do science fair projects on ultraviolet light and pimples. The very word *pimple* has much more of a comic book feel than a science journal. I hate being here almost as much I hate my bad skin. Terrible posture and teenage acne—let me count the ways I can disappoint my dad. I am saved by the metallic ding of the timer on the boxy ultraviolet machine.

That night at dinner, I look at Tommy's perfect three-year-old skin. It is so unfair, an imbalance in God's plan, because it just makes perfect sense to me that babies and young children should be dotted with this hateful acne when they're too young for this indignity of nature to matter. Too, since they're so short, mirrors are out of reach for them, but again God does not consult with me.

In spite of going every Tuesday for two months, I never get comfortable at Dr. Hollander's and my skin never gets better. Anyway, it costs way too much money for my dad with no results, so I stop going. When I later read in a crawl-paced book by William Faulkner about the old-fashioned Southern custom of covering mirrors up after a death, I think this practice might be a good trick for teenagers with bad skin.

31. Sweet and Sour Times

Easter, the Election, and (Step)Mother's Day

MARY IS QUITE proud, I can tell, of how she has put together a serving tray for Easter with jelly beans, mostly black and green, which I hate, marshmallow chicks, and chocolate aluminum foil-wrapped eggs. For neatness sake, she portions out the fake grass, which gives the tray a bare, skimpy look.

"Joe, Michael, Carole, and Danny are just too old for Easter baskets so I thought I'd put together a tray for Easter," Mary announces in a pleased-with-herself voice to my father.

"You're in charge, Mary," he answers flatly, barely looking up from his newspaper. The decision that I am suddenly too old for Easter baskets makes me want to yell, to stamp my feet and pound my fists. There must be a Peter Pan streak in me that does not want to grow up, that wants to cling to the threads of childhood. In my head, I want to beg for a spring-colored basket with that shiny green grass. I hate being told I'm too old almost as much as I hate being told I'm too young. I remember when I was ten, and my mother told me I was too old to sit and cuddle in my dad's lap, and how I felt ashamed but didn't know why. Then, right after my eleventh birthday, my dad called me in from the backyard and told me I was too old to play football with my brothers. I did get him to give in, and he said I could play touch football every now and then, but no more tackle. I told him I was better than they were anyway.

The Easter tray didn't make any difference in the end, because, as the bigger kids, we all just stole our favorite candies, yellow and red jelly beans for me, from the baskets of the little kids when they were watching television. In our family, a lot of sugar sneaking goes on. As usual, Gerry is the best sneak, pointing to a nonexistent robin at the window to distract Bobby while he slips a chocolate egg from his basket, but Danny is the best liar, convincing Stevie that he would never go near his candy, while sugared marshmallow brushes the corners of Danny's lips.

*   *   *

Danny's blood, like mine, is fired with political ambition. On the first warm April night, with the sun still yawning in the sky, my dad is spooning fudge ripple ice cream into bowls for us when Danny announces to my father, "Yeah, I'm running for class president. The election's in another week."

"My son, the candidate," my dad beams, sealing the cardboard lip on the Friendly's container. "The Kennedys are going to have to watch their backs," he says with a smile.

"After I've already paved the way for him," I chime in tartly, vying for a niche on the family ladder.

"You have hardly paved the way, since girls at Cathedral cannot run for class president," Danny jeers with equal sarcasm, pointing his empty spoon at me.

"The rule that girls can't be president or vice president is just so unfair."

"A girl as president? That's laughable," Danny sneers.

"Well, I'm running for student council treasurer," I answer, peering at the stripes of chocolate fudge on the rim of my dad's dish.

"Which means nothing. Another job for a girl. Another job without power."

"Now how do you know that?" I ask in a confrontational tone.

"Trust me, will you? I know a few things." Danny always sounds so sure of himself I half-believe him, picturing Cathedral High School secrets tossed about the boys' locker room after football practice. "I've got to make a few calls, get things rolling," Danny says, striking a political pose, his arms outstretched, candidate-style. I flash the two-fingered "V for Victory" sign when he leaves and yell after him that the Kennedys are safe for now. "The Kennedys," I say to my father, rolling my eyes.

"It seems as if politics are flowing in the O'Malley blood. Maybe you did pick up a tip or two from that visit to Matty's office. It should go easier for you, Princess, now that you hold a class office," he continues, commenting as if this were a race for the Massachusetts State Senate. "So have you put together a team again? The way your brother is?" he asks, taking his reading glasses off to look at me.

"Dad, this isn't a big deal. I'm just putting up a few posters. I think I overdid it last year with all the signs."

"Hey, you won. You needed to get your name out there, get known."

"The election's in two days. There's not a lot I can do about it now."

"You sound a little blasé," he says, sticking the empty ice cream bowls in the dishwasher. "Do you have any kind of an election strategy?" In a way, I wish he weren't peppering me with questions, showing an interest in me.

"Well, it doesn't sound as if Danny's rallying the ninth graders to vote for me."

"I'll say something to him later, if I get the chance," he offers.

"If you think he'll listen to you." I watch him sponge off the kitchen table. "OK, Dad, if you really want to know," I confide, "my whole strategy boils down to walking around the halls at school, smiling at everyone."

"Already at your age you know the secret to getting elected to politics," he says and runs water in the sink.

"Style and smile, that's pretty much the secret to campaigning in high school, anyway."

"Style and smile, I like the rhyme," he replies, after a minute.

"I thought you would."

During fifth period on Friday, Sister Mary Eugene announces the election results.

V-I-C-T-O-R-Y for me and Danny. Although I had fake-smiled my way to another victory, a victory completely ignored by the cheerleading squad, I don't feel like celebrating the way I did back in ninth grade. Maybe, I am older and, come to think of it, I didn't really celebrate much in ninth grade either. At dismissal, I call my dad at his office, rehearsing a two-word victory speech, "I won," when his secretary, Estelle, perky as ever, answers the phone.

"Carole, I worry so about you, kids. You're doing all right, aren't you? Everything's OK, isn't it, with you and your brothers? I think of you so often." Since her voice drops from chipper to shaky, like Mrs. Meade when she discusses the O'Malley children, I try to comfort her, tell her we're all fine, thinking all the while, just put my father on the phone. Please, don't cry on me.

"Your father's not here right now, Carole. He left the office early this afternoon," Estelle explains, coughing and clearing her throat. "He said he had a few errands he needed to get done." She no longer sounds chirpy.

Robot-like, I manage a quick thank you and a hurried goodbye, and hang up. Streaks of sweat from my hand are lining the back of the telephone, and I wipe the receiver down with my blazer sleeve, thankful the hall outside the auditorium is empty. The hall's light, dimmed by tall gray shadows as the sun fades beyond the floor-to-ceiling window, feels comforting, a place for me to hide. Outside, I see the school's parking lot and the green pond beyond, peeking through a border of trees. After a moment, I pick my book bag off the floor and walk out of the building, all the while replaying Estelle's words in my mind. At the bus stop, Margaret Sullivan and Mary Anne Langone all but slap me on the back as they congratulate me, saying they voted for me, they can pick a winner, and tell me to congratulate Danny on his election as class vice president. I thank them, thinking how my father will be pleased with the O'Malley landslide. Then, despite my protests, Mary Anne corners me into tutoring her in geometry, a high price to pay for a vote. When they leave, I again begin wondering about my phone call with Estelle, unable to decide if she is covering for him, unable to decide what she said that's bothering me so. As my bus pulls in, I realize that before today my father has never left work for errands. Could errands be a cover-up? For what?

The election results, like the honor roll, get lost somewhere in the family hubbub. My dad doesn't mention them again and neither do I. At home, lately, silence seems safer.

At William S. Young, the religious bookstore, I buy a new Saint Andrew's daily missal for Mary, a gift from Michael and me for Mother's Day. Because Mary talks so much about God, almost as if she's having regular phone calls with the Supreme Being, I decide on a new daily missal to replace her old, falling-apart missal which she has said is just an "embarrassment" to her. Besides the gold Roman lettering on the cover, I wonder what the difference is between a Saint Joseph's missal and a Saint Andrew's as the thin-haired clerk wraps it. The missal is not cheap, so Michael better pay me for his half. There goes my babysitting money. But the missal was the easy part, because I have now spent fifteen minutes reading every Mother's Day card in Johnson's bookstore, and none of these cards work. Not even the Hallmark. Marilyn Martin's father works for

American Greeting cards, and Marilyn is nice enough and funny enough that maybe I could say something to her.

"Marilyn, would you tell your dad I'm having trouble finding a Mother's Day card? None seem to work." Since we can't talk in study hall, I could pass her a note, but if cagey Father Murphy intercepted the note, he might decide to be funny and read it aloud. "What's this note, Miss O'Malley? And now, besides running the sophomore class, you're trying to run the greeting card business as well?" I can hear him saying that in his booming voice and laughing at himself. Whatever I buy, it won't be right anyway, so I should just close my eyes and pick a card. Mary is "special," that is for sure. "Special"—the way she yells less when my dad's around. I wish my dad were around more. He gets home later now, and Mary yells even more. She never yells at my dad because she "LOVES" him so much. I cringe when she gets all goo and mush. Maybe my dad does too.

I pick a big card with a rainbow on it with the inside saying something about her being the pot of gold at the end of the rainbow. "Fool's gold," I think meanly. In Father Manning's religion class, he taught us about "mental reservations," which technically seem like lies to me. I will reserve mentally the "fool's gold" thought in my head and still be able to give her the card and be free from sin. I have to be able to live with myself, although I wonder what's the difference between a mental reservation and a sin of omission.

"A missal? Now why would you give me a missal when I have a perfectly fine missal?" Mary asks us. Michael casts his eyes down and waits for me to answer since the missal had been my idea.

"Well, I thought you said you were embarrassed by the condition of your missal," I explain weakly.

"What ever gave you that idea?"

"I thought I heard you say that."

"You heard no such thing."

"It's a Saint Andrew's, like your old one."

"Why would I ever want two identical missals?"

"I can take it back."

"No, that's fine. It will do." She picks the missal up and races out of the room without a thank you.

"Great idea, Carole," Michael taunts me.

"You still owe me the money," I answer back.

"Put an IOU in your accounting book," Michael says with a phony chuckle, storming off. Alone, I look out the back window and see the tiny green buds on my mom's lilac bush. I know Mary said she wanted a new missal.

In late May, in the Literary Supplement to the *Chronicle* is a short essay, *Mother,* I had handed in for an English assignment. Sister must have submitted some of our classwork to the paper so I'm surprised to see it. Reading my words in homeroom makes me feel like a phony.

Mother

The locksmith that holds the key to happiness . . . the dishpan hand that guides you . . . the artist that draws out your problems . . . the chambermaid that irons out your worries . . . the comedian that loves to hear your laugh . . . the chauffeur that drives you to do better . . . and the housekeeper that lives within your heart.

I don't even have a mother.

32. Fifteen Forever

THE SCHOOL YEAR ended in a yawn, and now it seems as though August 20th will never come. I will be fifteen forever. I am too old to ride a bike and can't get my driver's license until I turn sixteen in August.

As bad as an entire summer is without being able to get around, I can't get a summer job either. The law in Massachusetts says you must be sixteen to work, but I could get a job in the tobacco fields in Enfield, Connecticut. No laws for farm workers. When Mrs. Patterson down on Hartley Street ran away last fall and got remarried, my main babysitting job disappeared right along with her, and I need money.

"No daughter of mine is working in the tobacco fields," my father says. "What will you think of next?"

"Ann Culloo might do it."

"I don't care what Ann Culloo might or might not do. You're not," he orders me.

"Why?" I'm surprised he even cares these days.

"It might be a good idea for her to find out what real work is," Mary adds, on my side for once. I feel a sliver of gratitude.

"Mary, let me handle this. You know the kind of people who work in the tobacco fields."

"You know best, Cleon." I count the wrinkles on her forehead over her magic marker half-moon eyebrows. "It is not safe for a teenaged girl to work in a tobacco field."

"What do you mean it's not safe?" He heaves his shoulders when I ask him. "I can take care of myself."

"You probably can," my dad says. Mary purses her lips.

"Well, that means yes," I answer and run out of the living room. In the kitchen, I hear him yell after me, "I said 'No.'" Like the cilia on a paramecium, I am fluttering between Mary's unexpected support of me and my dad's remark about safety. When I learned the term "laissez faire" in history class, I thought of my dad and the way he lets things slide. He's hardly an autocrat, so when he says "no," it sticks with me. Besides, deep down, so deep I can't even say it aloud to anyone, I sense Mary wants to get rid of me.

"You let her get away with murder, her running out like that," Mary says, her words colliding with Ella Fitzgerald singing, "How Long Has This Been Going On?"

I pretty much do take care of myself, I think, as I walk up Liberty Street, kicking rocks along and watching them ricochet off the curbs. When Michael graduated, my dad called Eddie Boland and now Michael works the night shift at the Post Office. I'm wrestling with my jealousy when a car full of boys pulls alongside me and slows down.

"You want a ride?" a boy in the front seat asks. A redhead in the back seat leans out the window and makes kissing noises at me. I just keep walking faster now and don't turn my head to look at them.

"Stuck up, huh?"

"She thinks she's too good for us," they yell at me and speed up the street, smoke pouring from the exhaust pipe. "You're ugly, anyway," one screams out. The muffler drags along on the ground, yet I hear the "you're ugly" clearly over the clanking noises as the car rattles up the street. Up ahead, Gerry and Billy Metzger are sitting on the cement wall outside Cal's Variety flipping through Superman comic books.

"No one sent you here after me, did they?" Gerry asks by way of a hello.

"No, but it is getting dark," I say and point to the just lit street lights.

"How about getting me and Billy popsicles?" Gerry asks.

"I'm getting a magazine. I won't have enough money."

"Not one of those teenage girl magazines?" Billy asks with a look of out-and-out disgust on his face.

"Exactly. I'll send it over to you when I finish reading it." I zing him and see the wooden popsicle sticks next to them. "You've already had popsicles."

"One popsicle is good, but two . . ." Gerry says, extending his hands like Father Power carried away with a Sunday sermon. The screen door slams behind me, jostling the leather belt of bells nailed to the top of the door announcing a customer. I buy *Seventeen* and a fudgsicle, interrupting Cal's owner, Cal, Mr. Cal, Calvin, who is listening to a Red Sox game on his radio.

I take the long way home, up Newbury Street, down Thornfell. Those boys just called me ugly because I wouldn't get in the car with them. I'm sure of it.

My fifteenth summer drags on like the days before Christmas to a second grader. When I agree to drop the idea of working in the tobacco fields, my dad forks over the money for six lessons at Belmont Driving School. Finally August comes, and even my birthday comes, and I pass my driver's test. But by September I wonder what good did it do me to get my driver's license when I never get to use the car? Still, although my dad and Mary go out practically every night at the end of the summer and take the car, I secretly like it when they go out. Then I don't have to worry about Mary launching one of her temper tantrums that flare up without warning like a pimple on my chin. She and I can go as long as four days without a major attack. In our Cold War, that's the record—four days of peace.

⌐‾‾‾

33. The Ambush

I'M BREEZING THROUGH junior year. As an eleventh grader and student council treasurer, which no one else but me seems to know or care about, I feel as if I rule the school. Finding the chapel, the library, the school store, and the chemistry lab is a finger snap for me. I have the Cathedral High School lingo down, and by now I know the nuns' nicknames, "Big Al," "Patty Joe," and the names of many of the seniors, the girls anyway, and the boys by sight. That one academic year and calendar edge make the senior boys more mysterious, more desirable than the junior boys who, I admit, seem to be doing a good job of covering up any interest in me. But the senior boys have a reputation for wildness.

On the Monday morning after our first football game, the sound of static from the wall intercom floods our classroom. "Is this microphone working?" the crisp voice of Sister Mary Eugene, the principal, asks. My hand is covering the page summing up the uses of the French subjunctive when Father Leary's voice assures Sister that the microphone is working and that the students will hear her. In her deep West Point, fear-of-God voice, Sister Mary Eugene announces that a dozen senior boys have brought shame to Cathedral High School by their behavior Saturday night. Hugh Owens, red-headed and angelic, who sits next to me in homeroom, looks up from studying his black and white saddle shoes and I stop memorizing the subjunctive.

"These boys will not be expelled. They will be on permanent probation." Sister enunciates each word slowly, which has the effect of extending the punishment. "Each of these boys will now apologize to the entire student body for their unacceptable behavior, behavior that has damaged the reputation of Cathedral High School." One by one, Sister calls each boy to the microphone. With each apology, more students close books, put down pens, and stare at the intercom speaker. A seriousness spreads through the room, filling the pinholes in the acoustic tile. Bloody scenes from movies, crime scenes with violence and weapons, butt against one another in my mind until Sister Mary Eugene, back on the intercom, interrupts my plot lines, telling us to proceed at once to our first-period classes. What had these seniors done? I wonder. Who would know? I am excited, afraid, intrigued, but more than anything, I'm curious. How bad are they?

By mid-October, on weekend nights, hordes of Cathedral High students, mostly juniors and seniors, and scattered groups of Technical High kids drive through the parking lot of East Longmeadow Friendly's, scanning for classmates of the opposite sex. If the parking lot is empty, we circle right through it and head to the South End to check out the scene at Ray's Grinders. With the car windows down and the radio blasting, we sing and seat dance, yelling out to passing cars crammed with classmates, "Anyone at Ray's?," "Friendly's is dead," "Turn around. Meet us at Ray's." When Margaret Sullivan's dad, an Air Force colonel, grilled her on how she could possibly run up 100 miles in one night, she had her older brother, Johnny, teach her how to disconnect the odometer.

Right after the first marking period, six of us squeeze into a booth at East Longmeadow Friendly's on a Friday night, staking out our territory, and place our orders of burgers, Cokes, and, to extend the time, junior hot fudge sundaes. Sodas in hand, couples who are already "going out" pair off in the parking lot and stand in long adoring silences. Tonight, I am eyeing the senior boys, milling around the take-out counter. The five other girls wedged into the booth are dressed in our unofficial weekend uniform of dark crewneck sweaters, loose enough to conceal our parochial schoolgirl breasts, wool Bermuda shorts, and suede gumdrop tie shoes in assorted colors. Mine are a wild red.

"Aren't they the boys who apologized?" Jean asks with a slight nod in the direction of a crowd of senior boys.

"Yes, but not all of them did," Maria answers. All-knowing socially, she tells us who each boy is. Unlike my brother Michael, the swimmer, cranky and dateless, Bumpy, Maria's brother, captained the football team and dated Carolyn Vose, the captain of the cheerleading squad. It left me breathless. Some of that fraternal couple power has rubbed off on Maria and, even though Bumpy has graduated, Maria still knows everything about everyone.

"That's Kevin Gokey, Holy Cross parish. You know he's captain of the basketball team?"

"I didn't know he was captain," Dotty says. "He's tall anyway." I recognize the basketball players leaning against the freezer. Had the entire basketball team apologized? I wonder.

"He must be smart because he was dating Carol Kane and she's in the National Honor Society," Maria says. So am I, I think. If I had thought membership in the National Honor Society led to dating, I would have celebrated it more.

"They broke up about two weeks ago." With Maria, I almost expect the exact words of the break-up scene. She adds, "I heard he's funny, smart, but, you know, he's one of the senior boys who had to apologize." We sit in a respectful silence, awed by the apologies and apologizers.

"It's like Hawthorne's *The Scarlet Letter*. They all should be wearing red As. Instead of adultery, it stands for apology," Jean says at last, putting a napkin to her lips.

"They wish it stood for adultery," Maria answers, and we all laugh although I'm not sure why. Pat suggests calling them the Hester Prynnes.

"They'd like that," Dotty says, draining her Coke. "If that isn't a straitlaced New England name, I don't know what is."

"It's like this big secret. Does anyone know what they did?" Jean asks. "I get chills when I remember Sister Mary Eugene's voice."

"Who doesn't?" Dotty nods in agreement.

"Well, Bobby and Paul would have been there, but they were out with the twins," Maria says, tossing her curls in the direction of the parking lot where Monica and Veronica with their football player boyfriends are standing under the streetlight. Saved by dates, I think.

"If ever there were an argument for dating, that's it," I say. "Date me and stay out of the principal's office."

"I heard there was a whole gang of them drinking over at the park . . ."

"What park?" Jean asks, seeking accurate details.

"Nathan Bill," Maria continues without a hitch, "and they broke into the field house. One of them may have had a key, I don't know how, so they didn't technically break in, or they would have been in more trouble. Anyway, the cops saw the lights and heard them yelling and hauled them off."

"I thought there was more to it than that," I wonder skeptically. "I guess if there is any more to it, they're not talking. A vow of silence. Like cloistered nuns."

"I got it, Malsy, we can wear signs, 'Date me. No apologies necessary.'" Dotty says, appropriating Michael's high school nickname for me.

I am licking the traces of hot fudge from the teaspoon when Barry Crowley, a bench sitter during basketball games, walks over to our booth. "My friends and I are wondering if we could meet you. Formally, that is. We're a very formal bunch," Barry says.

"We'll have to think about it," I say, unwilling to expose my neediness. Then I feel a kick under the table.

"No, we won't. We're a friendly group. Bring them over," Maria and Jean answer, their words overlapping one another, both gunning for a Miss Congeniality award. Barry raises his arm, signaling the half dozen senior boys now at the cash register. Barry knows our names, or acts as if he knows us, chatting as his friends approach our booth. After a few minutes of bantering, he introduces us. At me, he says, "Well, you know who Carole is, don't you?" And I feel afraid. He could say she's the one whose mother died, eight kids, stepmother. Instead, Barry chants, "'Rally for O'Malley.' She's Carole O'Malley."

"The one with the signs? The signs were everywhere."

"There was no escaping them," Franny Lynch says in mock pain.

"And now you're student council treasurer. Big job," Barry says, bobbing his chin up and down.

"What do you do? Handle all the funds? Because I've got a project . . ." The senior Maria pointed out as Kevin lets the project idea dangle.

"Because Sister Mary Eugene is about to let you have a penny of school funds," Barry says, rolling his eyes.

"I'm not on her list of favorites, for the moment," Kevin answers. "But that could change."

"Not likely," Barry replies. I like the easy way they tease one another. I feel lighter, that I could work less.

"So what do you do at student council?" Kevin asks again. Is he interested or looking for a target?

"Well actually, the meetings are open. You could come." He and Barry look at one another and shrug, waiting for me to go on. "We don't discriminate."

"You mean there are no rules against pariahs. Didn't know I knew words like that?" Kevin asks. "I'm clearly college material, in spite of Father K." Father K, we all know, is Father Kroyak, nicknamed "The Mouse," bald, barely over five feet, with a reputation for discouraging all who shuffle into the guidance office.

"The nuns do everything. I really don't do anything beyond go to meetings." He had probed, prodded me on, and I realize now how true it is, how little I do. Saying I did nothing, I hope, takes me out of the anointed sphere of class leader, and puts me more on his level.

"A political sinecure," Kevin says. "There's just no stopping me."

Jean translates it directly from the Latin, *sine cura,* without care, a job with nothing to do, and as a group we share a vocabulary bond, laced with a twinge of pride, all courtesy of ninth-grade Latin I.

By ten-thirty, Barry has made a date with Jean and Kevin Gokey, a senior and captain of the basketball team, has made a date with me for the following night. Since Kevin doesn't drive, we will be doubling. A double date on a Saturday night, me. The stuff of miracles!

At the football game the next afternoon, Barry stops by to yuk it up with Jean, neat in her drill team uniform, while Kevin only nods to me. I'm sensing this date is mostly Barry's idea. I hope it's still on.

It is a few minutes before eight, and Frank Sinatra's crooning "My Way" in the background. On the night of my first date with Kevin, Mary and my father are sitting in the living room together, just like Anne Sullivan's parents. There is no party planned, no dinner reservation at the Fort. I look at myself in the medicine cabinet mirror and pinch my cheeks. If effort counts for anything, I have done the best I can with Clearasil and pink hair rollers. The house seems quiet, too quiet. I peer out the front window, leading my dad to comment on my anxiety.

"Looking out the window won't get him here any faster. Now how do you know this boy? He's not from Our Lady of Hope. What parish is he from?" my father asks. It had been months since my dad had asked me any questions about my coming and going, so his interest surprises me, catches me off guard. I have grown used to calling my own shots, no questions asked, no need for reporting, especially now that my friends can drive me. I start with the most impressive fact.

"Kevin's on the basketball team. I think he's captain."

"How does he do academically?" Is my father really asking me this?

"Dad, I didn't ask to see his report card. Do you hear Gerry's voice is coming from in front of the house. He's up to something."

"As my good friend Pat Amodeo says, 'Don't worry about nothing.' Take it easy, Carole." I peer out the slit between the curtains.

"Carole, please straighten the drapes the way they were," Mary says. I line up the hems and pat the opening shut.

"Dad, Gerry's out in the yard with the little kids and the Metzgers. Could you tell them to come in? I don't want them in the front yard. He's planning something."

"Your brother Gerry? He's a candidate for sainthood."

"No, forget the sainthood, this is one of those 'bad boy homes' times." When my mother was alive and Gerry was eight or nine, on the occasional Saturday afternoon my mom and dad used to threaten to send Gerry to the bad boys' home. We would all get hysterical, beg them not to send him away, and he would stand there saying, "Go ahead." While he had given up the fresh mouth, he still loved to pull a prank.

"Oh, great, here's the car. You could try to stop them, Dad. Where are they?"

"Carole, relax. They're just kids," my dad says. I stand behind the wing chair, my fingers feeling the brocade edges.

"For heavens sake, Carole," Mary says, contempt seeping into her voice. Don't let her get angry, God, not now. My dad's here. It will be OK. Then there are the sounds of warriors' yelling, high-pitched shrieks, coming from the front yard. "Geronimo!" "Full speed ahead!" "Ready! Aim! Fire!" Gerry has led his neighborhood gang into an all-out ambush on the front sidewalk.

"See. I knew he'd pull something. Do you hear that?" I ask as the doorbell rings. I open the front door, make a fast introduction, deferring to Mary, and watch my dad stand to shake hands with Kevin as Mary pats her lacquered hair. My dad apologizes for the "military action" and explains how hard it is to control Gerry's behavior. I keep quiet, holding back the accusation that he did not even try to discipline him.

"He'll have a future at West Point," my dad quips as we close the door. On the porch, before I even say anything, Kevin says, "I've never been greeted quite like that before. They jumped out from behind the bushes and then ran off. There must have been eight of them."

"My brother must have organized every kid in the neighborhood under the age of twelve as a welcome. He thinks he's funny."

"Well, I was on my guard." On his guard why, I wonder. "When I saw the sign on the tree," Kevin continues, "I figured something was up." He points to a shirt-sized cardboard sign taped to the tree bordering the street. Perched against the bottom branches, in letters unevenly lined up in thick black crayon, the sign read, "Carole O'Malley lives here." I am grateful for the night sky and the October darkness, hoping they cover my flush of shame. Kevin is looking around the base of the tree.

"I guess he came back and took the flashlight. A few minutes ago, it was all lit up."

"So I missed the full effect." Kevin opens the car door for me, and I ask Barry if there had been outdoor advertising at Jean's house. He tells us his welcome was tame by comparison.

God may be getting back at me for the summer night of kisses with Jay Vecchiarelli back in sixth grade because Kevin and I have now been going out for five weeks and he has yet to kiss me goodnight. Jean and I toss around theories for his lack of romance, from brothers popping up from behind evergreens to the nuns' dating lectures. I may have to start thinking about swigging my dad's mouthwash.

Betty O'Malley, Connecticut, circa 1940.
Courtesy of Gerry O'Malley.

Drawing of Joe O'Malley by Art LaVove, October 17, 1945.

Left: Joe and Betty O'Malley out for an evening, early 1940s. Courtesy of Gerry O'Malley.

Right: 21 Lynwood Terrace, early 1950s. Front row: Gerry, Betty holding Stevie, Carole holding Joey; back row: Danny, Michael, Joe. Courtesy of Gerry O'Malley.

Top: *Backyard, Springfield, Easter 1952. Left to right: Michael, Danny, Joey, Stevie, Carole, Gerry. Courtesy of Gerry O'Malley.*

Bottom: *Point O'Woods, South Lyme, Conn., mid-1950s. Betty O'Malley holding Gerry, Joey on the right, raft in the distance.*

Top: *21 Lynwood Terrace, early 1960s.*
Front row: *Joey, Gerry;* middle
row: *Bobby, Carole, Tommy, Stevie,
Mary;* back row: *Michael, Danny,
Joe. Courtesy of Gerry O'Malley.*

Bottom: *21 Lynwood Terrace,
December 1958.* Bottom row: *Stevie,
Bobby, Tommy, Joey;* top row: *Danny,
Carole, Michael, Gerry. Courtesy of
Gerry O'Malley.*

Carole and her date, John Burke, at the Senior Prom, May 1963.

Top: *Carole at a friend's house, May 1963. The graduation gown arrives. Courtesy of Maria Scibelli DeAngelis.*

Bottom: *Baccalaureate at Cathedral High School, June 1963. Carole in front. Courtesy of Maria Scibelli DeAngelis.*

Carole's graduation picture, June 1963. Courtesy of Maria Scibelli DeAngelis.

34. Planning for the Future

MY MOTHER WAS never sick in bed even one day until her cancer, and then she died; but Mary runs to doctors so often that she drops their names in conversations as if they are family members—Uncle Bill, Dr. Baltrucki. Only doctors understand her; I could not. With the back of her wrist to her forehead, Mary announces over a dinner of pork chops and Mott's apple sauce that she needs an operation. My eyes glaze over when she lists her weekly ailments, involving body parts and conditions I had overlooked in tenth-grade biology. When Mary mentions her pain, I blank out. I cannot fix pain. A willing, obedient patient, she seeks out doctors she can charm or manipulate until she finds one who listens to her ailments and agrees to do whatever it is she wants. Doctors who dismiss her concerns she condemns as unfeeling, unprofessional, and a long litany of failures that she links in a vague way to the Hippocratic Oath.

What the doctors she favors do best is cut. She is now scheduled for a hysterectomy. Last year, right after the wedding, she had a hiatal hernia. Michael, Danny, and I joke she is only on the letter "H" in her medical symptom book. Like her white mohair coat, Mary wore her hypochondria proudly.

As we wait for the elevator in the lobby of Saint Francis Hospital, my father turns and asks me not to say anything that might upset Mary. After all, this is their one-year anniversary and here she is in the hospital. What better place? I think. If there were a list of unacceptable topics that could get Mary going I would avoid them, steer away from them, but the way I figure it, I just never know what topic will get Mary going until we are smack in the middle of it. I have a better chance of ordering an eighty-degree day in a Springfield winter than I do of controlling Mary's reactions to me, to what I say or do. Tonight I promise myself to adopt a respectful silence. What harm could there be in silence? I reason; yet I know Mary could attack my quiet, could say that I really do not want to be there visiting her, that I want to be hanging out with my high school friends. Mary could spit out the words *friends* so that Jean, Pat, Maria, Margaret, Mary Anne, and the twins might just as well be vagrants I'd picked up at the Peter Pan bus station on Main Street.

Her green striped cosmetic bag is zippered shut on the bed stand. In spite of pain medication, *Where is that nurse when she needs her pain medication?* Mary's lips are painted that perpetual pink, the eyebrows that same perfect umbrella-shaped black.

"Joe, the roses are beautiful. They were here in the room when they wheeled me in from recovery," she says weakly, wiping away a tear and reaching for my father's hand. I sit quietly, reviewing in my head how many lines of Virgil I have to prepare tonight, grateful for the translation book I had bought at Johnson's Bookstore. According to the Baltimore Catechism, since visiting the sick is one of the corporal works of mercy, my divine tally sheet should jump up a notch or two with this visit. Out in the parking lot where I can unclench my fists, I realize that this night anyway, there were no skirmishes, no battles, as Mary lay sedated in the hospital bed.

As the car crosses the Enfield line and I spy the "Welcome to Massachusetts" sign, I start breathing normally again. The green and white road sign seems friendly, hopeful even. But when my dad pulls our station wagon into the driveway, he grips his hands around the steering wheel and sighs.

"I've been meaning to talk to you." He sounds serious, almost sad. "You're dating that boy Kevin now. And, and I don't want anything to happen to you."

His tone is scaring me. "What do you mean? Nothing is going to happen to me."

"I don't want you getting pregnant." Has he lost his mind? I'm not sure what's involved in pregnancy, but I'm not even close.

"Dad, Kevin hasn't even kissed me good night."

"Never mind. He will," he answers with a conviction in his voice I don't often hear.

"I won't get pregnant. I'm a junior in high school."

"Your cousin's pregnant and married now, and having a baby any day."

"Pat's pregnant?" No, I thought, it can't be. This was a stomach punch. My grandmother had raised Pat after her father disappeared and her mother, my aunt Grace, had decided that motherhood hampered her fun lifestyle.

"Yes, she was pregnant the night of her high school graduation." It feels as if he's battering me with this news.

"But I'm going to college," I sputter, suddenly sure of it.

"You are? And where will you get the money for college?" he asks with a hint of amusement in his voice. Quiz show appearances and picking tobacco jump around in my mind.

"I'll get it."

"You probably will. I can't help you with money, not with eight kids. I should have invested in real estate, in apartment buildings, and not bet on the horses. But you'll end up like your mother, a housewife. What do you need college for?" he asks in a mocking tone.

"I don't know. I might teach high school. Do Michael and Danny know about Pat?"

"No, I didn't tell them. Don't disappoint me."

"Dad, I won't." His suggestion just seems so preposterous.

"I won't always be here. Just don't get pregnant." His words chill me, make me hunch my shoulders even more, hide my breasts, want to disappear as I open the car door. But wait. What does he mean—he won't always be here? His drinking? I'm too afraid to ask. Arma virumque cano—I sing of arms and the man. Am I losing my mind?

Christmas comes and goes with more toys, clothing, and sporting equipment than ever. The crumpled wrapping paper, the empty cardboard boxes, the orphan gift tags always give me an eerie, grand finale feeling. This year it feels as if my father is on a retail mission to make up to us for the craziness that goes on every other night at supper. By now I can tell if Mary is taking her tranquilizers, sometimes Valium, sometimes Librium, because she rages less when she takes her brightly colored pills. My brothers and I signal one another, by a grimace, or a nod, or a hand gesture, on a constant red alert for her dangerous moods. With Mary it's her pills, but with my dad it's his drinking.

I've gotten so I can tell by the cadence of my dad's voice whether his drinking has put him over the edge. Ever since that night in the car, the night of my sex education talk, when he said he may not be around forever, I've been filing little signs away in my head: the way he rarely eats, how he pulls the bottle down from the shelf before work, how he gets sick in the bathroom. His drinking disgusts me, the way it changes him and me, making me want to hit him, to belt him in the stomach, to punch him until my frenzy blinds me, to shake him until I can make him see how he is killing himself. My fingers are trembling so I press my hands on the kitchen counter. All of the carving knives are in the drawer in front of me. I'll just look at them. Maybe, if I held a knife, I might scare him, make him stop the drinking. With my fingertips I caress a long blade, thinking how easy it would be, so easy, to slash Mary's scarecrow neck. My body is on fire, my eyes ablaze, and I slam the drawer shut. Wrapping my arms around myself, I rock back and forth. What is happening to me? Who am I?

35. Lil' Kiss

MY BROTHERS HAVE been calling me crazy as long as I can remember. It is easier for them to call me crazy than to listen to me, but I have to try. It's a Wednesday night in mid-January, and Mary and my father are out. Snow has been falling since late afternoon and a two-day blizzard is predicted. Michael, Danny, and I are in the kitchen.

"The snow is really bad," Michael says. "Dad shouldn't be driving in this weather."

"There aren't any other cars out driving in this blizzard," Danny says.

"Look, as long as Dad's got her out of the house, and there's no yelling and screaming, I don't care what they do," Michael answers.

"I'm more worried about Dad's drinking than his driving in the snow," I say.

"You worry too much," Danny says as he opens the refrigerator. I'm feeling desperate. I've got to get them to listen to me. If only I can find the words. I let out a breath.

"Do you think Dad is an alcoholic?" There I've said it. Both of them look at me, as if I've gone too far.

"What television show are you getting that from?" Michael asks.

"He's not an alcoholic," Danny says. "After all, he's still working. Alcoholics don't hold jobs."

I divulge my worst fear. "He's an alcoholic, and I'm afraid he's going to die."

"Now you're really crazy. Dad's not going to die." Michael says, dismissing me.

"He's getting sick a lot more," Danny says.

"And he doesn't eat anything." I add, trying to convince Danny.

"Maybe he's afraid food makes him sick," Danny offers.

"It's not as if the food around here's really worth eating," Michael complains.

"Michael, it's not the food."

"Carole, you have a way of creating problems where there really aren't any," Michael answers.

"What if I'm right?"

"What? Dad's going to stop drinking because you tell him to?" Danny asks.

"Well, we have to try something!" I am imploring them.

"I'm not doing anything. I think you're getting carried away, playing God." Danny, my last hope, dismisses me. We hear yelling from the other room and Gerry comes running out.

"No public or parochial school tomorrow. A snow day." He looks at us. "Carole probably wishes there was school," he jibes and runs off.

"Where are your old term papers?" Danny asks. So much for the problem of my dad's drinking.

"Danny, you can't turn in one of my old papers."

"Why not? I just want to see what you did. I thought you'd be flattered."

"I know you think the honor society is not cool, but I don't want to get kicked out of school."

"First of all, I'm just looking for ideas, for inspiration. You can understand that, can't you?" Danny manages to sound reasonable. "And second, no one will ever know or care."

"I'll know."

"How's it feel to be a saint, Carole? To be better than everyone else?" Danny asks, knowing I have no answer. "I'm just asking to look at it," he continues. "I've got a lot going on right now."

Like what, I wonder, but he's worn me down with the saint remark. Only here, with my brothers, with Danny anyway, is it wrong to be right, bad to be good.

"Check the bottom drawer of the desk."

"What did you get on that World War II paper?" he asks from the stairway.

"A minus," I answer, thinking I've disappointed him, even as he gets exactly what he wants.

"I can't find it," he yells down. I turn up the volume on the radio so I won't hear him.

Outside, the cotton candy snow covers the front yard and is creeping up the low wall of hedges. With sculpted hats of sugar-coated snow, the tree branches droop in this Christmas card fairyland where all are safe from danger and evil. But I don't feel safe. The streetlight casts flats of yellow on the matte snow. I watch the flakes falling steadily, rhythmically against the globe of the streetlight and glance again at the wall clock: 10:55. As family "saint," which saint? Catherine of Siena, Teresa of Avila? With a need to check off the O'Malley family attendance list, I am staying up until Mary and my father get home. From other nights, I know that Mary does not drink as much as my father when they go out. But while she nurses her Scotch sour, she teams up with my dad in their drinking game. Admiring his capacity for whiskey, subtly encouraging his socializing with barroom cronies, Mary with her watery, adoring eyes, keeps the drinking going. Tonight, it is eleven-thirty when they get in, and Mary, red-cheeked, is holding the car keys as she brushes snow away from her coat. A few steps behind, my dad stands on the porch, stomping the snow from his shoes and flicking it off the brim of his felt hat.

"Look at that snow come down, kid. Look at that snow come down." A variation on his *Look at that rain come down* couplet, but tonight there is no smooth flow to his words.

"I had to drive home in the snow. Joe just insisted," Mary, giddy with Scotch, reports with pride.

"Hey, maybe I can't drive, but I can still sing. Mary, Mary, sing with me in that pure soprano of yours," he pleads. *"Heart of my Hearts, how I love that melody. When we were kids on the corner of the street, we were rough and ready guys but, oh, how we could harmonize to . . ."* he croons in his deep baritone. For me, his singing always created slices of happiness, but now what I'm listening to is a drunken duet.

"Oh, Joe, we'll wake the kids," Mary whispers, putting her finger coyly in front of his lips. Then, as she loops her arms around his neck, they fumble for each other. When they linger over a kiss, I close my eyes in disgust.

"Oh, come on, Joe, a real kiss," Mary teases in a babyish voice and pulls my dad to her. Seeing from the corner of my eye, I am swept with an avalanche of embarrassment as they slobber over one another. Although their making out has cast a spell of loathing over me, I am frozen still, unable to move. Abruptly my dad takes Mary's arms from his neck, turns to me, and asks, "How's the Princess doing? How about a lil' kiss for your old man?" When he steps toward me, he stumbles and grabs a kitchen chair, knocking over another chair. "Princess Summer Fall Winter Spring, a kiss," he repeats, "right here." Detesting them both, I back up and bend to lift the chair. Smudges of Mary's pink lipstick are staining his cheek, and his eyes are a terrifying shade of yellow bile with laces of red veins, a project for an entry in a science fair.

"Dad, I'm not kissing you. You're so drunk you can't even stand up straight."

"This kitchen's spinning," he says with a chuckle, opening his liquor cabinet. Ever so carefully, he pulls a whiskey bottle down.

"Dad, do you need to do that, now?" I can't help asking.

"What are you trying to do? Deprive your old man of a lil' nightcap?" he asks, slurring his words. "Don't worry about nothing, Princess. Give your old man a little kiss."

"Here, Joe, let me get you a glass," Mary says, clinging to his arm. "And you, young lady, you watch your mouth."

"You're wunnerful to me, Mary." As they trip over one another, I run out of the kitchen, hating them both.

In my room, I sit on the floor, my back against the door, my fingers taut against my widow's peak. My breath comes quickly as I picture his sick eyes. What will I do? What will I do?

36. Skidding

THE SNOW LASTS two days. No school Thursday and, a winter gift, no school Friday as well. The only black spot is that the Friday cancellation means the one and only scheduled student council dance, a sock hop, is canceled and, at sixteen, I am too old for sliding on Thornfell Hill. Although most kids' parents won't let them drive the car in the snow, my dad gives me the family chariot. It should have been no surprise to me, but East Longmeadow Friendly's is church-quiet, and I come home early, disappointed more of my friends had not seen me behind the wheel. As I pull in the driveway—shoveled courtesy of a team of complaining brothers, a task I escape—the back door entry light is on and Joey, coatless and shivering, stands on the top step.

"Where were you? They needed the car tonight," Joey says accusingly. "Gerry was hit by a car on Liberty Street. He's in the den."

I know Gerry is in pain because he's quiet as he lies on the sofa. No jokes. No talking. He has a hot water bottle filled with ice cubes on his knee. Steve and Joey vie with one another to tell me the story. Gerry had been playing CYO basketball and was walking home. Barely a block away at the corner of Tourigney Street, right in front of the Marcheses' house, a car skidded and nailed him to a snow bank.

"He'd have been really hurt if he didn't fall in the snow bank. He told the driver he was fine, but the man drove him home and dropped him off anyway." My dad called Dr. Blackmer, who advised raising the injured knee, icing it, and checking in with him tomorrow. Neither my dad nor the family doctor saw a need for any more than a duty phone call on a snowy Friday night at nine-thirty.

"I don't know why you're all making such a fuss. He'll be fine," Mary says from the bedroom doorway. "No one seemed to care much about me when I had my operation." A drink in his hand, my dad appears at the doorway and looks around at all of us and then Gerry. As he stands there wordlessly surveying his brood, I imagine in his eyes a lost, sad look.

"You're tough, Myers," my dad finally pronounces, using Gerry's nickname. "Your knee will feel better tomorrow." Gerry has tears forming in the corners of his eyes.

"Now that the car's home, you could take him to the emergency room," I say, worried by the falling tears and my father's quiet appraisal.

"It's all taken care of. Gerry, you'll sleep here on the sofa tonight," my dad says, then turns and walks into the bedroom. One by one, at ten-minute intervals, we slink off to bed, leaving Gerry to his pain.

By Saturday morning, Gerry's injured knee is bigger than an end-of-season cantaloupe. Like Danny's curls, Gerry's fine blonde-haired legs are a source of envy for me. He will never need to shave his legs, and yet I will always hear Robert Kupka taunting me with "Gorilla Legs," adding to the misery of my sixth-grade year. Give me Nair and bloody razor nicks, though. I wouldn't want Gerry's leg now for anything.

When Mary returns from getting her hair done, my dad and Gerry leave for the emergency room. The doctor with the unpronounceable name gives Gerry crutches and tells him he may have a torn cartilage. By two-thirty, each of us has had a turn hobbling around the den on the crutches.

A little before eight that night, I stop in the den, carrying my loden coat on my arm.

"In heaven with Kevin tonight?" Gerry asks. A sign he's getting better.

"Yes, I have a date," I answer.

"I'm not going to be able to play basketball for the rest of the season," Gerry says, pointing to his knee. "Even you get to play basketball." He picks at the rubber cushioning the handle on the crutch.

"I'm not sure the Cathedral High School girls' basketball team really counts. We have a six-game schedule and two have been snowed out."

"Ask Kevin if he's had any injuries. Will you?"

"You could ask him. He'll be here soon."

"Nope, I don't want to see him." I see a grimace of pain creep across his face as he tries to lift his leg.

"Where's Dad?" I ask.

"He and Mary went to a party at Judge Clancy's tonight."

"Where's Michael? Did he go out?"

"He's at a hockey game. I'm in charge."

"At least now, you have an excuse for everyone to wait on you."

"True." Just last week, Gerry had called me into the den, and I went, thinking he needed some sisterly advice or was going to confide some secret to me. My younger brothers surrounded him on the couch. I stood in the doorway, as he paused and asked me to change the television channel. He had set me up and zinged me.

Kevin's acceptance to college had been an easy lay-up.

"Mouse Kroyak is sitting in the guidance office, scratching his bald head, trying to figure out why Saint Michael's College accepted me," Kevin says, leaning over the front seat between Barry and Jean.

"Kevin, you weren't a desirable candidate? College material?" Jean turns and asks in mock surprise.

"Kroyak and Marie de Lourdes did not paint a rosy future for me. I showed them," Kevin points his index finger to his chest and leans back against the cold leather seat.

"I'm not doubting your academic abilities," I say, and Kevin cuts me off.

"I would hope not."

"But it sounds . . ." I plow on, but Barry interrupts me as he flips on the turn signal. Fiddling with the toggle pull on my loden coat, I can tell there is a secret joke going on between them.

"Shall we tell them?" Barry asks.

"All right, Barry, but just don't let that fusspot Kroyak find out."

"Find out what?" Jean and I both demand.

"Kevin's uncle, raised by Cy Gokey after their parents died, is the dean of the college."

"There was no way I was not getting accepted," Kevin smiles, pleased with the ace hidden up his sleeve. Kevin Gokey, man of mystery, I think to myself as Barry turns his dad's Chevy into my street. I glance up at my house through the car window and see all the lights on, and at once I know something is wrong. With a quick goodbye, I jump out of the car and run up the driveway. "Dad's home," I think to myself as I rush past his car. Before I have my coat off, I see the whiskey bottle on the kitchen counter and I hear my father's voice in hushed tones behind the bedroom door talking to Mary.

"Cleon, I don't know how much more I can take," Mary cries. "There,

there," soothing sounds from him. I walk into the den, take one look at Gerry's tear-stained face and ask him in a whisper what's happened. He says he'll tell me tomorrow and, pointing to the bags of ice on his knee, jerks his thumb toward the bedroom door.

Since Danny and Michael are both at the Coliseum at the hockey game, I run upstairs and stand in the doorway of the bedroom my younger brothers share, Lingering, I debate whether to wake up Joey when he sits up suddenly.

"Carole," he calls out. "I wasn't sleeping. I was faking. You missed a scene."

"What happened tonight? Why is Mary crying?" A tightness creeps through my chest, and there is a feathery feel to my breathing.

"Gerry's knee was killing him, so he asked me to find Judge Clancy's number in the phone book. Then he called Dad and Mary at the big party at Clancy's house."

"Yeah, go on."

"Well, they left the party and came home. Mary went in, yelled at him never to call them when they were at a party for any reason, and slapped him across the face."

"Wait, she slapped Gerry?"

"Yeah, and then she started crying."

"What did Dad do?"

"I don't know. He might have given Gerry a glass of whiskey."

"Why?"

"For the pain, he said. Dad was leaning against the walls and his talking sounded funny, like he couldn't get the words out. Gerry told me he was drunk but I think he was just mad. Then, Mary started threatening to leave so he's been trying to get Mary to calm down." I wish she would leave! I thought to myself.

"I wish she would leave!" Joey said, echoing my thoughts. Starting around the holidays, always when my dad was at work, if a pair of boots was on the porch or a jar of peanut butter left out on the counter, Mary would threaten to leave us. Then, she'd add, "if it weren't for your father." About the twentieth time she threatened to leave us and "get the hell out," I wanted to yell back, "Go ahead, leave!" With all her sicknesses and frail health and doctors' visits, I wondered why she just didn't die.

Although I am kneeling next to my bed, I can't pray. With my intentions nothing more than a confused mess, I don't even know where to start imploring God. Besides, can't God see what's wrong? My bedspread has a white background with cheerful red chenille polka dots. Twisting the chenille tufts in my fingers, I poke a hole in a corner of the spread and feel hatred welling up in me, running every which way, settling in my hands. Life is just not supposed to be like this, God. It's not. Let Gerry be OK. Give me a television life, not this madwoman-saint and my dad, drunk, again. For the last month or so, my dad seems to have given up trying to calm my stepmother down, given up even a swipe of an effort to protect his children. One minute, with whiskey tears streaming down his cheeks he would repeat how much he loves us, and five minutes later he would watch in silence as Mary raged insanely, the face slap her predictable weapon of choice. When he cries so helplessly, the little girl hidden in me wants to suck my fingers and curl up under the bed, but the warrior princess orders me to swoop down and save my dad before he becomes like one of the Bowery bums I see on television and loses his job. Then what would happen to us? Where would we all be? I have to do something, find the magic words, the right prayer. If my dad is going to act like a child, then I can't.

37. Snowbound

"IDLENESS IS THE devil's workshop" is a long-favored threat of the Sisters of Saint Joseph, at both Our Lady of Hope and Cathedral. Sister Patricia Joseph utters this warning if she so much as sees a student glance out the classroom window. Platitude Patty, Michael calls her. Now, with his knee cramping him, Gerry is a sitting target for Satan and his evil ways, especially with a week-long winter vacation and two days of heavy snow. The younger kids have been sliding at Thornfell, making snow families, and waging more than a few snowball fights ending in tears. Gerry is perched in front of the television set waiting for Steve, Bobby, or Tom to tire of winter's cold appeal. By the way Joey and Steve stop talking when I come near the den, how they try to keep straight faces, and how they are pretending an interest in detergent commercials, I can tell that Gerry is hatching a plan, hand in hand with the devil. I know some scheme is in the air, but I can't pin it down.

"What are you writing, Gerry?" I ask when I see notebook paper and a yellow pencil.

"I'm trying to write down the words I remember from John Greenleaf Whittier's *Snowbound*." Gerry sounds so affected that he laughs at himself. Joey runs out of the room laughing, a clue that Gerry is not taking up poetry to replace basketball. "John Greenleaf Whittier," he pauses, "Gerald Frederick O'Malley. Do you notice the rhythm, the sound, Carole? There's something about the number of syllables."

"Yes, I do. So what have you written down?" I ask, sitting on the arm of the sofa. Gerry holds the paper in front of him. "*Snowbound* by John Greenleaf Whittier," he reads aloud, pausing after each word, and stops. Steve begins laughing. "That's all I have for now, but I have all afternoon."

"I just remember the title, too. Maybe it falls apart after that title."

"I'll let you know how I progress." His phony poet act with no poem is a good routine, and he's pumped up by it.

An hour later, I race downstairs for a phone call. The receiver sits on top of the dishwasher and the kitchen is empty. We are a family who listen to one another's phone calls, grabbing snatches, eavesdropping. Telephone privacy as a concept in the O'Malley family does not exist.

"Carole, what's happening at your house?" Kevin asks. There is no alarm in Kevin's voice, and I think I hear him chuckling. Kevin himself is funny and, like Gerry, can milk a situation. On our fifth date, when he next saw my father, my dad had asked him about his report card. Back in the car, Kevin said he was glad my dad had not pressed him for details, since he described his report card as a full house, 3 68s and 2 85s. An only child, Kevin could not grasp the chaos of my family. Now I hear Barry talking in the background.

"Gerry?" I ask at a guess.

"A clown. Five minutes ago, he called me and sang a song he had written." So much for John Greenleaf Whittier.

"And how does the song go?" I demand when Barry grabs the phone.

"I was here at Kevin's as a witness. Good thing Clare's getting her hair done or she'd have had a collapse."

"Is it as bad as the front yard ambush, Barry?"

"If you think 'Kevin and Carole walking in the hall as Kevin dribbles a basketball' is a song lyric, I leave it up to you. I have to hang up now and call everyone."

"Thanks, Barry." I put the receiver back, cover my face with my hands, and push my fingers from my thick eyebrows up to my hairline. Then, imagining the song, I smile. No one, but no one, has a twelve-year-old brother quite like Gerry.

In the den, Gerry straightens a pillow under his head and assumes an angelic pose.

"So Kevin called? What'd he have to say?"

"You can't guess why he called? He said you talked to him earlier."

"Well, yes. I got bored with the snow and all and my leg. Do you want to hear the poem, Carole? It may be more of a song. I think you'll like the way I rhymed hall and basketball. I have you and Kevin holding hands in the hall." Gerry couldn't get the words out fast enough. "Do you and Kevin hold hands over at Cathedral?"

"Sister Mary Eugene frowns on hand holding." Sister Mary Eugene's patrician nose could sniff out hand holders in the halls of Cathedral High School faster than week-old fish.

"Well, it's an image. Do you think I can make any money with this? I'm pretty good at it."

I shrug.

"I think I'll put a swimming pool in the backyard," he says. Before I could call Jean to tell her about Gerry's newfound literary gifts, she calls me. Barry is out there, spreading the word. Gerald Frederick O'Malley, poet.

While Kevin and I may see each other after a Friday night basketball game, our official "date" night is always Saturday. In tonight's overtime game against Commerce, Kevin scored 22 points, squeaking out a victory for Cathedral. Jean and I are making our way down the bleachers through the sell-out crowd when Barry approaches.

"The advantage of suiting up and not playing is there's no need for me to shower. Kevin's back in the locker room listening to Coach Connery rant about next week's game with Saint Michael's in North Adams, a road trip I may not be making." Barry reaches for Jean's hand and looks around the field house.

"Carole, there are two people here very interested in meeting you," he says. "Don't move. Stay right here." Jean and I look at each other.

"What's he doing, Jean? Did he say anything to you?"

"I have no idea. You know Barry," Jean answers, shrugging her shoulders.

"Oh, no, Jean, look, Barry is bringing over Kevin's parents to meet me. Kevin will kill him." Kevin's father and mother, Cy and Clare, dote on him and never miss one of his basketball games. They are distinguishable at the field house by his mother's thick white hair and his father's Harris tweed hat and slouch, perched against a railing at all the games. All Kevin's friends call the Gokeys by their first names, but during Barry's very formal introduction I stick to the more formal, safer "Mr. and Mrs. Gokey."

Half an hour later, in the Friendly's parking lot, while Kevin is inside at the take-out counter, Barry confides in Jean and me that Cy, Kevin's father, used to drink but doesn't anymore. "Doesn't anymore." My throat tightens, and I wonder if Kevin suspects anything about my father and his drinking. A friend of my uncle Bill's has stopped drinking, "doesn't anymore," and goes to one of these new Alcoholics Anonymous meetings. When my dad and uncle learned of his "tee totaling," they raised their shots of whiskey and toasted him, saying, "To Bud—a man who has found religion in church basements. Let him have his AA." Their mockery delighted me.

"I wish you two would," Aunt Madeline had whispered under her breath. Now, in the parking lot, I feel the familiar fear choking me, the fear of my father's drinking and the vise it has around him and all of us, but I smile, acting as if there is nothing more on my mind than tonight's two-point victory over Commerce.

───

38. Down the Drain

AFTER A TWO-HOUR minstrel show rehearsal in Ellen Seymour's wood-paneled basement, the twins drop me off at home on a Friday night. When I pleaded with my dad this morning to let me borrow the car, he gave me his customary refusal, a look of pain in his eyes. Rarely do my dad and Mary spend a weekend night at home anyway, so I'm not sure why I bothered to try. From the back porch, I wave a goodbye to the twins, who are backing out of the driveway. Although a light is on in the kitchen, the rest of the house is in darkness. My hand grips the cold doorknob and, pausing in the damp night air, I make a decision. When I open the door, Michael is standing at the refrigerator.

"We have to do something about Dad, Michael." I plunge right in, though my stomach is lurching. He squints, his ragged eyebrows forming a line.

"Use a glass, will you?" I say, like sand in his sock. He sneers at me and pulls a glass from the cabinet, slamming the near-empty gallon of milk on the counter.

"Yes, Saint Carole," he answers. "What do you think we can do?" There's an undertone, an unspoken "You fool, Carole" in his question.

"What about Dr. Blackmer?" I suggest.

"He's as bad as Dad."

"You're right. You're right." I give in. Our family doctor, another of my dad's drinking cronies. Done with me, Michael refills his glass.

"Go easy on the milk," I say, unable to stop myself, not caring about the milk. Danny slides in on his crew socks and does a hockey stop in front of the kitchen chair. I turn to him, seeking an ally.

"I heard Dad getting sick in the bathroom this morning. Did you hear him, Danny?" My desperation and a scrap of hope spar with each other. How many times do we need to go through this?

"No, but I heard him getting sick yesterday," Danny says and reaches into the cabinet for a handful of Oreos.

"See, Michael. Yesterday. Today. It's happening more and more." I offer up the evidence. "Dad's drinking in the morning now, and he never did that before."

"When was he drinking in the morning?" Danny asks.

"Monday before he went to work."

"Just let him alone," Michael orders and wipes the milk from the corners of his mouth with the back of his hand. "He's just throwing up from the booze," Michael says.

"Just, just, just. I'm telling you he's sick." There must be a way I can get through to him. "Dad's an alcoholic." This is not the first time I've called my dad an alcoholic, but when I say the word "alcoholic" now, a razor-edged shame cuts its way through my body and settles in my gut.

"You know, Carole, you watch too much television. Dad's not an alcoholic." Michael, the expert.

"No, what is he then?"

"Don't call Dad an alcoholic," Michael orders me.

"Why not? That's what he is."

"And what medical school did you get your degree from?" So now Danny chooses and decides to side with Michael. I'm losing.

"He's going to die just like Mom. Then we'll be left with Mary."

"Just because you don't get along with her."

"You do?" I snap back.

"Carole, there's nothing you can do if Dad wants to drink himself to death."

"So you believe me then?" I ask. "Michael, you think I'm right about Dad?"

"No, I said if. You're wrong as usual. He is not drinking himself to death."

"You're crazy. You worry too much." Danny gets in the last word. They leave me alone in the kitchen. I am not crazy, I think, and I pull a kitchen chair over to the cabinet. Panic has its hands around my throat. Opening the door, I reach into the top shelf and grab a full bottle of my father's whiskey, the last bottle. Crazy, crazy, crazy whirls through my head, and I pour the whiskey down the drain.

The snow falls in broken lines, diagonal flakes lit by the glare of the street-lamp. Back in fifth grade during a snowstorm, Sister Mary Ephraim told us that each snowflake is unique, further proof of God's divine plan, and in art class she assigned us to draw different snowflake designs. When it snows, I always think of Sister and wonder about the snowflakes. In her sweet, calm voice, Sister would say that God could do anything, God was omnipotent, and even as a ten-year-old, I knew Sister had more faith than I did. Ever since God ignored my prayers and let my mother die, I'm superstitious about praying and accepting God's Divine Plan. I keep saying that, but it sticks in my head like chewing gum on a sneaker. What if I pray now that my dad will stop drinking and he gets worse? Should I risk calling God's attention? What if my dad loses his job? What if all my friends find out my dad is an alcoholic? The shame of his drinking creeps in and takes a center seat in my broken soul. Will my dad understand why I had to pour the whiskey down the drain, understand that I am trying to save him? But what if, in spite of everything I do, he dies?

There's a gap in the living room curtains where I can see the street outside, still visible beneath the snow. Driving should be easy with this soft snow, but there's no sign of them. Over an hour ago, Danny, hunting down another cookie, found the empty bottle in the trash and yelled in to me he didn't want to be there when Dad found out what I had done. Danny's words race in my head, and I decide I better go out in the kitchen and bury the bottle at the bottom of the wastebasket. No, I'm not afraid. Why should I be afraid? My dad's only been angry with me once, unlike Mary, whose rage ambushes me two, sometimes three, times a week. With Mary, anger is always unexpected, like stepping on a piece of broken glass. Even when my dad's gonzo on the booze, he just cries a lot and gets mushy, not angry. One angry maniac per family, and Mary is ours. It's after eleven and they're still not home. Michael warned me I better be up when they get home and not sneak off to bed. I'm not blaming this trick of yours on anyone else, he said. There's a car rounding the corner from Liberty, it's our station wagon, and Mary's driving, not a good sign for me if my dad's too drunk to drive. Each week his drinking changes things, like Mary driving. Would it help if I wrote down the drinking changes to show him in a sober moment?

"Joe, I did not hit the bushes on the way in. You're teasing me." Mary's playful flirting is just another step in their dance of drink as they help each other into the house.

"You can see scratches on the car." His words spill over into one another with no beginning and no ending. "What the hell, what difference does it make?" One long slurred phrase. Syllogism as taught by Father Manning in religion class: When my father is drinking, nothing makes a difference. My father is drunk. Therefore, the empty whiskey bottle will make no difference.

"Goddammit, wheresawhiskey, Mary? Haddabottle. Right here. On this shelf." Funny how the missing bottle cured the slurring. Michael clears his throat in the den. Better talk fast and keep moving. Plan an exit. Can't have Mary at my back. Clear path.

"Dad, there is no whiskey. I threw it down the drain." I'm talking as fast as I can, but he turns on me.

"You what?"

"I threw the whiskey down the drain. Your drinking . . ." I swallow the saliva in my throat.

"You had no right to throw away my whiskey!" His eyes, all pinpoints of anger, flash at me. He steps toward me, and I can smell the whiskey, his Old Spice a morning memory. His fists are inches from my mouth, my cheeks.

"You drink all the time, Dad. I hear you getting sick."

"My drinking is of no concern to you. I'll do what I want."

"Do you want to die? Is that it? Join Mom in some barroom in the sky?"

"Carole, how dare you?" Mary screams at me. Just hearing the word "Mom" fires up Mary's jealousy, and she jumps on me, telling me I have no respect. No, Mary, I don't, I want to yell, but it's too late as my dad hunches his shoulders and covers his ears with his hands.

"Stop it, both of you! I never want you to touch my whiskey again. I don't want to hear from you about my drinking." He clenches his teeth as the cold anger seeps out of him. He turns to me and says, "Christ, you're sixteen. What do you know?"

"I know you're an alcoholic!" The words fly from me, and I want to duck.

"Never say that word to your father!" Mary raises her hand to slap me, and my father grabs her hand back. The furrows on his forehead line up, and the back of his hand is in my face. About to strike me, he stops himself.

"Never do that again, Carole. That is my whiskey." My body is a bundle of knots as he dismisses me. Upstairs, alone in my room, I think how my father has never threatened me before, but I know one thing now: He does want to die. In some sick, booze-romantic way, he's decided to join my mother. When he says how much he loves us kids, it's just the booze talking. He's made his choice. He will drink himself to death, and I feel so desperate and so alone in my failure. But I won't give up. I'll think of something in a day or two. The secret of my father's drinking, the way he drinks, is bigger than I am, and my calling him an alcoholic has changed nothing. I can't even tell if I'm angry or afraid anymore, but right now saying that word, "alcoholic," only makes me feel small.

39. Hold the Fort

"CAROLE, YOU MESSED up on the dance steps. You put your back against your partner's back on the line 'Then, I'll never grow up . . .' Have you got that?" Ellen has singled me out and is instructing me as if she's Margaret Curry, our physically unfit gym teacher arranging a Scandinavian folk dance, but I can't blame Ellen. My mind keeps wandering off to 21 Lynwood, and I have started pinching my wrist to force myself to pay attention to our "I Won't Grow Up" routine from *Peter Pan*. My mind wanders in school more, too. When I'm away from home, I worry about yesterday's skirmishes and the battles that haven't even happened yet, but I know will. With all the snow of the last few weeks, my brothers have been cooped up more and fighting one another over television shows, comic book ownership, and who had what seat on the couch. "Aw, shut up!" has become the way we talk to one another. I'm right in the middle of it, too, and my brothers have given me a new nickname, Acid Tongue. Gerry might have coined it, but it's caught on much better than Kitty ever did. In the O'Malley family war zone at 21 Lynwood Terrace, I choose words as my weapons. Sarcasm is the weapon of the weak, according to Sister Patricia Joseph, but it's unlikely that she and Sister Rose Carmel are yelling "shut up!" at each other between the decades of the rosary over at the convent on Surrey Road.

*   *   *

After the Saturday afternoon rehearsal, the twins are ferrying me home again when I see my dad and Mary driving up Liberty Street with Mary at the wheel. Suddenly I feel my stomach tighten. If one of the twins asks me where they're going at 3:30 on a Saturday afternoon, I'm ready to lie, not that my dad or Mary would have felt the need to tell me. If I have no idea of their destination (though I'm guessing the lounge at the Sheraton), why should the twins?

Right away, the low murmuring of the television set in the den seeps its way into the thick wall of silence in the empty kitchen. The lack of other noise and the uneasy quiet make me tense, and my left shoulder hunches forward. Warming my cold hands on the hissing radiator, I calculate how long until I am the magic age of twenty-one, and as the heat spreads into my fingers I latch onto the slim hope that for Carole the adult, Carole the grown-up, all will be different.

"Where were you this afternoon?" Michael asks. His question has the sting of a face slap. Both Danny and Michael fold their arms and stand in the doorway.

"I was at minstrel practice. Why do you care?"

"You're never here when something happens."

"What happened? Did anyone get hurt?"

"You're out with your friends 'rehearsing' your silly show," Danny adds, "when we're here putting up with Mary and Dad." The kids are all right, I think. Whatever happened involved my father and Mary.

"The minstrel will be over in two weeks. Will you just tell me what happened this afternoon?"

"It was all Michael's idea." My eyes dart from Danny to Michael.

"No, it wasn't my idea. You were in on it. Don't try to blame it all on me."

"Blame what?"

"We poured water into Dad's whiskey."

"You did?" I couldn't help smiling at the trick.

"It's not funny, Carole. Danny poured it. Dad took one sip, said this wasn't a joke, and he and Mary got in the car and took off."

"Did he get mad?" I ask.

"He told us to give him some credit. Said he was still able to tell watered-down whiskey, then they just got their coats on and left."

"He's following her out the door, turns to us, and says, 'Hold the fort.'"

"Yeah, hold the fort." The three of us let a moment of quiet pass. From the den, Bobby is crying because Steve took away his toy plane, and Danny studies his reflection in the kitchen window.

"You tried, anyway," I offer. Danny's finger-combs his hair, fighting the curls I wish were mine.

"He's drinking all the time now," Michael says with a sniff of defeat. "He's throwing up blood. That can't be good."

"You've seen it?" I ask, shaken by the word "blood," but Michael keeps pacing in front of the door and doesn't answer me.

"Dad pretends his getting sick every day is nothing, like it's no big deal. Mary doesn't say anything," Danny adds.

"Yeah, just yells at us. Me, anyway." Her voice has squirreled itself into my brain, my cerebellum, my medulla oblongata, my cerebrum. Would Sister Mary Arthur know which section of my brain Mary's reproaches settle in like moss-covered stones in a running brook?

"Carole, you've never liked me. Can't you just once think of me? You should know better, especially with the way I'm feeling." Danny imitates the tone of her lecture voice so that I cover my ears, but I smile anyway, surprised at his mimicry, surprised he could read my thoughts. Every conversation ends back with Mary. I reach down for a saucepan from the cabinet and with my back to Danny and Michael say again, "You tried anyway."

I push the white eyelet kitchen curtain aside and glance through the window at the winter sky. Inside me, I have a secret vault where I throw the drinking scenes, the stunted words and messy pictures, onto a scattered pile. Outside, the sky is the color of ashes, the sun a long-departed guest. It's not yet supper time and not yet the end of a slow, now-lonely afternoon.

That night as soon as the doorbell rings, I grab my loden coat off the chair and hurry to the door, yelling a goodbye behind me, anxious to be out of the house, anxious that Kevin not ask where my parents are. My goodbye weaves its way into the TV room and is answered by Gerry's "Give Kevin a kiss for me tonight."

The car inches toward Liberty Street and Kevin taps Barry on the shoulder.

"Barry," Kevin says, "I told you not to introduce them." Then to me: "Now Clare wants to take you to tea. The woman is unstoppable."

The tight-lipped waitress sighs as we order our hamburg specials and seems impatient with our French fry decision. Barry taps his fingers on the counter, waiting for her to leave, and runs his hand over his mouth, holding back a laugh. "I think you set a record tonight, Jean," he says, folding a paper napkin into an airplane.

"Yeah, a record for gutter balls," Jean answers with a half-smile.

"If you do the math, Jean, the chances of your—" She interrupts Kevin before he can make a calculation.

"Kevin, please, I'd rather you didn't do the math."

"Or turn it into a word problem," I add, taking Jean's side. As Kevin and Barry had toted up spares and strikes, Jean had rolled gutter balls. Kevin had commented that there was something to be said for her consistency. Discouraged, publicly humiliated, Jean had not given up trying.

"Back to the movies for the four of us," Barry says and pats Jean on the arm.

"Speak for yourself, Bar. I came close to breaking 200," Kevin smirks.

Since Kevin and I have never advanced to anything more than a peck of a kiss, and even that had taken long enough, I notice any gesture of Barry's that borders on affection. While Kevin had scored twenty-eight points in the Saint Michael's game, Barry, fresh off the bench, threw the ball into the opposing team's basket, scoring two points for Saint Michael's, yet both he and Jean with the bowling fiasco seem so comfortable with themselves. I seem brittle, always on guard lest it seem I care about anything. In nonchalance, Kevin matches me.

40. Imperfect Prayers

ALTHOUGH MY DAD might throw up every morning, he never missed work. At eight-fifteen, after he had dropped the little kids off at school, he would drive down to his office at Aetna on State Street. But on Ash Wednesday, March 7th, he was too sick to get out of bed.

It is a little after four, and Gerry is telling me all he knows.

"Mrs. Metzger knocked on the window when I was coming through the backyard, like she was waiting for me. She wanted me to bring Tommy back home." Gerry takes a gulp of milk, and I watch his Adam's apple dance. He shakes the milk at the bottom of his glass exactly the way my dad shakes the whiskey in an old-fashioned glass.

"So what did she say?"

"She said Tommy would be better off over here with us."

"No, not about Tommy. What about Dad?"

"Nothing. Dad went to the hospital in an ambulance this morning while we were all at school. Mary will call us."

"I guess we'll have to wait," I manage to say with a calm air.

"Where are your ashes, you heathen?" Gerry asks.

"They fell off. They always do," I explain while I examine the black smudge on his forehead. "Are you sure you didn't use a crayon on your ashes? One of Mary's eyebrow pencils?"

"And risk my life. I'm not that crazy."

For supper, after I set up the assembly line of bread for grilled cheese sandwiches, I nudge the soup can under the electric can opener. As it whirrs, I remember how after a Friday night at the track my dad showed up with this "new, improved" electric can opener, and my mother asked with a trace of exasperation in her voice, "What now, Joe?" Of all the gadgets my father bought—the meat slicer, the private telephone line, the garbage disposal, the dishwasher, the floor buffer, the mangle for pressing pants—nothing would ever compare with the magical day he showed up with our first television set. I would sit riveted to the *Howdy Doody Show,*

Tarzan, and *Kukla, Fran, and Ollie,* feeling what a lucky little girl I was, lucky my dad loved gadgets the way he did, especially since back in kindergarten, I was the only one who owned a television set. But with him in the hospital now, I'm feeling anything but lucky.

With the saltines doing a dead man's float in the tomato soup, we wolf down the grilled cheese, our favorite meatless meal, and watch as buckets of snow fly by the kitchen window. After the usual Ash Wednesday debate over whether to give up candy or comic books for Lent, my brothers scatter. Another hour passes, and Mary still has not called. At eight o'clock, my aunt Madeline calls and speaks with me, and then Danny. In a tight voice, she tells us both that my father is very sick, Lew and Mary are with him, better for us not to visit tonight, and asks us to pray. My uncle reached Michael at the Post Office. My blood is bubbling, pushing against my skin. God could not have singled us out again, could He? Refusing to let myself think of my father's sickness, afraid that, as before, my prayers have no sway with God, I decide to pretend my dad's at the bar at the Student Prince having a "few." What else can I do?

Bedtime prayer is hit or miss for me. But tonight, instead of yelling at the little kids to get to bed, I go upstairs with them. We kneel down at the beds, make the sign of the cross, place hands heavenward, and say an Our Father and a Hail Mary. Bobby and Tommy twitch and throw in made-up words to these prayers they do not yet know by heart, and into my mind flashes a picture of Father Power lifting his eyebrows at these imperfect prayers. As if we were building to a crescendo, we ask God to make Daddy better.

"Is Daddy going to die?" Steve asks, tears puddling on his scabby knuckles. I stop breathing, searching frantically for a quick response to lessen the words, "Daddy" and "die," when Tommy pulls at my blouse.

"Will I have to stay at the Metzgers' tomorrow? Jimmy doesn't share his toys when I'm there."

At nine-thirty, Mary Ann Langone calls, begging me to help her study for her geometry test after school tomorrow. We joke for awhile, but she wears me down and I agree. It was easier for me to say yes, easier than saying my father is in the hospital. I had to keep that hidden because I had no answers for any questions she would ask. No answers, and, worse yet, just terrifying questions of my own. Why did I say yes? Shouldn't I be visiting my dad in the hospital? I hate geometry almost as much as I hate the hospital.

Mary sweeps in at ten-thirty, her face the color of flour, her lips a smudge of coral. When he hears the porch door, Danny leaves the TV room and joins me in the kitchen.

"You kids better get down on your knees and pray for your father." The accusation and blame in her voice freeze me, and I am treading in this pool of finger-pointing, surfacing only to ask about my father. She locks her blazing eyes with mine, her hands now shaking, and says, "If you know what's good for you, you'll pray." Then she runs down the hall and slams the door to her bedroom, where she wails and cries ghostly sounds we have never heard before.

"I'm going to the hospital tomorrow after school," Danny says.

"Do we need to check with Auntie Mad?"

"Like I care." Part of me envies the way Danny thinks nothing of breaking rules, when rules hold me in their tentacles, strangling me in a soft sea of easy answers.

I try to sleep, to block out Mary's cries, to tell myself that she is allowed to moan and wail, but I resent the way she takes all the room, all the feelings. All anger, all hysteria. God, please don't let my dad die. My feet touch the cold floor, and I stare out at the streetlight as if God were hidden somewhere in that white brightness. A transparent, tissue-paper cloud rolls in front of the full moon. Please, God. Please, God. God, please. After a few minutes, Mary wears herself out and the house is quiet.

I must have been in French class studying verbs with *être, mourir*—to die, *naître*—to be born, the black and the white, when the ambulance came. Then I remember tomorrow is Tommy's fifth birthday, and I picture a cake with five lonely blue candles. My mind keeps racing—birthday, cancel the tutoring, hospital. Let me slip away into the dark, welcoming arms of sleep so I can forget how I accused my dad of wanting to go to that "barroom in the sky." Please, God, don't let him die.

41. A Yellowed Cheek

LATE THURSDAY AFTERNOON, my aunt reports that my father's improving, may return home as soon as tomorrow, and suggests we not visit him. We'll have Tommy's birthday when my dad gets home. Afraid Tommy would feel cheated, I duck into Liberty Bakeries on my way home from school on Friday and pick up a dozen cupcakes. After a supper of tuna sandwiches, we sing Happy Birthday as tunelessly as ever.

Squeezed into a booth at East Longmeadow Friendly's later that night, I have just set it up that Dotty Homan, Big Black Dot (my brothers' nickname), will pick me up at eight tomorrow morning for a National Merit test. Dotty is saying she has no idea why she is bothering to take the test when Anne Sullivan taps me on the shoulder.

"Carole, the waitress over there is calling your name," Anne says. No one ever gets a call at Friendly's. The chilling fear of this summons flashes through me, paralyzing and energizing me at the same time. At once, a phantom-like body of fright, bigger than I am, pushes me toward the waitress. My friends are watching me.

"Your brother, Michael, said for you to call home. It's very important," the waitress says, straightening her white apron and fluffing her hair. "Please use the pay phone." She clicks her tongue and points to the wall phone. How do I get there? Do I slip the dime in? Are those my fingers dialing the phone? Is that my voice sounding so normal? I, Carole, have entered a zone where only my body functions. Breathing quickly, inhaling, inhaling, I cannot talk myself out of the panic bubbling up in me—I know what I am going to hear.

"Dad's dying and you're at East Longmeadow Friendly's. Have one of your friends with a car drop you off at Mercy."

"Right now?" I ask as if Michael's words have not registered. In the zone, comprehension and reality do not exist.

"Yes, now, if you want to see Dad while he's still alive." I am not here at this hangout; I am in a horror film, aware of a stirring behind my back where four or five friends form a semicircle around me, alarmed at the phone call. Pat Smith hands me my coat, Dotty will drive me, and Maria offers to tell the twins I've left early. As with the drinking, my friends know nothing of my father's hospitalization, another twig in my nest of secrets. Why am I so humbled by their small gestures of kindness? The freakish air of normalcy to these arrangements only confuses me.

Tubes in his nose, tubes in his arms, oxygen tank next to the bed, eyes closed and yellowed skin. This is not my handsome, well-groomed father but a species of my father the hospital has created. Unwilling to step into the smells and colors of that room, I linger in the doorway while my aunt and uncle look up at me, nod somberly, and stare back again at the creature in the hospital bed. Down the hall, Mary is half-held by Dr. Blackmer's bearish arms with Michael and Danny on either side of her like bookends. Dr. Blackmer lets Mary go and approaches me. I draw in a breath.

"This is it, Katsy, time to say goodbye. Your old man doesn't have much longer." Dr. Blackmer's words, spoken as if he were discussing the mildness of the March breeze, hammer me. At thirteen, I never heard the words, time to say goodbye, but at sixteen, this hateful phrase dances through my head, making me want to rebel, to yell, to question God, all actions that would displease my father.

"But he, he," I stammer in disbelief, "was at work on Tuesday." My breathing is shallow, catching in my throat.

"I don't know how he made it to work." Brutality and honesty drip from his dry, white lips like icicles from a rooftop in late March.

"My aunt said he was getting better." Am I trying to argue Dr. Blackmer out of another death sentence? If he sees me trembling, will he pull out a hypodermic?

"Go see him now." His hand centers on my back. Like a grotesque ball-room dancer executing a waltz step, this bear of a man pushes me into the room.

Inching my way to the bed, I take in my father, his crew cut with its patches of gray, his slack arms, his expressionless face, his pale lips. "Dad, please, Dad," I beg, "don't die." His eyes stay closed. "Don't die on me." My hands won't touch him. My chest is heaving through my sobs and my tears fall, leaving a wet spot on the hospital sheet. Terrified of touching a tube, I place my trembling hand on the tips of his lukewarm fingers. When he opens his eyes a slit, he seems so sad, so spent, as if he can no longer bear this world, and he is so weak he can't turn his head to see me.

"We're here. I love you, Dad. Don't leave me. Stay," I plead desperately. "Don't give up. What about us kids?" Lost in my choked sobs, in my shaking, frenzied body, the words are scrambled. My aunt puts her arm around my shoulder and in a soft whisper tells me that I should kiss him goodbye. But if I kiss him, Auntie Mad, don't you understand I might hasten his death? Is there no hope, no chance? No talk of prayer?

"Carole, it's time for you to kiss your father goodbye." Slipping back into the zone again, I do what I am told. I lean in, frightened by the choppy rhythm of his breathing, kiss my father's yellowed cheek, and bolt out of the room, gasping for air. In the hall, I slump against the wall for support. I can't hold on anymore. A smothering heaviness surrounds me, making me shrink. I can't hold on. I can't bear this loneliness, this agony.

But, that night, ten days shy of his forty-eighth birthday, he died.

"It happened again. It happened again," Michael storms up the stairs, yelling. "The hospital just called. Dad's dead," he sputters. "It happened twenty minutes ago at four this morning." Michael stands in the hallway separating my room from my brothers' room, his forehead against the doorway. When I push the rumpled bedspread back, my aunt's voice from my mother's wake echoes inside me, "You've got to be strong, Carole, for your brothers' sake." I stand up and flick pink rollers from my hair. At the hospital last night, I did my falling apart, but I can be strong now, find the energy to fake it, to play the fraud, all tricks I used after my mother died. I am becoming nothing more than a skilled hypocrite.

"What will we do? What will we do?" Michael's voice is laced with tears and panic. Terror is contracting and shrinking me, shutting down a soft, gentle part of me, a luxury that I can no longer allow, no longer afford. As the only girl, I am different, and now I'm supposed to know what to do.

"There's nothing we can do now. Let the little kids sleep. They'll find out in the morning. We'll get through it."

"But . . ."

"Michael . . ."

He takes two or three steps down the stairs and then says, "Carole, you were right. He drank himself to death."

I lie in bed thinking how I knew he would die and how it had made no difference. This pickax of death is shoveling out the pieces of my soul, leaving a ragged hole in me. Sucking my fingers, I curl up like a fetus, put my arm across the pillow, my hand under my cheek and fall asleep as if everything were perfectly normal, knowing full well I would never be normal again, wishing there were a place I could go where no one knows me.

The next morning, I jump when the phone rings. It's Dotty saying she is leaving her house to get me. My dad died. My dad died. I have to tell her, to say it, to get it out, but it is just so hard. My dad died.

"No, don't pick me up. I'm not taking the test, Dotty. My father died last night. Please tell everyone. Tell Jean to tell Kevin," I say quickly in a jumbled spurt, and hearing it out loud for the first time makes his death so much more real. With the phone like a dead weight in my cold hand, all I feel is a shoulder-sagging relief that Dotty will tell my friends and I am spared this shred of pain. After a minute or two, I find the courage to place the receiver back as if the tragic O'Malley children, now orphaned, could somehow handle contact with the world outside.

Food comes pouring into the house. Sugar lovers, we poke to the bottom layer of Maisie Marchese's chocolate cake for loose crumbs, but snub Kay Vecchiarelli's sausage lasagna. We vie with one another over the baskets of fruit for green grapes and tangerines. Always, the older kids have the edge. The Student Prince, my dad's favorite restaurant, sends platters of German food. If food were money, then we would be rich.

Soon I stop answering the door as people walk in, nod, and help themselves to a drink, as directed by my uncle Bill.

My father's death feels more like a party.

42. Cashmere Sport Coat

"HE SO LOVED this cashmere sport coat," Mary says, stroking the sleeve. "I can smell his after shave," she says, inhaling and closing her eyes. Two dark business suits and my dad's sport coat are draped over a kitchen chair, picked from his closet by my aunt and uncle. Mary's birdlike body begins to shake with low moans, and she puts her face down on a shelf of her folded arms. My uncle murmurs soft words and casts a helpless look over Mary's bent head at my aunt. Without looking up, she says, "Bill, you and Mad pick something out for Joe to wear. You know how he loved clothes." Her voice is clear and strong as she speaks, but she breaks down again, ending the discussion of what my dad should wear in the coffin.

"You knew what he liked better than I ever did," she says and raises her face, waiting for a response.

"Mary, that's not true," my aunt protests, but Mary dismisses her with a wave of her hand.

"Do you want Bill to bring the suit and shirt to Sampson's?" my aunt asks, her fingers picking at a thread on the white starched shirt. Before Mary can answer, the doorbell rings and she dabs at her eyes, stands up, and opens the door. From grief-stricken widow to gracious hostess in a split second, she welcomes the neighbors who have gathered in the driveway.

By late afternoon, the only signs in the kitchen of my father's death are the casseroles, cakes, pies, and fruit packed tightly on the table. The neighbors have eaten, drunk, cleaned, and gone home for their family dinners, and we are left by ourselves, which is the last thing I want. I felt safe and faceless and comfortable in the crush of people, but now Tommy and Bobby circle the table, eyeing the desserts. Breaking a brownie in two, I hand them each a half.

"I'm five now and didn't have a birthday cake. I should get a whole brownie," Tommy argues.

"Here, birthday boy." I slip him a brownie.

"That's just so unfair, Carole," Bobby complains. In the O'Malley family, we keep a dessert scorecard, so I slip Bobby a brownie too. Tonight supper would be an afterthought, and a brownie is as good as a slice of canned ham.

The setting sun falls on the liquor bottles lined up on the kitchen counter, making tawny parallelograms on the refrigerator door. With the shadows, I make a rabbit and a dog with my hand for Tommy and Bobby, who spend five minutes trying the shadow play for themselves. Quickly bored, they scoot off for a television show, leaving me alone. The bottles make me think of my father. If he were here, two or three bottles would still be open, and there would be puddles of mixer and liquor on the counter. Now the counter is dry, and I shiver with a worm of relief. How hateful am I to be relieved, not to have to worry anymore . . . worry about the Bowery . . . the job loss . . . the sickness? It is over. All over. The yellow man on the hospital bed is gone. I am worn out.

They recognize us at Sampson's, but as experienced wake goers we know what to do. The receiving line. The handshakes. The nodding—all just the same as my mom's wake. What is different is the number of people, as if Mayor Tommy O'Connor had issued an edict that not only everyone on Hungry Hill, but everyone in the City of Springfield also had to pay respects. I never knew my father had so many friends, so many people whose names none of us know. The March air is cold with the winds tossing grayed litter up in funnels from the curbside. The sky is a perfect Crayola blue, a blue my dad might have noticed with a sigh. But at this wake I can't help feeling the O'Malley family has become a freak show, parents dead, eight kids, stepmother. . . . People want to see us and then—what?—feel better about themselves? feel better that they are not recognized at Sampson's? The size of the crowd makes eavesdropping difficult, but I do hear ". . . those poor children" and "will she stay? The stepmother?" Thankfully I do not hear the word "alcoholic."

During the wake, each of us had had one major breakdown, prompted by the tears or words of a friend, often, oddly, not even a close friend, not even words we remembered; but now on the morning of the funeral we are all tight inside. A black-suited man reads names from a list, and the mourners stand, make the sign of the cross, and leave for their cars. When only the family is left, Mr. Sampson folds his hands across his chest and nods toward the casket. We line up, youngest first, to kiss my dad goodbye for the last time. While I wait for my turn, I start picturing us all in waist-deep water at the beach and lock that image in my mind and stop paying attention. Mr. Sampson touches my arm, bringing me back, and I hurry to the coffin. Beneath my lips, my dad's cheek feels like clay that has been sitting on a windowsill. We follow the man who is leading us to our limousine when Mary's piercing cries begin hitting us in the back.

Outside the church, the limousine driver slides the window separating the front and back seat area and instructs us that he will tell us when to go in. The limousine with Mary and my aunts and uncles rolls up in front of us. A crowd has gathered outside Our Lady of Hope—my brothers' grammar school classes, friends from Cathedral in small groups, parents, couples, businessmen, all staring at the black limousines. While people are straggling up the stairs through the church's heavy bronze doors, the driver walks around the car and opens the door for us. My uncles are helping Mary from the car in front of us when the funeral director hurries over and lines us up with Mary at the very end.

Another grim-faced Father John J. Power, another requiem high Mass, just like my mother's with altar boys carried away swinging the incense burners.

On the long ride to the cemetery, my cousin Billy asks why there is a flag over the casket. "My dad served in the war." "He was in the army." "It means he was a patriot." Michael, Danny, and I answer together, our words spilling out. Billy sits there, mulling, and then says, "Uncle Joe wasn't a patriot. He was a Catholic, just like my father." Michael, Danny, and I chuckle. Joey knocks on the driver's window and kneels up on the seat. When the window slides down, he asks the driver if he would let him wear his uniform hat.

"I could get in trouble for this."

"For letting me wear your hat? I won't hurt it," Joey argues and the driver passes his hat back. The hat falls over his eyes, and Steve begs for a turn to wear it. After a few minutes, Joey caves and hands the hat to Stevie. Gerry, who has been pretending to be uninterested, swipes the hat off Steve's head and places it carefully on his own, sits up straight, puts his arms out, and turns his hands as if he is driving the limousine. When we laugh, the driver says he needs his hat back. The minute Gerry hands him back the hat, our laughter stops, replaced by threads of embarrassment, guilt, and shame holding us in place until we reach the cemetery.

After the burial, people crowd into our house, drinking the last of my dad's liquor and heaping their plates with cold cuts and potato salad. There is a forced loudness to their jokes and stories, as if everyone is afraid a silence might give room for quiet thoughts. Unlike my mother's party, no one is in a hurry to leave, and men carve hams and turkey while the women keep refilling the trays. After two hours, my mother's family, relatives we never see anymore, file out and neighbors follow in clumps. It feels as if all the jokes have already been told, and there is now more staring at the floor. Jake Richmond, a white-haired Jewish lawyer in his seventies, corners Michael, Danny, and me.

"I loved your old man. Look, I told Mary this, but she may be too upset to listen. If you kids need anything, legal advice, help with the estate, Christ, money, come to me. If you ever get in trouble, I want you to call me." He opens his arms and stands for a long minute, hugging the three of us. His words make the finality of my dad's death real for me. I can no longer pretend this is just another Wednesday, and I start crying. Michael and Danny are shaking too. He clasps his furry hands around ours, squeezes our fingers, and sighs. "You know the story about your brother's name, the bet I had with Joe?" We all knew the story and loved it. "Your mother was pregnant and I told your father I'd give him a thousand dollars if he named the child, presumably a boy, Myers. Myers O'Malley—if he could stick that Irish name of yours with a first-class Jewish name. Well, your father thought about it and said he couldn't do it. So Betty and Joe named him Gerald, but he said they considered naming him Jeremiah, which was as close as he was going to get."

"You know we call him Myers?"

"Your dad told me that, but I was never sure if he was needling me." Danny motions for Gerry to come over and asks him to tell Jake his nickname. A look of confusion crosses his face and he answers, "Myers." We chuckle while Gerry scoops a few pieces of coconut off a plate and jams them into his mouth.

The pallbearers, my dad's best friends, leave next. Mary falls into their arms, weeping and shaking and kissing. I watch, embarrassed, and notice how she acts so helpless and vain with men. Just as Jake Richmond had, the congressman and Matty Ryan, the D.A., offer us their help, but Mr. Richmond is the only one who mentions money.

43. Dr. Blackmer's Magic

ABOUT A WEEK after the funeral, I wake up with a sore throat and a high fever. Not counting my stitches, I'm never sick, and now I don't even know what day it is. Three days later, Mary calls Dr. Blackmer, who pulls up in his black Lincoln, diagnoses strep throat, stabs me with a shot of penicillin, and tells me to stay in bed until the penicillin kicks in. Closing his black bag, he hums the music from the Dodge car commercial, and I'm too sick to smile. While I am home with strep throat, Tommy stays with me while Mary goes to see Matty Ryan about "our future" and her old boss in Hartford. When I begin to feel that I won't be heading up to Sampson's Funeral Parlor myself, I walk out of my room to find Tommy sitting by my door as if he were a sentinel on guard duty. Already at five he has lost faith in Dr. Blackmer's magic.

Yes, Mary would be back. I would get better. Are there any cartoons on now, Tommy? Do you want to see if there are any pussy willows out in the backyard?

In the kitchen, I hoist him up to the counter, and together we scan the backyard, muddy with melting snow, for branches of pussy willows. There, by the fence. Well, the white buds feel like fur. A sign that winter is over and spring is right around the corner. Right around the corner—my dad's phrase. I did miss Saint Patrick's Day, didn't I? You did wear green. The song Daddy always sang about the band? *My name is MacNamara and I'm the leader of the band . . .* My dad's song and the pussy willows get us through, somehow.

Delighted with their willingness to take her back, Mary returns a week later to her old job of bookkeeper at Travelers Insurance in Hartford, a thirty-mile commute. She leaves the house in her expensive knit suits (she still favors pink) before seven and returns at five-thirty. My brothers and I have committed her schedule to memory and adjust our routines. Michael is still working the night shift at the Post Office, the job my dad and Eddie Boland found for him. So, although he might be sleeping, he is around during the day if anyone draws blood while Mary is at work. We are pretty used to fending for ourselves. In the late afternoon, Danny, Gerry, or I prepare the house for Mary's return. Never once do any of us whistle while we work. We blame and shirk and point fingers at one another, all in an effort to avert an onslaught from Mary. My brothers and I have learned the fine calibrations of her mood, and we can gauge by her behavior whether or not she has taken her Librium. If she has popped her pills, she is less likely to rage. But she is always a time-bomb. All I can predict is her anger; I just never know when a surprise attack might hit.

Mary assigns us older kids weeks where we clean the kitchen up after supper, and this is my week. Since the funeral, the relentless teasing during supper has lessened as if we no longer have the spunk for it, but tonight Gerry is telling a joke from *Reader's Digest* and Joey is chomping on a cornflake-coated chicken leg.

"Joey, I want you to take this cake plate back to Mrs. Marchese right after dinner," Mary orders. "It's been here since your father's funeral." Mary thrusts the cake plate at Joey, who throws chicken on his plate, scattering crumbs, and runs from the table in tears.

"Joey, get back here," Mary demands, her eyes afire.

"Get someone else to go. I'm not going to Marcheses," Joey yells down from upstairs. "Christine Marchese is in my class at school."

"I don't care who is in your class," Mary yells from the hallway, her cheeks flushing a bright pink.

"Mary, let one of us take the cake plate back," I say. "It doesn't . . ."

"Don't you dare defy my authority!" Mary turns on me. "I'm running this house since your father died and you'll all do as I say. Do you understand?" she asks, looking around the table.

"I'm sorry," I answer, unsure of why I'm apologizing.

"You're not sorry. I don't know why I even stay. Do you know where you kids would be without me?" She throws a sponge into the sink, and water squirts up. "Do you have any idea of where you'd be? And this is the gratitude I get."

"What difference does it make who takes the plate back?" I can't let it go, as if I am some caped superhero protecting my ten-year-old brother, as if I alone am capable of making her understand fifth graders. Then her hand whips across my cheek. The blazing eyes and what might come next frighten me more than the face slap.

"Stop it. I'll take the stupid plate back." Joey, in the doorway with his winter jacket on, walks over, takes the plate, and is opening the back door when Gerry says, "Wait. I'm getting my coat on and I'll go with you."

"You'll do no such thing." Leaning over, almost losing her balance, she backhands Gerry across the face. He throws his hand up, covering his cheek. Crying, spent, she runs into her room, slamming the door, and yelling, "You kids!" from behind it. Afraid and cowed, we look at one another, all wondering, what if she does leave? Would I be able to manage?

A week or so after what Gerry dubbed "the cake plate episode," Mary did leave. When my "fresh mouth" set her off into a rage, she grabbed her car keys, slammed the door, stormed into the car, and sped away. What had I done? What had I said? When she left that night, the house was trembling. Stevie cried, Bobby blamed me, and Tommy asked if Mary was coming back. Joey said he didn't care, which started the little kids off all over again. Two hours later, Mary swept in as if she had been to Cal's for a gallon of milk. Shaken by her going off that night, I begin to construct scenarios of my taking over the family, but I can never get any of these to work.

In English class the next morning, Sister Patricia Joseph is discussing symbolism in *The House of the Seven Gables* as I doodle in my notebook. Halfway through class, she announces that we are to continue with our reading assigned for homework. An in-class reading with Sister Patricia Joseph—this has never happened. From her desk, she then says, "Carole O'Malley, please come outside with me into the hall." Pools of sweat run down my arms, and I am grateful for the green wool blazer with its Pro Deo Pro Patria emblem. Eyes look up from their reading as I walk awkwardly to the front of the class. Sister steps over to the door and closes it behind me, signaling for me to follow her. With my back to the lockers, I put my hand behind me and flatten my fingers against the cold metal. She straightens the bib of her habit and studies me with brown-gold eyes.

"Now, Carole, I know you were sick last week."

"I made up all the reading, Sister."

"It's not that. With your father's death, I am just wondering how things are going on at home." She puts her hand on my sleeve, and I feel tears creeping into my eyes. I am afraid to breathe. The cake plate? The threats? Just never knowing how to please my stepmother? Even in class, I feel most comfortable with one-word answers and shy away from discussion questions as if I will be pounced on. In that hall, a bright orange sun fills the two-story window overlooking the pond. If I could only point out the sun to Sister, say something Nathaniel Hawthornish about its saffron orb, maybe I could duck her question. I run my fingers around the combination lock.

"Things are all right," I answer in a jumble, looking down at my knuckles. She places her hand under my chin and stares at me with a kindness I have never seen before. She asks again, "You're sure?" I nod my head, but tears wash slowly over my face.

"Remember I'm here. The Sisters are all concerned. Now, stay here for a minute, Carole, and then come back to class." She waves away a Student Patrol member from his corner post. After she has gone, I lean back against the lockers and feel overwhelmed, that I have betrayed my brothers with my silence. Sister Patricia Joseph had given me a chance, and I had thrown it away. I so desperately want things to be different than they are, and feel a cotton ball at the back of my throat. I slam the lock against the locker door. Wiping my face with my sleeve, I slip back into class, hoping no one will stare at me. What could Sister have done anyway? And Mary could put on her public sainted face that fooled everyone.

44. Job Market

THAT SAME AFTERNOON after the Patty Jo incident, while standing at the bus stop, I vow to arrange my life so that I will never ever have to ask Mary for anything. Within a few days of my father's funeral, Mary, cheeks ablaze, had launched a lack-of-money tirade, in which she ranted that we would all be out on the street and then what would we do?—a speech that terrified my younger brothers and made me go numb. Although my uncle had told us that my dad had left a "substantial" life insurance policy and we would be fine, I don't dare bring that up with Mary. Do I need to hear from her how selfish and inconsiderate I am and do I understand how things are different now? To protect myself from her, I need to find a job. Turning around, I leave the bus stop, doubling back on Main Street. In the middle of the next block, there is a "Help Wanted" sign in the window of Lobel's Children's Clothing store.

"I saw the sign in the window, and I'd like to apply for the job," I say to the short man with the crew cut and yellowed sawed-off teeth behind the cash register.

"Are you in school?" he asks, spit forming at the corners of his mouth as he studies me.

"Yes, I go to Cathedral. I'm a junior." I'm wearing my school uniform.

"Is that the Catholic high school?" he asks, opening the cash register drawer. His wife walks over to him with an armful of organdy dresses and nods a "Yes" to him.

"You understand it's just until Easter? Every day after school, Thursday nights until nine, and all day Saturday, that's fine with you? Our business falls off after that. You can start tomorrow. The pay is ninety cents an hour. What time can you be here?" It's that easy. Not even a form to fill out. I'm hired.

At 21 Lynwood, Gerry is bumped up to after dinner cleanup and retorts in a mild protest that his eighth-grade friends are too old for the little kid clothes at Lobel's, a weak putdown for him. He also suggests I think about paying him for the kitchen cleaning, a remark I ignore. Adding figures in my head—I never was much for pencil and paper and the evidence it produced—I calculate that since I will no longer be going to Big Ben's, the weekday downtown after-school hangout, I could easily buy a dress for the prom, two paychecks, and then start saving for college. When I tell Mary about my job, she sniffs and says she doesn't know how we'll manage and don't come to her for any money.

Only Mr. and Mrs. Lobel touch the register, and each checks the sales slips so carefully that a starting spot on the Cathedral High School math team seems a possibility for them. I watch overly made-up mothers and sullen daughters argue over twelve-dollar Easter dresses, help customers with sizes and merchandise, and write out error-free order slips, which pleases the Lobels. Little boys rarely shop; instead, their mothers mechanically pick out shirts, jackets, pants, and clip-on ties as if in a dazed state, a faraway look in their eyes as they pine for the ruffles, patterns, and flowers that a daughter's dress demands. The Monday after Easter, as he hands me my final paycheck, Mr. Lobel smacks his lips and says, "Business falls off. You did a good job, but I don't have the business. Good luck." Mrs. Lobel had not come in that day, so I waved goodbye and walk over to the savings bank to open an account, wondering why Mr. Lobel had never once called me by name.

After the bank, I go to the employment offices of first, Steiger's, and then Forbes, where I fill out forms, listing with near pride my three weeks at Lobel's as experience, only to be told by both that they are not currently hiring. I have fallen in love with paychecks and now sit on the bus trying to figure out a plan. Di's uncle has an "in" at A&P, and she's starting work at the end of the month, but it had taken weeks, months, of waiting for the job. I don't know if Di's uncle will help me, but The Great Atlantic and Pacific Tea Company, Di, its newest employee, reports, is currently not hiring. Like Di, however, I have an uncle too.

Like an animal adapting to the wiles of its predator, I linger in the kitchen that night until Mary leaves the house to pick up groceries before I can safely call my uncle. He picks up on the second ring and seems relieved that I'm only asking him to help me find a job. The plan is for me to meet him after school tomorrow at the statue in Court Square, where he will "personally" handle my job campaign. Unafraid to bring up phrases peculiar to my dad and a few of his friends, my uncle assures me, "Katsy, don't worry about nothing. Getting you a job is nothing." The heartiness in his voice calms me, but I can tell he's been drinking.

By 4:15, my summer job is all set: I will be a junior clerk in the county treasurer's office and making fifty-eight dollars a week, a staggering amount. The interview with Dan Walsh, the county treasurer, lasts the same three minutes as my interview with Mr. Lobel, but Mr. Walsh has the advantages of better teeth and knowing both my father and mother. As we walk across Main Street, my uncle says, "Like I said, nothing to it. Was there, kiddo?"

"Thank you so much. Uncle Bill?"

"What?"

"I need a job for now, like the Lobel's job. The treasurer's job doesn't start until June."

"You're quite the hustler," he replies with a smile, and I can smell the whiskey on him, just like my dad.

"It's just I don't want to have to ask Mary for any money." He looks at me sharply and asks, "Bad?"

"Bad," I say.

"What was your old man thinking?" The sting in his question is softened by his broad smile. "Let me call Matty about a job for you." While he's on the pay phone, I watch the pigeons snuggling under the benches in Court Square and think about what my father had been thinking. Not that I would ever tell my uncle or aunt, but I think he planned it all along. Find someone to care for us and ease himself out of this life with Frank Sinatra and Nat King Cole crooning songs of lost lovers as background drinking music.

With barely a word for me, but with a big smile for my uncle, Matty's secretary ushers us into his office. Motioning for us to sit, Matty is on the phone, barking out a yes-or-no. My fingers grip the cracked arms of the maroon leather chair. The wood-paneled office with the shelves of orderly matching law books humbles me. Had he read them all? Skimmed?

"Carole, where do you want to work?" Matty's brown eyes lock on mine when he flicks off the phone. From the journalism interview, I remembered how quick and impatient he was, but I had half-expected a "hello."

"I tried to get a job at both Forbes and Steiger's, but they told me they weren't hiring," I stammer, feeling like a failure. He waves his hand as if he were shooing away a house fly.

"Pick either store. They owe me."

"Didn't you just handle something for Al Steiger?" my uncle asks.

"You don't want to know, Bill," Matty answers. "So?"

"So, what about Forbes? Forbes and Wallace."

"Wait outside, Carole," Matty directs, "and let me make a call."

Forbes or Steiger's? Back in eighth grade, right around the time my mother first got sick, she would ask me to take the checks for the electric and phone bills to the Steiger's business office each month. I remember how efficient I felt when I handed my mother back the receipts stamped "paid," but maybe all along I had resented the waiting in line, shifting from foot to foot, while the clucking battleaxes in charge of the utility bills always let the grown-ups pay before me.

Five minutes later, Matty opens the door and waves me back in. My uncle is looking out the window with its view north of City Hall and the courthouse.

"It's all set. Ask for Mr. Elliot in Personnel. He's waiting for you."

"Thank you for your help." Just like that, I think, impressed.

"Just a phone call. Heard you were sick a few weeks ago. You OK?" The quick change of subject surprises me. "Lew come?"

"I had strep, but I'm fine now."

"Mary was in last week and she can be a tough lady, but you can deal with her, can't you? Don't let her get to you. Now you and your uncle get out of here and let me get back to work. Bill, send Eileen in, will you?" Matty shakes my hand with a politician's firmness while he and my uncle exchange looks. In the elevator, I wonder how Matty knew I was sick. Do he and Dr. Blackmer talk about us? And his telling me to not let Mary get to me makes me think he understands what a witch she can be.

I have these three-minute interviews nailed. Mr. Elliot told me I would be working in a general auxiliary position relieving people for dinner and their breaks, and to start on Saturday, April 28th. My schedule would be from four to nine on Mondays and Thursdays and on Saturdays from eight forty-five to five forty-five, and I should report directly to Mr. Howard, my boss, Saturday morning. Eighteen and a half hours each week, I calculate at one dollar and five cents an hour I will be making almost twenty dollars a week. As I wait for the bus, I mull over how Matty was able to get a job for me when two days earlier I was told there were no jobs. I sure wish people owed me favors.

"Your uncle had no right to ask for Matty's help. Here's Matty helping me with the VA, Social Security, and the fact that your father died without a will, and isn't that enough?" Mary yells at me, her anger catching me off guard. "Your uncle just had no right. He and your aunt Madeline cannot run my life."

"Well, Matty said if we needed help to call him," I argue back. I feel a sharp kick on my shin under the table and look over at Gerry, who is arching his eyebrows in a warning gesture. "I'll be making my own money."

"You are never to ask your father's friends for help. Do you understand?" I will never understand her. Knots are forming in my shoulders. When I apologize, it is for her reaction, for my upsetting her. Besides me, my uncle is now in trouble with Mary.

When my uncle calls me later for an update, Mary yells, "Let me get that phone." She grips the phone like an assault weapon and says curtly, "Bill, before you talk to Carole, I don't want you turning to Joe's friends for help. Do you understand me?" I walk behind the refrigerator where I won't have to see her.

"You don't see anything wrong with it?" she screams into the receiver. "Well, I do." She slams down the phone, glares at me, and orders, "I don't want you talking to your uncle or your aunt tonight." Matty Ryan may have had a way of dealing with her, but I don't. Can I do nothing right?

45. Bargain Tables

STUDYING THE CURRIER & Ives calendar on the kitchen wall, I notice how Ash Wednesday was March 7th, the day before Tommy's birthday, and Easter this year was April 22nd, the day before Gerry's birthday—odd how they overlapped—and there are only two weeks left until the Junior Prom. While I have asked Kevin to my prom, he has not asked me to the Senior Prom, so after school today I hung out at Big Ben's secretly hoping he might be there. No one was there so I hit every department store in Springfield—Peerless, Forbes, Casual Corner—and found my prom dress on the second floor at Steiger's, in exactly the same department where I bought my eighth-grade graduation dress, my lucky department. The dress is blue, the color of clouds, with a lace fabric covering the long-sleeved top and a shiny blue umbrella skirt. A tiny blue satin ribbon runs along the neckline with a matching blue satin ribbon at the waist. I love the lace and thin satin ribbon and withdraw the twenty-one dollars from my savings account to pay for it. With my first paycheck from Forbes, I'll buy the shoes.

For my first day at Forbes, Mr. Howard, my new boss, a white-haired man with a pin-dot scattering of dandruff on his dark suit coat, explains everything to me about my job in ten minutes, then assigns me to the bargain sales tables scrunched between the escalators. The time at work crawls as slowly as if I were enduring one of Father Thrasher's monotonous chemistry lectures. At five forty-five, when the store's closing bell chimes, I weigh my expenses. Bus fare, thirty-five cents. Employee cafeteria—I could bring my food. While Di makes a dollar thirty-five an hour at A&P, she does work fewer hours and says there are never any openings. Besides Di, I don't know anyone else who has a job yet. Forbes and Wallace will be OK. I can't think of any other part-time job, and it is eighteen hours where I'm safe from Mary. Disappearing at work for me on Monday and Thursday nights and all day Saturday will be a blessed escape.

That night in the car, Kevin fakes disappointment that I hadn't bought him a bargain-table sweater. The last few Saturdays when the four of us went out, we tried to act as if everything was the same, but everything was different, for me, anyway. In line at the movies, when Jean asks me about my new prom dress, Kevin's eyes glaze over when I mention the lace top. But as he was leaving the back steps after our ritual kiss, he averts his eyes and asks me to the Senior Prom. My hand on the doorknob, I feel like a sad afterthought, an also-ran.

In front of the medicine chest mirror, I stare at the dots of Clearasil I have just caked on my spray of pimples and wonder whether Barry had made Kevin ask me? Continue the foursome? How could Kevin break up with someone whose father had just died? Am I just someone to feel sorry for? I brush my teeth hard trying to make my gums bleed when I hear a car screeching to a stop in front of the house, followed by the sound of doors slamming. Fearing Mary might wake up, I tiptoe into the kitchen where I see Danny standing on the back porch with his best friend, Dan Kelly, the blonde Dan, right behind him.

"Those girls were all over us," Dan Kelly brags with a half-laugh. "Were they even in high school? How old were they anyway?" My brother is fumbling with the doorknob when I open the door.

"Old enough to drive," I answer crisply. "Come in, be quiet, you two, before Mary hears you."

"Oh, she's on her sleeping pills. She's out for the count." The two Dans chuckle softly, covering their mouths. The way they put their hands over their mouths alerts me: Do I smell anything?

"Were you two drinking? Danny, what would happen if you got caught?" I ask, frantic. My brother says nothing, but lets Danny Kelly do the talking for them.

"Carole, I am offended that you would think that of us, with me the champion breast-stroker," Kelly protests.

"The swim season's been over for a month."

"For me, it's never over. I'm a dedicated swimmer." He makes it sound as if he was a member of the clergy, but, dedication or not, I am not falling for their innocent act.

"Lay off, Sister Belle, we were not drinking. Christ, we're only sophomores," Danny finally says with a testy anger in his voice.

"All right. Let me smell your breath." Kelly puts on an air of exaggerated hurt and breathes, laughing and giggling.

"I'm not letting you smell my breath. You're such a skirt," Danny sneers and brushes by me. Although Kelly's protests of innocence have a false ring, I can't smell beer or whiskey on either of them. Slinking off to the back bedroom, they lift their feet and shush one another. Leaning back against the kitchen sink, I stare at the rooster clock as if it could tell me whether they had been drinking, as if it had answers for me. Mary's sleeping is a gift, like a heavy rain putting out a brushfire. How does Danny know Mary is taking sleeping pills? Like me, Danny is playing detective nosing around at the scene of the crime. Climbing back up the stairs, I wonder what kind of a locker room putdown a "skirt" is.

46. Beautiful

AS A MEMBER of the Junior Prom decorating committee, though one with limited artistic talent, I stop by the cafeteria after the student council meeting and am amazed by the transformation rolls of multicolored crepe paper make. Pastel paper roses hang from the ceiling, decorating the mirrored columns and the base of the statue of the Blessed Virgin Mary. I, the visiting drone, compliment the buzzing worker bees and search for a suitable task. Gathering the scissors, tape, wire, and leftover crepe paper, I carry them to the secretary in the principal's office. When my crepe paper roses are laughed at and rejected, the chair hints that there is nothing more for me to do, so I skip out and take the after school bus downtown for my appointment to have my hair done.

On the fourth floor of Peerless, Bruno, Mary's hairdresser, a miracle man who manages to keep her happy when it comes to the all-important topic of hair coloring and style, jumps to the task of creating pouf with my mass of limp, fine hair. In an hour, Bruno works his magic on me. Coiffed, sprayed, my stiff hair rubbing against the collar of my blazer, I catch myself admiring the reflection of my puff-head, half-afraid a robin might settle in it, in the window of the bus.

The dress. The hair. The shoes dyed to match. When I walk into the living room, Tommy rounds the corner, stopping in the entryway to gawk at his Cinderella sister. He approaches me slowly, looks me up and down, steps back, and whispers, "Carole, you look so beautiful." I feel the edges of an ice cube inside me softening with the "beautiful" from my short-legged admirer, and I pat his hair, the crew cut tickling my fingers. In their white tuxedo jackets, Barry and Kevin glide up the porch stairs on patent-leather shoes with Jean in the middle holding their arms. Mary takes pictures of the four of us, pretend grown-ups, in the living room with Jean's camera. The red carnation I stick in Kevin's lapel falls to the sidewalk on our way to the car.

At work on Saturday morning, guarding the bargain tables, I file sums away in a rivulet of my brain where only I know the totals, the real figures. The prom's sneak expenses cost me more than two weeks of work, but I will just wear the same dress and shoes to the Senior Prom. At lunch in the employee cafeteria, I look down at my knees and spot varicose veins on my legs, just like my mother had during her pregnancies. Although I stand at the bargain tables for eighteen hours a week, I am shocked that a sixteen-year-old could get black and blue pathways of varicose veins. Cruising the hosiery department for the ugly, thick support hose, I finish up my lunch break. Ugly and expensive stockings, stockings the nuns might wear, is not the way I want to spend my paycheck, so I decide to let the stockings go for now and hope the veins will disappear. Tonight, I, no longer "beautiful," will stay at home. Although Jean and Barry have a date tonight, Kevin told me he was just too worn out from sitting at the prom. At the prom, Barry and Jean had danced, while Kevin and I had sat in an awkward silence.

Back in January, Kevin and a group of seniors had decided that the minstrel was beneath them. The minstrel is scheduled for four nights, May 8th through the 11th. Ellen had whipped us into shape; the coed number, my favorite, of "I Won't Grow Up" from Peter Pan and the girls-only Russian dance number "Midnight in Moscow" are peach-fuzz smooth. For the Moscow number, Ellen became breathless when she talked about the costume we would wear, purple cossack pants and an apricot collarless shirt. For me, the costume is just another costume and another paycheck. When I had asked Mr. Howard for permission to have Thursday night off for the minstrel, I felt a redness crawling up my neck and my voice squeaked. He could have cared less, just pointed out I would not be paid. Why is it so hard for me to ask for anything? At the dress rehearsal, girls were whispering backstage how their parents were muttering about the costumes' cost, but I had hung back, saying nothing. I hide from my friends that I pay for everything now so that they won't connect money, or my lack of it, with my father's death. Each of us was allotted two tickets for the minstrel: two tickets I'd give away. In November, when my dad was still alive, he and Mary went to a cocktail party on the night of my induction into the National Honor Society, so I'm used to going to school functions alone.

After the final Saturday night show, the cast members, some still in costume and stage makeup, head for East Longmeadow Friendly's, honking horns whenever another car full of minstrel performers passes us on the way. When I walk by Kevin in the Friendly's parking lot, I wave to him, but he either doesn't see me or is pretending he doesn't. Since his prom is only a week away, I guess I'm still going with him, but there is a dull foreboding spreading in me like the lyrics of the new Neil Sedaka song, "Breaking Up Is Hard to Do."

47. A Ten-Second Phone Call

SISTER WALTER MARIA, a French teacher and the head of the school's memory book, is fond of flirting with the boys. And maybe it is her romantic French accent, but Sister is good at it. On the Tuesday afternoon of Senior Week, Sister is speaking French with Klaus Shigley, her favorite, in the corridor before unveiling to us the school's first memory book. Just as Father Leary runs the student council at Cathedral, Sister Walter Maria has controlled the memory book, but I have been the one to give it a name: *Pantherpix.*

Since the thin, purple spiral-bound books are ready on time for the Senior Week deadline, the memory book committee members are distributing copies to senior homerooms. As I count and stack the books into piles of forty-two per homeroom, I weigh sneaking a look at Kevin's picture. But I am afraid of running the risk of being caught in the act by the sports editor breathing through his mouth on my left or the clubs editor standing on my right. With the whole committee in Sister's homeroom, we empty the boxes, and within an hour the committee has handed out eight hundred books. So delighted with the first *Pantherpix*, Sister Walter Maria claps her hands and gives us her *mercis* and *au revoirs*. How I wish the French words would slide from my lips with the same ease they fall from my pen.

The Senior Prom is the high point of Senior Week. Back in the blue dress I so love, I slink down in my seat when Kevin and his friends ridicule the memory book, and its name in particular. "Who named it? Pantherpix? What is that?" they demand of one another, and I whisper under my breath so that no one would hear, "I did." I try to explain that "pix" is a journalism term, at least Sister Edward Agnes had said it was, referring to a group of pictures. But the seniors avert their eyes, a sign for me to hold off on my feeble explanations. I sit there, pulling off the brown-end petals of my wrist corsage, rubbing the soft petals between my fingers, crinkling them into tiny pieces. While the orchestra plays, Kevin is talkative and funny, but aims his wit to the group at the table and has little, if anything, to say to me. For Kevin and me, the Senior Prom feels like an ending.

Kevin's ten-second phone call, *I think we should date other people,* came two weeks after the prom. Hurt, but not surprised, since I had guessed his not calling me post-prom had meant the end, I mumbled, *Fine.* His breaking up with me stings, and of course everyone (maybe even Ray, the manager) at East Longmeadow Friendly's knows I am the rejected, the tossed, the dumped. If only I could be in a place where no one knows me, I might feel lighter, less humiliated. This time, sensing my discomfort, Gerry writes no ballads about scorned lovers.

In March, there had been an article in the *Chronicle* critical of the "do nothing" student council, and I had found myself silently agreeing with its slant. When spring came, bringing with it the annual election hoopla, I was not nominated, nor did I ask anyone to nominate me, so I am left a lame duck, a term my father had taught me. I wondered if I'd miss class office the way I missed Kevin's taking me out. My never-ending supply of school spirit has dried up like a puddle in a driveway under a July sun.

48. Rich Woman Someday

STANDING ON THE wide stairs of the Hampden County Courthouse at eight-twenty on the morning of my first day of work, Uncle Bill is busy nodding to passersby like a candidate running for office. Behind him, the square courthouse, built of a rusticated gray rock with three curved arches spanning the entry, has a look of propriety and respectability. When my uncle kisses me on the cheek, I sniff the pine of his aftershave, my dad's smell, and notice the fine red veins, map lines on his round cheeks.

"Ready, Katsy? You'll be fine. Dan says Margaret Hoey runs the office like a well-oiled machine. She's a character, and you'll be covering for everyone during summer vacations. Dan doesn't get back from Black Point until late morning so I'll make the introductions."

"Do you know them?"

"Well, I stop by to see Dan every so often. As the boss's cousin, they're cordial to me," he says with a wink and turns into the first office on the left where three middle-aged women, chatting in low voices, stop their talk to gaze at me. My uncle introduces me to Mrs. Hoey, whose steel-blue eyes survey me from my Breck hair to patent-leather flats. The flash inspection over, she then introduces me to Louise Geisel and Helen McQuade.

"We'll keep her busy. See if she's any good. I'm a very stern taskmaster. Isn't that right, ladies?" She looks across her desk at Louise, who raises a white eyebrow in agreement, and then turns around to Helen, who buries her head, hiding a red-lipstick smile. With her chin jutting out, Mrs. Hoey folds her hands, her chubby fingers interlocking, a signal that she is now in charge.

"Take good care of her," my uncle says from the doorway. Mrs. Hoey and I watch him walk away. Slapping her hand on the counter, Mrs. Hoey sighs deeply as if she has already decided I will be a burden to her, clicks her tongue, and says, "Now I suppose I'll have to find a place for you to sit unless you plan on standing all day. And then I'll have to find some work you're capable of doing." She has a joking, ironic tone, but I remain unsure; so I say little and wait for her direction. Mrs. Hoey's bluster and efficiency remind me of one of the nuns who teaches in the commercial program at Cathedral, and I imagine her in a habit as she leads me to a back windowless cubbyhole. I hope Mrs. Hoey thinks that, like my uncle, I am related to Mr. Walsh, the county treasurer.

On the first day, I check payroll reports for error, find two discrepancies and, like a puppy retrieving its first ball, report them to Mrs. Hoey. Peering at me through her steel-rimmed glasses, she tells me to leave the papers on her desk. In the afternoon when I work for Helen McQuade, I calculate back earnings and retirement contributions for all the county employees while Mr. Walsh reviews and directs business with Mrs. Hoey in his office. Later, on his way back to his Main Street insurance office, he stops in the entrance to my cubicle to say he hopes all is going well with me. As he's leaving, I hear Mrs. Hoey saying to him, "Mr. Walsh, frankly, I'm worried. I think that new girl, Carole O'Malley, is after my job." His deep chuckle floats into my cell, landing on a pile of retirement index cards.

At a little after three, Mrs. Hoey and Louise are discussing recipes, groceries, her diverticulitis, and vegetables that do or do not agree with them when I walk into the front office. In the tail-end of a lecture on fried foods, Mrs. Hoey asks me what it is I want. Stammering, I explain about my part-time job at Forbes and how I need to leave fifteen minutes early on Mondays and Thursdays. The words spill out as I wrap one leg around another, awaiting her verdict.

"Oh, you do? And we have to accommodate you, I suppose?" she asks, examining her squared-off fingernails. I hold my breath, wondering how I could have phrased my request more smoothly.

"Mr. Walsh told me all about your leaving early, and he's the boss. If it's all right with him, then I guess it has to be all right with me." There is no sigh, only a pained expression in her unlined face, the expression I am coming to expect, an expression that changes when a bald, pear-faced man with kind eyes walks slowly into the office. "Larry, I'd like you to meet my replacement," Mrs. Hoey says. "Carole, this is my husband, Larry. He's on the custodian staff in the courthouse." I smile and say hello and then, sensing my dismissal, disappear into the back office.

The walk by the Congregational Church through Court Square Alley past City Hall takes me six minutes. As I punch in at the employee time clock at Forbes, I think how unlike my father I am. While my dad was always late, I am always early, as if I have decided to be different from him, to be punctual. On the bus ride home, I look away from my reflection in the window and slump down in the seat, relieved that I'm able to keep my part-time job at Forbes and Wallace, a job I'll need my senior year.

Mid-morning Tuesday, I am filing retirement papers while Larry and a chuckling Margaret, heads together, whisper at the counter. When he leaves, she turns to me and demands, "Carole, how did you get to work today?"

"I rode my bike."

"Well, the custodians had a pool over which county employee was biking to work. Pat Shea thought it was the college boy over at the Registry of Deeds, but I told Larry it was you. I knew it."

"Well, I don't have my other job tonight," I explain.

"You're familiar with the Wilbraham Road bus? That it drops you off on Main Street?" she asks me.

"Yes." I picture the nearing-two-hundred-pound Mrs. Hoey, her face apple-red, pedaling my bike down Main Street. "If it's not allowed . . ." I start to say when she interrupts me.

"No, it's allowed, Carole. You'll be a rich woman someday." She picks up a sheaf of payroll reports and sits down again. It's not that I don't want to be a rich woman one day, but out of plain old spite, I ride my bike less and the bus more. It's mostly uphill on the way home anyway.

My monastic cell provides such an excellent cover that they often forget I am there.

After the first week, I ask Mrs. Hoey for permission to make a telephone call. She puts her arms on her waist, harrumphs, and grants me permission, skipping the lecture I half-expect on office etiquette. So each afternoon, I call home, talk to Danny or Gerry, get a report, and remind them what they need to do for dinner.

Like an anxious squirrel frantically flitting about for fallen acorns, I store my paychecks in the Springfield Institution for Savings as if I, too, am terrified of a barren Massachusetts winter. While my college fund is inching along, Michael is hatching his own get-rich-quick schemes. But when his horses fail to win, place, or show, his eye keeps landing on my bank book.

"Carole, just loan me some money. It's only for three days. I get paid on Thursday. I'll pay you back then," Michael begs me. "I promise you. I'm good for it." He paces back and forth in the kitchen, wringing his hands, then stops to look out the kitchen window as if half expecting some enforcer to be outside in the driveway waiting for him.

"But, Michael, I'm saving the money for college," I protest.

"Didn't you hear me? What does college have to do with it? I said I'd pay you back on Thursday."

"Why do you need the money?" I know why he needs the money, but I'm stalling for time. The summer before, my dad, Uncle Bill, and Michael went to Hinsdale, a horse track right over the New Hampshire state line. Now Michael drives to the races on his nights off and whenever he has a chance. He bet and he lost. A gambler.

"I just need it. You wouldn't understand." Will some bookie hurt him? Do I have to fork over money from my savings to him? Do I believe him when he promises to pay me back?

"Will you stop pacing? You're making me crazy." I haven't yet said yes.

"You don't want Mary finding out," he pleads, emphasizing each word. His eyes dart around the kitchen as if a hit man were squeezed behind the refrigerator.

"Finding out what?" Although my father had liked the horses, gambling now did not fit in with Mary's view of what "good" people do. I just thought of betting on a horse, always a "sure thing," as lighting a match to your money.

"Just never mind. Are you going to loan me the money or not?" His chin thrusts forward in spite of years of wearing elastics on his teeth.

"How much?"

"It's only a hundred dollars."

"Only a hundred? Michael, that's more . . ."

"Just until I get paid."

"You'll have to wait until tomorrow when I can get it out of the bank."

His gambling scares me. I am becoming Silas Marner frugal, Molière's l'Avare, keeping only enough money from my Forbes paycheck, my smaller paycheck, to hang out with my friends. And he's pushing a new role on me—Shylock.

"You don't have any money upstairs?" Michael demands, not happy with my bank answer. I picture Michael with a shovel digging up Silas Marner's dirt floor searching hysterically for the bag of gold, ripping up the floor boards in my bedroom.

"No, it's all in the bank. I don't want to be tempted to spend it." The bank with its vaults is a safe place; 21 Lynwood Terrace is not. "Michael, you have to stop gambling." If I'm loaning him money, he at least has to listen to me.

"I've got it in control," he says, lumbering off, jingling the car keys in his pants pocket.

After three weeks of my hounding him, always out of Mary's earshot, he pays me back half the money he borrowed. And he's gambling more than ever. So much for my sermon.

49. Handbag

IN JUNE, MARY announces that she can no longer afford to run the risk of Michael or me getting in a car accident, which would raise her insurance premiums, so we are forbidden to drive the family car. Now it's her car. Then, unsatisfied by our meek acceptance, she launches into her familiar lecture about money and being out on the street and where would you children be? Am I supposed to say thank you for not letting me drive the car? It's not as if we had said anything. What's the point? I want to hit her when she torments us with her "the wolf is at the door" routine. Besides, since marrying my dad, Mary is the one who has already been in two car accidents, a fact I secretly love, not that any of us would dare to mention it. Envisioning the station wagon with its torn-off door handle, the aftermath of a temper tantrum, and, later, the dented front fender is enough for me, and I shrug off her car edict. I begin to wonder why I had been to Belmont Driving School for my package of lessons, but at least I have my license. On his sixteenth birthday, when Danny decides that he'll just skip getting his license and keep getting his girlfriends to chauffeur him around, Michael and I are in a state of disbelief. In Springfield, getting your driver's license at sixteen is like having your first drink at twenty-one.

In the middle of a late-August heat wave, on a slow Thursday night, when men's sweaters top no one's shopping list, Maria and Ellen, carrying Casual Corner and Peerless shopping bags, yell down from the escalators a plan to pick me up out front after work. With Ellen tooling down Main Street in her dad's brown Impala, Maria turns from the passenger seat to hold up the Etienne Aigner handbag they had each just bought at Casual Corner. One look at the warm chestnut brown leather and brass clasp, and I instinctively know this bag is going to be the bag every girl, every cool girl, in the senior class will be carrying. In my head, I picture the entire cast of "Midnight in Moscow" lining up to buy this bag and decide I will abandon my lunch-hour summer reading tomorrow to jog into Casual Corner to check out the price. My money thinking has started to run like this: If I ask Maria and Ellen how much the bag cost, like everyone else does, then they might remember, "Oh, her father's dead, Carole doesn't have the money and she can't buy a bag like this," and they'd end up feeling sorry for me, especially if they remembered about my mother's death. I can't give anyone the chance to feel sorry for me, and I want everyone to forget my orphan status. Fifteen minutes later, cruising into the Friendly's parking lot, I spot Kevin talking to a blonde girl with dark roots in a madras plaid sundress. I wish I hadn't seen him. I try to block out the dull hurt by thinking of the Etienne Aigner handbag. I check to make sure the blonde with Kevin isn't carrying one. A junior hot fudge sundae with chopped pecans dotting the whipped cream turns out to be the sugary Band-Aid for the tiny hurts festering in my heart.

Crossing Main Street on the way to Casual Corner, I am weighing whether to buy the Etienne Aigner handbag, as I have all morning, and I make a deal with myself that if the handbag is less than my Forbes and

Wallace weekly paycheck of eighteen dollars, I will break down and spend the money. There the bag sits in all its magnificence in a glass-fronted case for every Springfield high school girl to covet. A matter-of-fact saleswoman places it on the counter, her hands on either side as if there is a danger I might slip it under my arm and sprint down Main Street.

"How much is the bag?" I hate asking, but her hand is covering up its price tag. Moving her hand aside, she lowers her glasses and tells me the price. Nineteen dollars and ninety-eight cents. Are her eyes saying, more than you can afford?

"I'm just looking. Thank you," I say, handing her back the bag and wonder if my "just looking" has disappointed her. I could afford it, but I stick to my deal. Besides, if Michael pays me the rest of the money he owes me, I'll buy the bag then.

The entire summer has passed, and on the Friday before Labor Day weekend, my last day of work at the county treasurer's office, Mrs. Hoey sighs theatrically, a deeper sigh than her everyday sighs, as she hands me my last paycheck and says, "I suppose you'll be back next summer to torture us."

"Is torture really the word you'd use?" I manage in a fake-pained way.

"You tell me." The day before, when Mr. Walsh was leaving for the beach, he had said how they all hoped I'd be back next summer. Grateful and relieved, I had murmured a thank you and shook his slim, dry hand.

"When does school start?" Helen asks me.

"I go in for an hour on Tuesday."

"Not much of a vacation for you, is it? Now, Carole, I suppose you'll be applying to college? Where will you go, the Elms?" Mrs. Hoey asks me, rat-a-tat-tat. The College of Our Lady of the Elms is a Catholic, girls-only college about a mile from my house. I could walk there. "You could live at home. Help out your brothers," she suggests.

"I'm not sure." Funny, how she doesn't mention helping out my stepmother. Maybe Mrs. Hoey shuns the word "stepmother" the way I do. Then Louise puckers her lips, pulls out her tortoise-shell compact, and waves her hair with her fingers. Louise treats me as if I were as welcome as a pea-sized wart on an index finger.

At the door, Helen tells me to drop in during my Christmas vacation, that she might have some work for me. There is something about leaving and saying goodbye, the sappiness of it all, I don't trust.

This time, Michael wants even more money.

"I paid you back last time, didn't I?" he demands. "You've got the money, don't you?"

"She's got every dime she ever made," Danny answers with a smirk.

"Why don't you loan him the money?" I ask, turning on Danny. "You bragged all summer about the money you made caddying."

"That money's gone," Danny protests. "Loan him the money before they break his legs."

"I thought it was so his car wouldn't be repossessed."

"Look, what do you want? Interest? Is that it?" Michael asks in a nervous giggle.

"That's not such a bad idea," I say. "I had to hound you for the money all of August. Once I give it to you, you forget all about paying it back." We both know I'm going to give him the money, but he has to know I want it back. "All right. I'll get the money on Saturday."

"Go after school tomorrow. I can't wait until Saturday," he says, desperation filling his voice.

"But, Michael," I inhale, "first, you're betting on the horses and now it's football games. You have to stop."

"I'll stop. I'll stop," he promises, a crazed look in his eyes as if legions of demons are surrounding him.

The next day, I hand him two hundred and fifty dollars.

50. Best Tunafish

SISTER ROSE CARMEL terrifies me. After a run-in Kevin had with her in the hall last fall, I remember his saying that if Sister could play defensive guard for the football team, they might win a game or two. In the opening minutes before the bell rings, she asks what we have read over the summer, and Gail Culver just about does cartwheels over *Catcher in the Rye* and *Rabbit, Run*. Although I had read nothing beyond the summer reading, I could recite the name of every town in Hampden County and many of its employees as well, a recitation that would not amuse Sister Rose Carmel. Suzanne Kean, another reader, throws the title of a novel or two into the pile. At the bell, Sister explains that in Honors English we will spend the fall term reading medieval literature—Beowulf, Chaucer, *Paradise Lost,* Dante's *Inferno*—and there will be a five-hundred-word essay due every Monday. A few brave boys, those as tall as Sister, groan softly. Ernie Croughwell raises his hand and asks her whether she had said "every." No one breathes while Sister stares him down, but the fool stares back. Sister drags him into the hall, and two minutes later a cowed Ernie slouches back into class.

Father Peter "Smacks" Loughran speaks in such a droning monotone that we can hear the saliva pooling in his mouth cavity. Students in his seventh-period American history class fight drowsiness as he lectures us about the Revolutionary War, the causes, the battles, the Tea Party, and the Freedom Trail. In his class, everyone sits in anticipation, waiting for him to smack his lips together. Father hardly ever gives homework and is thrilled when anyone knows an answer. Four or five boys have started to answer questions by smacking their lips together and despite the outbreaks of coughing when they do it, Father doesn't even get it. Sister Rose Carmel could give Father Loughran lessons on classroom discipline. Like everyone else, I start my other homework during his class. Seventh-period history is like a study hall.

Stuffed into my assignment notebook, I have an application for the University of Massachusetts in Amherst, which I slide out, relieved to see that it requires no application fee, but annoyed that I have to write an essay. Sunday afternoon is now my essay writing afternoon. Thank you, Sister Rose Carmel. I tuck the application back into my book and put my chin in my hand to keep from nodding off, staring at Father so he might think I care about the Articles of Confederation. Between the hissing noises from the radiator and Father's smacking, his class has a lullaby feel.

"I will kill or be killed if I don't get away from my stepmother." The University of Massachusetts is not expecting its applicants to be harboring thoughts of violence. But I am. Since the last family "explosion" (Gerry had come up with this word, more fitting than "fight") I have been trying to figure out a way I could take care of my brothers if Mary makes good on her threats to leave. Grabbing a handful of hair, I rub my head until I can dream up a more riveting answer on why I want to attend the University of Massachusetts. I don't think "nearby and affordable" indicate the intellectual curiosity the admissions staff is favoring. Leaning back in my chair, I look out the window at Tommy and Bobby jumping in a pile of blood red leaves. With Mary away for the weekend visiting her mother in a nursing home outside of Boston, a blessed peace has descended on the house.

The essay is not coming easily, but a confusing memory is. I remember the night sitting in the living room when my dad told me about my mother's scholarship to the College of New Rochelle, and how even with a scholarship she couldn't afford to go. From the armchair across the room, my mother had given him a resigned, tired look and stubbed out her cigarette. Like my mother, I can't afford to go to New Rochelle, and couldn't even if my father were still alive, a fact hard for me to admit. No class leadership positions for me this year, and still there's not enough space on the form for my extracurricular activities. Chewing the pen, I realize I'm not helping my brothers any and, no matter how hard I try, I only make the fighting worse. I can't be Saint George and fight the dragon anymore, and Amherst is less than thirty miles away.

I drop the completed application in the corner mailbox on Columbus Day, and a few days later the world begins to fall apart with the Russians setting up missile sites in Cuba. I wish my father were alive now. He had a way of calming us down. Mary pays no attention to it.

* * *

Two weeks later, on the Friday before Halloween, the University of Massachusetts accepts me. I figured I would get in, so the acceptance doesn't matter much. I am in the kitchen making a cup of tea for myself when Mary comes home, carrying groceries.

"You and your brothers get the groceries out of the car," she puffs, putting the bag on the counter. I round up Joey and Steve, though Gerry ducks into the back room, and the three of us unload the car.

"What did that letter say, Carole?" Mary asks as she puts away a box of Cheerios.

"They accepted me."

"And I suppose you're going? Don't expect me to give you any money. If you had any idea what groceries cost to feed you and your brothers . . ." She folds up a brown paper bag.

"I know. I'll have the money."

"The money your father left is for me to run this house. You and your brothers think just because he was in insurance he left me a fortune. Everyone in Springfield thinks that. Well, he didn't. You understand that, don't you?"

"I understand." The thing with Mary is she doesn't stop, just keeps right on hammering.

"You're just going to show everyone how smart you are. Isn't that it? Just want everyone to know how smart you are." She looks at me as if she expects an answer.

"Well, answer me. You just want everyone to know how smart you are."

How am I supposed to answer her? I never know.

"I guess that's it." I try to answer as if she has solved the riddle of the ages.

"Don't get fresh with me. You just hate me and want to get away from me. That's true, isn't it?" Mary pierces me with yet another question I'm afraid to answer.

"Mary, I don't hate you," I lie.

"You've never cared for me, have you, Carole?" she asks, and her eyes fill with tears.

"Mary, I care for you. Why do you say that?" Another lie falls from my cracked lips as Steve drops a bag of Wonder bread into the bread box.

"Will we still see you? Are you leaving us?" Steve asks me and hugs my waist. His voice has an air of loss to it, but he has rescued me. Mary bolts to her room, crying she's never done anything to hurt me.

"Steve, I'm not going away until a year from now. It's just twenty-five miles from here. I'll be home. You'll see."

"But you make the best tuna fish," Steve whispers. A voice in my head drowns out Stevie, ordering me to get away from here or I will fall apart.

The Central branch building of the Springfield Public Library, a straight uphill climb from Main Street, perches proudly at the intersection of State and Maple like a dowager hosting an afternoon tea. The white limestone exterior with its regal, yet welcoming air is flanked by patches of grass, now blanketed with layers of crisp red, yellow, and orange leaves. Leaving behind me a picture-perfect fall afternoon, I climb the wide, endless steps to the entrance and, once inside, hurry to the ground floor reference room.

On my third straight Sunday afternoon of poring through thick books on unclaimed scholarships in the library reference room, I slam the last book shut, violating the library's posted quiet policy. The four other people scattered at the long rectangular tables remain motionless, dozing or lost in thought, unfazed by my wayward behavior. Rather than risk a look from the hard-faced librarian, I stare out the State Street windows, frames for the half-dressed trees, basking in the late afternoon sun. Tapping the scuffed toes of my loafers against the highly polished green linoleum floor, I see a built-up ridge of old floor wax lining the perimeter of the floor moldings. The dark wooden shelves loom over me as if to threaten me with the continents of facts I will never know and scholarship entries I may have overlooked. No wonder these scholarships go "unclaimed"—to be eligible, an applicant has to be part Portuguese, or belong to a Youth Fellowship in Kansas, or both. On my sheet of notebook paper, I have noted: Football, American Legion, UMass. With entire sections in these books listing football scholarships, I have scribbled down, *Tell Danny,* who is again starting as a defensive guard for Cathedral. Because of my Forbes job, I miss all the Saturday afternoon games, so no one ever watches him play.

The American Legion entry I have circled with heavily marked stars. For the last two weeks, I, as the college-bound child of a veteran, have been working on my application for an American Legion scholarship, submitting an essay from sophomore English class entitled "What Is a Brother?" Although the head of the Women's Auxiliary had encouraged me to write on a more patriotic topic, I ignored her advice and stuck with the brother piece. When I was ten, I had begged my parents to buy a flag so we could fly it in front of the house on holidays, and they had said, "We'll see." Since we never did get a flag, I chose not to write about what seemed like a failure of O'Malley patriotism. By Thursday, I will have finished the forms for a UMass scholarship and will drop them both in the mail. Tapping the eraser against the paper, I write down *Michael* and three question marks after his name. While I haven't loaned Michael any more money, he hasn't paid me back either. I jot down three more question marks, making it an even half-dozen.

SCOTCH AND SODA—A TRANSCRIPTION

SETTING: Heritage Hall South, room 206, a health care facility in Agawam, Massachusetts. The present; a Sunday in winter.

(*Mary is sleeping. A tray of food sits on a wheeled table in front of her. Carole places a plant on Mary's dresser. She puts her coat at the foot of Mary's bed. Carole pulls out a disposable camera and takes a picture of Mary. There is no chair, so she places her handbag on the floor and waits for Mary to stir. Five minutes later, Mary wakes. In this transcript, many of Carole's lines, mostly repetitions and agreements, have been deleted.*)

CAROLE: Hi, Mary. I brought you this plant.
MARY: Pardon?
CAROLE: I brought you this plant, right here. (*Carole holds up a red flowered plant in a clay pot.*) Can you see it?
MARY: Yeah, what is that?
CAROLE: It's a . . . oh, what did the florist say it was?—it's a primrose. (*Pause.*)
MARY: How come you're so nice to me?

CAROLE: I don't know why I'm so nice to you. You're very lucky, aren't you?

MARY: Yeah, I'll say. (*Carole puts the plant down on a dresser next to a photograph of the O'Malley children.*)

CAROLE: Mary, you're not eating your lunch.

MARY: Huh?

CAROLE: You're not eating your lunch.

MARY: At Christmas, we went to that party, you know that, we went from one house to another. (*Pause.*) Can't remember anything else . . .

CAROLE: You remember going to Christmas parties? From one house to another?

MARY: Yes.

CAROLE: Do you remember me and all the O'Malley children, the boys?

MARY: Oh, I remember them.

CAROLE: I'm sure you do.

MARY: You know them, too?

CAROLE: I know them, yeah.

MARY: What is, what is your full name?

CAROLE: Uh, Carole O'Malley Gaunt.

MARY: Oh, Carole Gaunt.

CAROLE: Right, I married David.

MARY: Oh, I remember when that happened.

CAROLE: Uh-huh, you were there . . .

MARY: M-hum.

CAROLE: . . . Looking lovely.

MARY: Do you know if they have a baby now?

CAROLE: We have three grown daughters.

MARY: Oh, how, what does David have?

CAROLE: Uh—David has the same three grown daughters.

MARY: Oh, none of his own?

CAROLE: Well, they are his own, they are his own.

MARY: Oh, but not little kids?

CAROLE: No, they're grown up.

MARY: Oh. (*Pause.*) How is David?

CAROLE: He's good. He's good.

MARY: Yeah?

CAROLE: He's good.

MARY: So they're happily married then?

CAROLE: Yes. David's in New York. He's trying to exercise and stay healthy. He walks all over the city. We live in New York.

MARY: I haven't seen any of them in so long. I used to see them all the time. Boy, how things change, you know?

CAROLE: They do.

MARY: (*Happily.*) You know, one time I really knew so many people . . . I had a lot of fun, you know? Once everybody just gradually goes away . . . they all go away. And there you are up and left to the side. Sitting on the curbstone.

CAROLE: Did you . . . what did you do for fun?

MARY: Well, it was hard to find anything to do. That's why I was always glad I read a lot. I bought a lot of books. Went to the library and borrowed one.

CAROLE: So has Gerry been by lately?

MARY: He was here one day.

(*Staff member comes in and goes out.*)

CAROLE: I'm going to see him later.

MARY: Who did you marry?

CAROLE: I married David . . . David Gaunt.

MARY: David Gaunt, yeah.

CAROLE: Right. We've been married a long time.

MARY: You're married quite a while.

CAROLE: Yeah, we have. We got married at Our Lady of Hope.

MARY: How's David?

CAROLE: He's good.

MARY: That's good. He's a nice man, isn't he?

CAROLE: He is a nice man. (*Pause.*) You liked all of my boyfriends.

MARY: Pardon?

CAROLE: You liked all of my boyfriends.

MARY: Yeah, that's right.

CAROLE: (*Pause.*) Most men.

MARY: (*Threateningly.*) Careful now.

CAROLE: (*Backing off.*) Okay . . .

MARY: Don't go any further . . .

CAROLE: I won't.

MARY: I'll—I'll have to get up right out of this bed and break my neck and give you a wallop.

CAROLE: Uh-huh.

MARY: That ought to be fun.

CAROLE: Well, I don't think you're strong enough to give me a wallop right now, Mary.

MARY: No I—I'm not strong enough to even get out of bed. Ah, what a mess I am. (*Pause.*) I don't even understand how you can't walk after you break a leg. The attendant says to me, "Oh—Oh, you just like using that walker, don't ya?" And I just felt like saying, "You know, why don't you just turn around and get away from me, 'cause I don't want to listen to you anymore," because if he ever says it again, I am gonna say "I don't want to talk to you anymore."

CAROLE: The nurse? The male nurse?

MARY: Yeah. No. I—I don't know if he's a nurse or not. I've know him for a while, but . . . Jeez, I said, "I don't know how you can talk to me like this and pretend you're a friend of mine." He said, "Well, Mary, I think you're a fool" and I said, "Well that's your business, but don't try to push it onto me. I married him because I wanted to." (*Pause.*) And I don't think he lived very long.

CAROLE: (*Fearfully.*) He didn't live very long. He died from too much drinking.

MARY: Really? You know, I remember I think I heard that too. I knew that he drank when other people weren't drinking, you know, but I think that, you know, I think that everything just destroyed him anyway. He was, he was really a nice man.

CAROLE: He was a nice man, too.

MARY: Yes, he was.

CAROLE: (*Probingly.*) You and he used to go to parties a lot.

MARY: Yeah . . . partygoers.

CAROLE: Uh-huh, yeah partygoers.

(*Pause.*)

MARY: I sometimes wonder how I ever went to so many of those parties.

CAROLE: You liked getting dressed up and looking good and seeing other people.

MARY: Yeah.

CAROLE: Dad did too.

MARY: I think that once your—you break up with them—I don't think I ever broke up with them, but uh, once you get separated, they never bother coming back.

CAROLE: Yeah.

MARY: Like none of the kids I brought up all by myself.

CAROLE: You brought us up all by yourself, yeah.

MARY: They never come to see me.

CAROLE: They don't?

MARY: No. Some of them do. Of course now they, they live so far away they can't do anything about it anyway. They left for the Cape. And uh, what's his name, Tommy lives down in Florida, I can't remember his name but of course you don't expect to see him. But um, it's kinda disappointing, you know . . .

CAROLE: It is disappointing.

MARY: . . . Without me, they don't have a shot, think of what they'd be, if I didn't take care of them. (*Pause.*) Suppose they feel well, they, if she hadn't taken care of them, somebody else would have, and you don't know, you wouldn't think kids would think that way, but I think they do.

CAROLE: Why, I think they've all been pretty grateful and attentive, Mary.

MARY: Yeah.

CAROLE: (*Daringly.*) You used to get angry a lot.

MARY: Hm?

CAROLE: You used to get angry a lot.

MARY: Really?

CAROLE: Yeah.

MARY: With the kids?

CAROLE: Yeah. And me, too.

MARY: With you too?

CAROLE: Yeah.

MARY: Why was I angry with you?

CAROLE: I don't know.

MARY: Do you drink a lot?

CAROLE: No, not then.

(*Pause.*)

MARY: Oh, now you do, huh?

CAROLE: No, not now, not now. There was a time when I drank too much . . . for me anyway. But you don't drink? You stopped drinking . . . after my father died.

MARY: I can't remember the last time I had a drink. I enjoyed drinking though. Cause I, you know, I never over-drank because I knew I was gonna die if I did, and then I'd wake up with a terrible headache and I didn't need to have worse headaches than I had already . . . So I didn't—even now I can't remember the last time I had a drink. I—I always loved a scotch and soda.

CAROLE: Was that your drink?

MARY: Yeah.

CAROLE: Did you have a favorite kind of scotch?

MARY: Hmm?

CAROLE: Did you have a favorite kind of scotch?

MARY: I can't remember now.

CAROLE: Johnnie Walker?

MARY: Yeah, I had that too. People say they don't understand how anybody could drink it because of the taste—the taste is so terrible, but, see, that's when somebody doesn't know how to make it.

CAROLE: Uh-huh.

MARY: They don't mix it right . . . if you put the . . . the . . . uh, alcohol on at the top, they get all the drink of alcohol and nobody wants that, maybe somebody does, not me.

CAROLE: Yeah, but when you were taking Valium you couldn't drink— or the Librium or whatever it was, you know, that you took for your . . . was it for your headaches?

(Pause.)

MARY: What was that?

CAROLE: Valium or Librium?

MARY: Oh, yes.

CAROLE: Which one?

MARY: Valium, I think.

CAROLE: What's that sandwich there? Peanut butter and jelly?

MARY: I guess that's what it is. I have asked them so many times, please put it on white bread. When you have it on dark bread it takes away the taste of the whole thing.

CAROLE: I'll say something at the desk on my way out.

(*Staff member enters.*)

STAFF MEMBER: You want something to drink?

MARY: The only thing to take care of really is the bread. When it's on white bread it tastes fine.

CAROLE: We grew up on peanut butter and jelly sandwiches. (*Pause.*) Just like Elvis Presley, except Elvis liked peanut butter and banana.

MARY: Who's that?

CAROLE: Elvis Presley. Remember Elvis Presley the singer?

MARY: Yeah. What's new, anything?

CAROLE: No, nothing's new. (*Beat.*) I'm writing a book, and it might be published so . . . that's exciting.

MARY: Hmm?! What's it called?

CAROLE: Hungry Hill.

MARY: Sorry?

CAROLE: Hungry Hill.

MARY: Really?

CAROLE: Ah-huh. You're in it.

MARY: I am?

CAROLE: You are. (*Pause.*) My dad's in it.

MARY: Sold a few, huh?

CAROLE: Pardon me?

MARY: They sold a few?

CAROLE: Well, they haven't sold them yet . . . but . . .

MARY: Oh. This is just something you've done recently, huh?

CAROLE: Yeah, I'm doing it now.

MARY: Oh, oh, that's wonderful.

CAROLE: Took me a long time. I'm seeing some friends later.

MARY: Huh?

CAROLE: I am seeing some friends from Cathedral later.

MARY: Really? That's fun, isn't it?

CAROLE: It is fun.

MARY: Where did you go to school?

CAROLE: I went to Cathedral . . . and then I went to UMass.

MARY: At Cathedral, did they teach you any religion?

CAROLE: Yes, they did. It was one of the required courses.

MARY: Did they teach it good?

CAROLE: They were pretty good. How were they at your high school?

MARY: Oh, Buckley. I went to Buckley.

CAROLE: Were you and my mother in the same class? Betty O'Malley? Remember Betty?

MARY: Betty and I were good friends.

CAROLE: I know. You met in high school and then you both went to work at Travelers together?

MARY: Where is she now?

CAROLE: She died.

MARY: She did, oh, somebody told me that, but I didn't know when she died of course. What did she die of?

CAROLE: Uh, she had cancer. And you married her—you married Joe O'Malley. Cleon.

MARY: Cleon.

CAROLE: He didn't like that name though.

MARY: Huh?

CAROLE: He didn't like that name. Cleon.

MARY: He didn't like it?

CAROLE: No.

MARY: It's kind of nice, isn't it?

CAROLE: It's different.

MARY: Must be terrible if you don't like your own name.

CAROLE: Must be.

MARY: It's a funny world, isn't it?

CAROLE: It is a funny world.

MARY: It's not really funny. It's more cuckoo. Cuckoo. (*Beat.*) This bread is terrible.

CAROLE: You can't go to the dining room? (*Beat.*) You can't go to the dining room with the other people here?

MARY: If I go to the dining room, I have to use the walker. And I can't do anything about that. I don't like using that walker. Every once in a while I try to walk without it, they say, "Mary, don't forget that walker, you'll fall and break your neck." They say it right out loud. Everybody looks at you. Not much fun to have. They're wonderful to have, wonderful when they were made for people who have a need for them like I did. I felt like such a cripple, you know?

CAROLE: I like your jersey with the snowmen on it. (*Beat.*) The shirt you're wearing? They have such cute faces.

MARY: I think they're cute.

CAROLE: Did I give it to you or did Gerry give it to you?

MARY: Isn't it awful? I don't know.

CAROLE: Oh, it's not important.

MARY: All the cute little faces on it. They really make you laugh and smile. (*Beat.*) I brought up a lot of kids. I think I did all that and I never had one of my own.

CAROLE: I know.

MARY: I don't think that's fair. (*Mary laughs.*)

CAROLE: I don't think so either. (*Beat.*) You had that hysterectomy . . . remember?

MARY: Pardon?

CAROLE: You had that hysterectomy.

MARY: Yeah. Boy, you remember a lot of things, don't you?

CAROLE: I guess I do. Did any of my brothers ever fight with you?

MARY: Your brothers fight with me?

CAROLE: Yeah, did they ever fight growing up?

MARY: What was his name?

CAROLE: Any of them—Joey, Michael, Danny?

MARY: Well, all of those kids were named O'Malley. There was Tommy, Bobby, Stephen, Joey, Gerry, Danny, and Carole. Do you ever see Carole?

CAROLE: Yes, I do see her.

MARY: Somebody said she was going to come up. I haven't seen her in awhile myself, but they said she was going to come up this way. I knew Carole very well years ago.

CAROLE: What was she like?

MARY: She was nice.

CAROLE: You knew David, too.

MARY: They're still married, aren't they? Do they have any kids?

CAROLE: They have three girls.

MARY: That's right. I can't remember what their names were, but I remember when they were born.

CAROLE: Abby has your maiden name, Abigail Ford.

MARY: Ford, huh?

CAROLE: Ford.

MARY: Is that her mother's name?

CAROLE: No, that was your name.

MARY: Where did she get it?

CAROLE: From Carole. Carole named her after you.

MARY: Carole Gaunt?

CAROLE: Yeah.

MARY: Carole's name was Ford before she got married?

CAROLE: No, she was Carole O'Malley. Did she ever help you while you
were raising the boys?

MARY: Pardon? I don't remember.

CAROLE: No one cleaned the house like you cleaned the house, Mary.

MARY: Hey, I did so much work it's a wonder I didn't kill myself.

CAROLE: You don't like the crust?

MARY: Not really.

CAROLE: I'll take it off for you if you want.

MARY: I don't like it on this bread. You see it's such a tough bread. It
takes the taste of the whole thing away. Oh, dear. How many children
do you have?

CAROLE: I have three daughters.

MARY: What are their names?

CAROLE: Abby, Susan, and Victoria.

MARY: Abby . . .

CAROLE: Susan and Victoria.

MARY: They're all grown up now.

CAROLE: Yes.

MARY: Any of them get married?

CAROLE: No, no. Not yet. (*Beat.*) I wanted to name one Elizabeth, but I
was afraid to. (*Beat.*) I thought you'd get angry.

MARY: What?

CAROLE: If I named one Elizabeth.

MARY: Why would I get angry?

CAROLE: I don't know. Maybe you would have felt slighted.

MARY: I don't think everybody should name their children after me.
Who ever told you that?

CAROLE: I don't know. Maybe it's just something I came up with on
my own.

MARY: All the kids I took care of, and I never had a baby of my own.
I don't think that's fair. I'm going to talk to him upstairs someday

when I leave this place. Of course, I don't know whether I'm going to heaven or hell. I don't really think there's any such place as hell. It's hard for me to believe that the man who created all of this would let us burn. There are other ways to make people suffer without burning them to death. I don't think they ever found very much about it.

CAROLE: Yes, I think you're right on that. Guess it comes down to faith. (*Beat.*) OK, Mary, I think I'm going to go.

MARY: I knew this was going to happen. Oh, thank you. (*Mary giggles.*)

CAROLE: (*Carole kisses Mary.*) Enjoy the plant.

MARY: What is it now?

CAROLE: A primrose.

MARY: What color is it?

CAROLE: It's red. Can you see it?

MARY: Oh, that's pretty, isn't it? That was lovely of you to bring that. You're a real nice gal.

CAROLE: I try.

MARY: It was nice having you come and see me. It makes all the difference in the world when someone you know comes to see you, especially when it's someone you like very much.

CAROLE: Thank you. Let me take a picture of you.

MARY: Of me?

CAROLE: Yes.

MARY: You do it already?

CAROLE: I'm doing it right now. (*Carole takes her picture.*) OK, 'bye, Mary. I'll see you the next time I come up.

MARY: You live in New York?

CAROLE: I live in New York.

MARY: You're married to David?

CAROLE: I'm married to David.

MARY: He was a nice man.

CAROLE: He was a nice man. He still is.

MARY: Tell him I said hello.

CAROLE: I will.

MARY: It was lovely of you to drop by to see me. I really appreciate that.

CAROLE: 'Bye, Mary.

(*Carole exits and stops at reception desk. The staff member looks up.*)

CAROLE: Is it possible Mary O'Malley could have white bread for her sandwich? I know she doesn't like to eat the hot meal in the dining room.

STAFF MEMBER: We rarely have white bread. We just don't serve it here.

(*Carole walks down the long hall, weaving around the women slumped in their wheelchairs, and exits. Carole leans against the columns at the front of the building.*)

51. Only a Dish

THE TURKEY HAS been hacked to bits, stripes of baked-on squash hug the serving bowl, and squares of orange pineapple Jello wobble in the Pyrex dish. With a heavy grayness and little conversation, we have almost survived Thanksgiving, our first Thanksgiving with neither parent. Just let it end in peace, I pray silently. There is no hint of sun anywhere this bleak afternoon. With dessert yet to come, Mary starts to clear the table with me following her, when Michael hits his dinner dish with his elbow, breaking the plate in half.

"Mary, I'm sorry. It was an accident," Michael rushes to apologize, picking up the pieces of the plate.

"You clumsy fool! That was my grandmother's china," she wails.

"I'll buy you another dish, Mary. Just tell me where to get it." Voices murmur at the table—it was an accident, he didn't mean it, he'll get you another plate.

"The dish cannot be replaced! Don't you understand?" Mary yells, her eyes a familiar blaze. A tightening spreads through my body from forehead to ankles. "That's right. Stick up for one another. Don't even think of me and what I do for you kids." Her words are like bad reception on a radio. Michael blushes and stares down at the broken plate. I dare not say what I am thinking, it's only a dish, when Joey grabs the sides of his plate and says as if I had fed him the words, "It's only a dish."

"How dare you?" Mary's anger is an animal at that table and she lunges, slapping Joey across the face.

"Do you want me to break every dish at this table?" Joey picks the plate up in his hand, threatening her. Danny on one side and Gerry on the other reach for Joey's arms but he shakes them off. He and Mary stare at each other, their dark eyes flashing. No one backs down.

"Don't you ever hit me again! You're not my mother." Joey's voice seethes with anger as he slams the plate down and picks up a dinner knife.

"Joey, don't." "Put the knife down." "No, no, no." "Don't hurt her." Fear and panic hit me. Tommy and Bobby are crying uncontrollably. Mary runs from the kitchen into her room and slams the door. Joey runs from the table and slams his fist through a window in the kitchen door. Broken glass flies everywhere, and Joey escapes outside into the November cold.

While Michael and Danny sweep up the pieces of glass, I keep the younger kids away. We put cardboard over the broken window, sit back down, and Danny and I dole out Liberty Bakery apple pie for dessert when Mary, her eyes red, walks back into the kitchen.

"Did you forget there's pumpkin pie, too?" she asks and reaches for a bakery box on top of the refrigerator as if broken windows and knives meant nothing.

Although Joey has been missing for nearly three hours, Mary has forbidden any of us to look for him or to call anyone. "He'll be back, like a bad puppy. I couldn't be that lucky," she had said, unloading the dishwasher. Just as the streetlights are coming on, Joey sneaks back into the kitchen, wolfs down the last piece of pumpkin pie, and gulps milk right out of the bottle. As a clumsy relief lumbers into the dim kitchen, Danny and I warily badger Joey for some explanation or some pale sign of remorse for the knife, the escape, but he scowls at us blackly and refuses to let on where he'd been hiding. Michael just says, "Carole, can you blame him?"

Even if your dad is dead, what is Christmas without a party?

On Christmas Eve, I open the kitchen door where at the counter Mary is stirring pieces of Lipton's dried onion soup into sour cream transforming its whiteness into a marbled beige with each flick of her wrist.

"Take those packages you're carrying and put them in your room." As I cross the kitchen, she says in a rush, "The dip's always better if it sits in the refrigerator." Reaching into the refrigerator for a kielbasa, she orders, "No one touch this bowl." A corner of the kitchen overflows with bags of chips, crackers, and an assortment of cheeses. The little kids run in and out, hair still wet on the edges, dressed in their ties and pass-it-down-to-the-next-one sport coats. Every minute or so, another one will check the windows for cars pulling into the driveway. Climbing the stairs, I think how my dad loved parties and how he would love the open house Mary is having.

Forbes & Wallace had been a madhouse all day with last-minute shoppers, so desperate they almost wiped out our bargain tables of the rust-colored sweaters that would be returned before the New Year. There had been none of the usual standing-around-doing-nothing boredom. I change into the matching mint-green sweater and skirt set Mary had picked out for me for last year's Christmas, an outfit I love. When the doorbell rings, I put on my frosted lipstick, pinch my sallow cheeks, and run down the stairs, taking two at a time.

By seven-thirty, the kitchen and living room are overflowing with my aunts, uncles, cousins, neighbors, and friends of my dad. While I was at work, my brothers had invited their friends, so I go into the back room and call Jean. I listen while her mother tells her to stay home this one night. It isn't bothering any of these boys' mothers that their sons are partying on Christmas Eve, I want to protest.

Eddie Boland's mother leans on his arm as he slowly leads her into the living room. "Carole, what happened with UMass?" the congressman asks.

"It was your letter of recommendation. They accepted me."

"My letter had nothing to do with it. It was the easiest letter I ever had to write," he says with a wave of his hand. The three of us are in the archway. "Your old man would be so proud of you." I feel my eyes wash with tears because I'm not so sure my dad even wanted me to go to college. As I pass around a tray of kielbasa and mustard, a task to hide behind, I wonder if my dad had ever said anything to Eddie about me? About my leaving my brothers? I smile at Gerry, who is standing next to the stereo and mouthing the words as Nat King Cole sings "The Little Drummer Boy." Pa rumpa pum pum.

"Oh, Matty, you shouldn't have," Mary protests and kisses Matty Ryan on the cheek. "A kiss for you, too, Rosemary." She trips as she reaches down to kiss Matty's daughter. "Really, Matty, you've done enough. Your father's a bad boy." Mary shakes her finger an inch from Rosemary's face.

"Mary, we just wanted to drop that gift off. Peg's waiting at home."

"You're not even having a drink?" The hurt fills her voice.

"No, I can't. Too much to do tonight," Matty says with his hand on the doorknob.

"But, Matty, you haven't even taken off your coat."

"I've got to pick up my mother."

"Oh, all right, but promise me that next year you'll bring your mother," Mary says, her hand on his arm.

"I'll do my best. Merry Christmas, everybody," he yells from the door.

"That Matty's always running somewhere. He just can't stay still."

His daughter, Rosemary, turns and gives a faint wave. Mary's flirting just kills me, but it's Christmas.

With no knives and no hitting, no Tiny Tim hobbling in the door either, the open house ends with a feeling of peace and good will. Or maybe it is just relief. On Christmas morning before Mass, Mary gives me a royal blue sweater and skirt set from Casual Corner, which I can't wait to put on. Now I own two, a collection. I will say this for Mary—she spends money for Christmas presents, and she has a fun Christmas Eve party.

I slog irregular bath towels all during Christmas vacation. The shoppers are staying home roasting chestnuts on an open fire or making figgy pudding. But there is no figgy pudding at our house. As I walk in, before I even have my coat off, my brothers are circling me, whispering about the fights and battles of the day. The victims will show me their blood, head bumps, or black and blue marks, and I'll promise to talk to their torturer. "Did he tell you what he did to me?" "He's such a liar. You believed him?" "He started it." "Leave me alone." "You won't tell Mary, will you?" Cain kills Abel. But Thursday's Cain is Friday's Abel as they flip-flop back and forth between victim and torturer. During Christmas vacations when it's sub-zero and only a good snowfall will drag my brothers outside, the fighting always gets worse.

52. Term Projects

SISTER ROSE CARMEL plucks tortures out of the air on a predictable, seasonal basis. This winter it is public speaking. In late fall, for a project in medieval literature, she directed us to form groups of three or four and to integrate what we had culled from this stilted, heroic literature into a presentation to be made to the class. Gail Culver, the reader, Diane Scagliarini, the poet, and I met during lunch and hoped some Muse of Inspiration would join us in the corner chair. During the two-week period of preparation, Diane changed the spelling of her name to, first, Dianne, then the more unusual Dyanne. Her last name she can do nothing about, and behind her back Scagliarini has become "Scags." While Gail and I tried to persuade Dyanne that she should write an epic poem that we would put our names on, she looked down her thin nose and shook her head, unsure if we were ridiculing her, which we were not.

At the start of each class, Sister allowed one minute to discuss the progress of our projects. While we had nothing to say, Suzanne Kean asked if she could bring in and wear a suit of armor. Klaus Shigley piped up that he wanted to bring in a ship's model or chariot that they were making while Gail and I rolled our eyes over our blank slate. At lunch, Di, who had switched to a "regimen" of eating only vegetables, remained calm while Gail kept adjusting her knee socks and I patted my hand on the table. With her quips and hint of sophistication, Gail is fun, but Di is just bearable, and normally she and I would never sit together for lunch. Gail and I vetoed the idea of any project involving props—hard to top Suzanne's suit of armor, "from the Museum," we guessed. Gail suggested we do a *Time* magazine for a week in the late twelfth century, a variation on a tenth-grade assignment. The three of us tossed it around and finally put it in our maybe category when I hit on an idea. "Why don't we do a quiz show, like the *G.E. College Bowl* on television, and our one category would be medieval literature?" I spewed out questions, already thinking of class involvement. Always enthusiastic, Gail clapped her hands while Di put the corner of her napkin to her lips. Realizing how little work this might be, questions and opposing teams, I begged Di, convincing her to abandon her Chaucer mural project, and she consented with a sniff.

The night before our quiz show, *As Time Flies By,* I spent twenty minutes on the phone convincing Gail to wear a white beard she found in a prop closet, an idea we abandoned when we considered Sister's possible reaction. Having split the questions among us and organized teams, we presented our panel. The first minute was slow going, but the teams got carried away with the interactive aspect. With her arms folded, Sister smiled and said she liked the surprise of mixing ancient material with the new quiz show medium. After class, Gail and I hugged each other with relief.

For the public-speaking exercise, Sister Rose Carmel assigns the speech topic "My Most Unforgettable Character," just like *Reader's Digest.* The entire debate team, whose members like nothing better than to hear their own reedy voices discussing the events of the day, is in this class. It is a springlike Sunday afternoon in February, and I have been staring out my window at the melting snow waiting for inspiration when I see Gerry walking up the street, cheeks all red, his ice skates over his shoulder. I bolt downstairs so I can nab a Hydrox cookie before he gets to the half-finished package.

"You're back early," I say, savoring the white sugar filling.

"No one was at Van Horn. The ice had puddles."

"Well, it's too warm for February. It'll get cold again."

"You didn't take the last cookie, did you? You wouldn't do such a thing, would you, Carole?" He drops his skates on the back porch and grabs a cookie. "Where's the Queen?"

"She's visiting her mother at the nursing home in Framingham."

"Oh, good, we'll have peace for two hours," Gerry says, wiping cookie crumbs from the table onto his index finger and licking it.

"I like the Queen title."

"Yeah, I thought you would. I just came up with it yesterday. I'm pretty proud of it."

"Almost as good as the Mona Lisa," I say. Ever since Mary has asked us not to sit in the living room because she wants "to preserve the furniture," Gerry has started calling a wing chair the "Mona Lisa."

"Don't forget the couch," he says in an affected voice. "It's a Rembrandt." Gerry cracks me up, grabs another cookie, and heads for an afternoon of television. No sooner has he left than Steve, Bobby, and Tommy fly into the kitchen, demanding cookies.

"Two each," I order as they palm a handful, ignoring me and my rules, and race away. I sit down, scooping up the crumbs, and stare into space. From the TV room, Gerry calls me. When I go in and see Gerry lying on the sofa with the little kids sitting on the floor, he asks me to switch the channel.

"You got me. I always fall for this trick. And here I thought you needed my help, my advice, my wise counsel."

"Well, I did. I needed you to change the television station." The little kids howl, admiring the way Gerry has zinged me with this old trick of his. Back at the table, I scratch my ear and start writing, "My Brother Gerry—My Most Unforgettable Character."

Even Arthur Larvey, who solves physics problems for fun (Sir Isaac Newton is his unforgettable character), is chuckling. From the corner of my eye, I see the bib of Sister's habit shaking up and down as she chokes back laughter. When I finish, she, all red-faced, asks, "You said this wunderkind's in eighth grade now?"

"Yes, Sister," I answer as my index cards drop to the floor. Anne Kavanaugh reaches down to gather them and smiles as she hands them to me.

"And I suppose this unforgettable character will be coming to Cathedral High School in the fall?" Sister asks, swinging the black cord circling her tree-like middle.

"Yes, Sister, Gerry will be a ninth grader."

"The other Sisters and I," she says with a cackling sound in her voice, "will certainly be looking out for him, come September."

Got him.

53. Runaway

"I'LL SHOW YOU! I'm getting out of here. You'll be sorry, all of you!" Joey yells on his way out the door. From the backyard hedges, he shouts back, "You're all jerks anyway!" An experienced runaway, Joey has spat out the language of mistreatment and warning, but has ignored the lion/lamb March weather with its falling temperatures and risk of snow. Only in sixth grade, Joey has already taken off from home four or five times. Families of runaways on television always care about the "missing" child, call the police even, but Mary just said to let him go, and began coloring her hair. Michael and Danny agree that Joey will be back, and I only worry because I don't have anything better to do and have an overactive imagination anyway. But over two hours have passed, Mary's hair is now in curlers, and Joey is still not back. Now the house is tense, as we wait, not talking to one another, somehow afraid of words. I can't get used to Joey's running away.

"What if he hops a bus for Connecticut? He knows where the bus station is, by now," I fret, once Mary is tucked away in the bathroom.

"He doesn't have any money, so how far can he get?" Danny reasons.

"But it's freezing out again. He didn't wear any mittens." I am thumbing through the basket of mittens on the cellar stairs.

"So that'll make him come back all the sooner," Michael says. "He's eleven, how far do you think he's going to get?"

"Dad's Mass is tomorrow morning. What if he's not back for it?" I ask. Mary has arranged for a memorial Mass for my dad on his one-year anniversary.

"I'd skip the Mass if I could," Michael says.

"Michael." I raise my voice in shock. Then we are silent, alone with our thoughts. In the quiet, I can hear the clock ticking. "Michael, remember how Dad used to say we'd never visit his grave after he died? How on Saturday mornings he'd try to get us to go with him to the cemetery to put flowers on Mom's grave?" My dad had been right, I have not been back to the cemetery. I was no better than Saint Peter in the garden denying Christ.

"That was the only good thing about his getting married again. He stopped that cemetery ritual," Michael says, knitting his eyebrows into a ragged line. "Mary wasn't going to put up with any of that nonsense of his." Michael's pronouncements wear me down, strip me of any energy to contradict him. I say nothing, but secretly am frightened of how he has leveled my dad's trips to the cemetery with the word "nonsense." I imagine Joey running to the cemetery, scaling the wrought-iron gates, lost inside, frantically searching for the Saint George plot.

"He's probably over at Jeff Sullivan's house, all warm and watching cartoons," Gerry says.

"What about calling Jeff Sullivan's house?" I ask as Mary slips back into the kitchen.

"No, you are not calling anyone. The Sullivans don't need to know what goes on here. Your brother will be back," Mary orders. "It's just what your father would have done." I can feel myself shrinking, holding back. How does she know what my father would have done? I wonder.

"Well, Carole, it *is* what your father would have done." I hate her for reading my mind.

"You disagree with me, don't you, Carole?" Mary taunts me.

"I don't know what he would have done," I say, making an effort to keep my voice calm, but failing. If my tone so much as displeases her, I am readying myself for a slap in the face. But, no, Mary does not hit me, crying instead that I have never cared for her, that she has never meant anything to me. I lie and tell her that I do care for her, all the while feeling as if I am going insane. While Joey is roaming around Springfield in freezing temperatures, I am reassuring Mary of how much I care for her. I stoop to using her line, Where would we be without her? She makes herself a cup of Sanka, which "limits the effects of caffeine on my colitis," and scuffles down the hall to her bedroom. By now, I am playing mind games to get through the moment, games where I learn how to control my thinking in time segments. In two minutes, she will leave the kitchen. In ten minutes, the little kids will climb the stairs to bed. In twenty minutes, I will make myself a piece of toast. Am I going crazy?

The next morning I ask Joey where he had been, and he growls at me "to leave him alone." I'm not even sure I care anymore.

* * *

On the Thursday of Holy Week, the announcement is clearly posted outside the glee club room for everyone to see. Father Sears has done the unthinkable: He has rejected Ellen Seymour's minstrel show proposal, preferring instead Suzanne Fraska's Polish dancers. With no minstrel performance lined up for senior year, the clique whose outskirts I circle like a hummingbird is quiet, coping with the news. During third period, I am huddled with Annette Langlois, a ninth-grade girl I have been tutoring in Latin since January, in a corner of the school library when Suzanne Fraska approaches our desk and throws back her blonde hair. Normally, Annette and I welcome any interruption to our Latin drilling, a free service provided to students by members of the National Honor Society, but Suzanne's excited prattle about her dance number runs on too long, and I tap my pencil against the desk, hoping she'll take the hint. She doesn't. When a heady Suzanne struts off, I confide in Annette, a soprano in the glee club, how I wish I could sing or dance.

But my stage career is not yet over. In English class, Sister Rose Carmel surprises us with the news that our class will perform *The Barretts of Wimpole Street* for the senior class. Sister says it will be the highlight of Senior Week. For a second, I consider contradicting Sister and telling her that many of us think the Senior Prom might be the highlight of Senior Week. Sister devotes the entire class to casting the play, thumbnailing the roles, and my classmates decide that I will sparkle as "Bella," Elizabeth Barrett's flighty cousin with a marked speech impediment. Suzanne Kean will direct the play, a fitting role for the only Cathedral graduate ever headed for the lofty yet secular Smith College. After all the roles have been meted out, Suzanne tells cast members in a high-pitched cackle how her father and she stormed the bursar's office at Smith to plead for yet more scholarship money for her. And Smith had scraped its coffers and tumbled to the Keans' requests. Try as I would, I cannot picture my father ever appealing to strangers, especially when it came to money. I wonder if Suzanne's dad is strange, odd the way she is; yet I am painfully jealous.

On the kitchen table that night, there is a letter from the University of Massachusetts awarding me a partial scholarship for six hundred dollars. I calculate that by the end of the summer, I'll have enough money in my savings account for half of my sophomore year in college as well. Upstairs, I stick the letter in my desk drawer and rummage my desk for the application for the Irish Heritage scholarship I picked up last week in the guidance office, finding it stuck in an old copy of *Seventeen*. In two weeks, there will be a test on Irish history. Since my knowledge of Irish history is scattered lyrics from "Danny Boy," "When Irish Eyes Are Smiling," and my favorite, "Paddy McGinty's Harp," I'll pick up the books on the reading list at the library. Relieved about the UMass scholarship, I am worried that if Michael learns about it, he might pry some more money out of me. I should give him Suzanne Kean's phone number.

On a rainy Saturday in May, twenty applicants take the test for the Irish scholarship in a third-floor room in a building on Worthington Street. John Burke, an old classmate from Our Lady of Hope grammar school, is the only person I recognize. When the test is over, he catches up and walks out with me.

"What was that test? Besides my name, I didn't know anything," John says in a high voice. "Here, get under my umbrella."

"No, it's just sprinkling. I like the rain."

"Did you read the books?" he asks.

"Yes, not that it did me any good. I don't think I've ever had a test where I had studied and knew so few answers."

"You probably won it, if you read the books."

"I doubt it. It felt like Sister Marita Joseph's geometry class," I say. At Main Street, we wait for a light and compare test answers. He puts the umbrella over me.

"If I don't win, I hope you do," he says, walking me to the door of Forbes.

"Same," I answer and we wave goodbye. John is much cuter than he was in second grade, I think, as I walk down the perfume aisle, inhaling the flowery fragrances made keener by my dampness. When I get home, I'll call Pat Smith to tell her about John Burke's taking the test because at Cathedral she and John share unofficial couple status. Although Pat and John don't date, they joke around between classes and during study halls. Too, Pat's made no secret that she is praying John will ask her to the Senior Prom.

It is so slow at work that afternoon that I study my lines from the play and practice my lisp whenever I have a customer. My prayer is that my slapstick performance as Bella will inspire some boy to ask me to the prom out of pity. Carole O'Malley, pity date.

"Carole, you're one of the ten National Winners. I'm so glad you didn't listen to me. The committee at National loved your essay on your brothers," Anne Wanant, the head of the women's branch of the American Legion Auxiliary, chirps over the telephone. "We're putting it in the Springfield newspapers. We've never had a national winner, and the prize is for a thousand dollars." As she blurts out the words, I am happy, but suspended, as if this American Legion scholarship is really being awarded to another, better Carole O'Malley, and not me, the real me. I had written the brother essay back in tenth grade, before the gambling, the running away, the endless zingers of pain we level at one another. Making it sugary had worked, and I had hidden away the shady grays and dark spots of my brothers and me. But Mrs. Wanant is excited enough for both of us as she tells me about the regional awards ceremony which will be held in Swampscott in an old inn on the ocean. I act excited, knowing Mrs. Wanant expects it, but I could have been playing Bella for the acting I was doing.

Mary congratulates me and says, surprising me, that she will take the day off to drive me to Swampscott. The consensus among my brothers is that I should be giving them a share because, after all, I had written about them.

I lie in bed that night, sleepless, listening to the rain beat against the window, afraid of the long drive to Swampscott, trapped in a car for hours with Mary. I imagine how she'll act as if she's won the award. My throat is tight, so I just don't swallow. A sliver of me, the part that wants to be like everyone else, wants a parent there, a mother or father. Would my dad be proud of me or would he belittle the American Legion scholarship as nothing more than a handout? He could do that.

54. Prom Fever

HEPBURN AND TRACY hit the halls of Cathedral High School. Robert Browning, played by John Brody, and Elizabeth Barrett, played by Christina Lovett, are waltzing off to the prom together. It must be reciting all those flowery sonnets. Bella, played by me, has no date, and the prom is only a week away. It is hot and stuffy in the auditorium as the imperial Suzanne, our director, is trying to bar any audience, insisting on a government-like secrecy surrounding the production. Richard Trudeau dashes around the stage, setting props. Watching him, it strikes me that he will ask Suzanne to the prom. I pull out my page and study it the way I would the French subjunctive. Half an hour later, when I finish up my little snippets of comedy, my dozen lines, I sneak out of the rehearsals. By Wednesday, six days from now, *The Barretts of Wimpole Street* will be history.

For me, Sharon Ford's pre-graduation party is a last-ditch social effort to snag a prom date. The whispered word "party" had flown through the study halls, the cafeteria, and the homerooms of Cathedral to its caged seniors. By senior year, if you hear about the party, you're invited. So many cars are lined up and down Bay Street that Monica has to park the car on a side street two blocks away. In Sharon's crowded basement, girls outnumber the boys three to one since many of the senior boys are now dating juniors, and the few boys there hug the walls. Had they missed the social graces in Jane Austen and don't understand that parties mean dancing? In a unit, we head toward the chip table. Jean hands us paper cups of ginger ale, the only soda left.

"He called on a Saturday morning, before Easter even. I was vacuuming for my mother. I don't know what made me say it, but I told him I had other plans for the prom," Jean confesses. "I should have kept the vacuum on when I shot him down."

"Wouldn't the vacuum noise add to his rejection?" I ask, and we laugh.

"Who asked you?" Monica probes. His name has slipped by me too.

"I'm not saying. You don't want to know," Jean says with a tone of finality. I respect her protecting him, but am wondering if he, a discard on Jean's reject pile, might ask me. So Jean and the twins had been asked over a month ago.

"You were gutsy. What if Mr. X had spread around that you already had a prom date?" Veronica asks.

"Well, I didn't think he'd broadcast that I turned him down. I didn't really think about it. I just didn't want to spend four hours in his company." The "in his company" phrase has a refined, Austen feel to it.

"Is he here?" I ask, looking at the clumps of boys scattered around the basement.

"No, thank God," she answers with relief.

"Because if he shows up, maybe you could point me in his direction and I could snow him with my charm."

"Trust me on this one. You'd rather stay home," Jean says. The weekend Barry left for college, Jean had written him a *Dear John* letter. She had even kept a handwritten copy, having had a number of boyfriends. Jean is short, not even five feet, which I think helps, but the sad truth is Jean has a gift for flirting. When I bat my long, dark lashes in a come hither look, boys scatter. In the front seat of the car on the way home, I seat dance to Elvis, thinking that if I had a choice between a gift for Latin and a gift for flirting, I'd go with the flirting, picturing Elvis in his white-glitter suit as my prom date singing "Are You Lonesome Tonight?"

The Saturday morning before Senior Week, I am headed out for work when Mary tosses an envelope on the kitchen table.

"There's something for you. Are you going to open it?" Her questions sound more like commands. Her urgency, coupled with her impatience, makes me nervous.

"It's from the Irish Historical Association. I'm sure it's saying I did not get the scholarship," I say, staring at the return address.

"You don't know that," Mary says.

"I knew about three questions on the test," I say and run my fingernail under the envelope.

"Carole, you're ripping the letter," Mary says. I had wanted to save the letter and read it on the bus to work in privacy. She grabs the letter from my hand and hands it to me. A check is clipped to the letter.

"I won. It's a check," I say in disbelief. "I can't believe it. Everyone else must have answered two questions."

"You win everything, don't you?" Mary asks and reaches into the cabinet for a coffee mug. "You're a winner."

At the bus stop, I kick the telephone pole and wonder about John Burke and the scholarship. Does he need the money more than I do? Funny how Mary makes my being a winner sound as if I have done something wrong. I don't feel like a winner.

In late May, glass vases of sweet-smelling lilacs stand tall on the altar of the school chapel. With the rah-rah organized activities of Senior Week, only the chapel remains calm and serene. Outside, there is an emotional pitch to the raised voices, the declarations on yearbook pages, the heady excitement that subdues me. Yet, too, exams are winding down and classes are over. The last this and the end of that amount to small satisfactions. Either way, I'm not up to the hysteria or the finality and have slunk into a fog of suspended animation. Upfront, the mid-afternoon sun hits the stained glass windows and creates soft-edged waves of color on the hard-backed oak pews, giving me whatever it is that I need.

Hurrying through the halls, I arrive in a sweat at the library for my last tutoring session. Ten minutes later, while I am listlessly drilling a distracted Annette on the ablative absolute, a small dark-haired woman approaches our table and smiles. Fidgeting, Annette says to me, "It's my mother." Automatically, we both stand to greet her, and Annette mumbles an introduction. When I shake her mother's hand, I study the visitor's pass on the collar of her London Fog raincoat, a coat exactly like one Mary owns.

"Annette didn't want me to come. I realize parents don't often drop by the school, the interrogation they gave me, but I knew from Annette that the two of you would be at this table here in the library," she said in a quiet voice, her dark eyes surveying the library. Her remark catches me off guard because I had never thought that Annette would talk about our tutoring sessions at home.

"Do you have it, Mom?" Annette asks with more animation than I am used to.

"Yes, Annette," Mrs. Langlois answers, and she pulls out a gift-wrapped box, which together they hand to me. "I wanted to thank you for how much you've done for my daughter. Her grades have improved and you've convinced her she can do it." I manage a thank you for the unexpected gift.

"At first, Annette was intimidated by you since you're a senior," she continues, unaware of the way Annette is rolling her eyes, "but she's come to learn so much from you. Her father and I both thank you." I feel uncomfortable when I imagine the Langlois family discussing me over roast beef.

"Open it," Annette urges me excitedly. I rip off the flowered paper, and Annette reaches for the ribbon.

"A bottle of Shalimar. Thank you."

"Wear it to the prom," Annette suggests.

"If I get a date," I say, grimacing.

"Oh, you will. Some boy just needs to find the courage," Mrs. Langlois says confidently.

After a whirl of thank yous and goodbyes, I watch them leave the library, whispering the way friends do. I stuff the Shalimar in my book bag so I won't have to see it.

Courage was floating in the air when the phone rang later that night.

"Carole, it's John Burke. Just to prove I'm not a sore loser about the scholarship I thought I'd ask you to the prom." I say yes, knowing that Cornelius Cleary had asked Pat Smith two weeks ago and her mother has insisted she go with Corny. After thirty seconds, I hang up the phone and wipe the wet outline of my hand on a dishtowel. It will be another hour before I worry whether someone has put him up to asking me, whether I was his second choice.

Emptying my book bag, I pluck the bottle of Shalimar from the piles of loose papers and place it in the middle of my bureau. I study Annette's scrawl on the thank you note and begin weeping. In bed, I cry myself to sleep.

My friends rally. Panicked on my behalf, Mrs. Sullivan and the twins, envisioning my showing up for the prom in a shower curtain, convince me that I will never find a dress with only five days until the prom. Monica offers me the loan of a white satin gown with a Jackie Kennedy look she had worn to a dance at Holy Cross. I am set.

On Class Day, Leon Maynard, senior class president, is hamming it up as master of ceremonies for the awards program in the auditorium. Because of the play, I can only stay for the prophecy and class history part of it. Backstage, Suzanne, our esteemed director, the back of her pale hand to her forehead, is reading her pages of final notes with more drama and flair than is in the play itself. Every five minutes, I crack open the curtains to hear the class ballot until Suzanne catches me, shooting me an exasperated look, but not before I hear Jean's name announced as The Girl with the Most Enthusiasm.

"Leon's reading the class ballot where he . . ." I start to say, but she has no interest in the class opinion of our peers.

"Please, pay attention. The curtain goes up in fifteen minutes," she snaps in a cold voice. Her frown tells me that she thinks less of me that I might care about the ballot.

"What about the class jingles?" I ask. There is a faint chuckle from the cast which she cuts short with a deep sigh.

The Barretts of Wimpole Street begins in the darkened auditorium. The class titters as Robert and the frail Elizabeth court each other with poetry. I enter on cue, am so so "fwightening" with my speech impediment that my classmates nudge one another and laugh, grateful for the barest hint of comic relief. Elizabeth's offstage dog, "Flush," produces even more laughs with its toilet references, causing a blank look on the director's face. Halfway through the play, the audience begins coughing, and the coughing, like yawning, becomes contagious, causing the nuns to rise from their seats and patrol the aisles. They glare at boys with well-honed reputations for troublemaking, who under Sister's gaze sit there innocently, in an assumed saintlike posture, with eyes now straight ahead. The play ends to wild, undeserved applause, culture's prisoners freed from a theatrical event, never staged before and never to be staged again by the Honors English classes or the Drama Club. Elizabeth Barrett, the sick and feeble poet, fails to capture the hardened hearts of the graduating seniors of Cathedral High School on Class Day, who could care less about her daring elopement and lovesick sonnets. In class, when we read the final lines of her famous Sonnet XLIII, ". . . and, if God choose, I shall but love thee better after death," Sister raved about the ethereal beauty of the lovers' attachment. But the false hyperbole of the couplet fell shrill on my ears. I'm no Victorian because, to me, there's nothing romantic about the dark, cold, empty room of death.

Backstage, I pull the hair pins from my Victorian updo and my hair right along with them. I stare at the black strands clinging to my fingers and decide it is time for me to abandon my stage career now that the Bella "wole" is over and done. I couldn't sing anyway. No stage-door Johnnies, no candy, no flowers . . .

Finally, after work, when I, deprived by those simpering Barretts, can no longer bear not knowing my place on the class ballot, I call Jean who mercifully is home. A school night date would have undone me. It bothers me that I am letting the ballot mean so much. There are no awful categories, like Girl with the Messiest Bedroom or Girl with the Most Persistent Acne. After a few minutes of trashing the play, I congratulate her on selection as Girl with the Most Enthusiasm, finessing my way into the ballot.

"You know what this means? You should have been a cheerleader," I said.

"You think so? I think so too. Too late now, I guess."

"Hardly a very enthusiastic remark. What was I in the class ballot?" I blurt out, stiffening as vague, unflattering labels flit through my head.

"You don't know? Right, you were backstage. You were Girl with the Best Sense of Humor so when you came on as Bella, you just confirmed it."

"Well, it's not Prettiest."

"Did you hear about Rose Carmel?" she asks, ending the ballot discussion before I find out who was the Boy with the Best Sense of Humor. "Bucko Fitzgerald was acting up during the play. So Rose Carmel found him in the hall after the play and said, 'Mr. Fitzgerald, if I had a gun, I would shoot you.'"

"Oooh. Not good."

"Wait. Then she said, 'But I wouldn't want to waste the bullet.' Bucko said he's thinking of skipping the rest of this week or he'll be dead by graduation."

I make the mistake of announcing to Danny and Gerry that I have been voted The Girl with the Best Sense of Humor. Gerry replies that I'm not funny, compared to him anyway, and Danny mouths off that the class ballot means nothing, the nuns probably run it, like they run everything else, and what difference does it make anyway? When I leave the kitchen, I yell back, "Jealousy!" In my room, I kneel down and pray, asking God to let me ignore this fusillade of Danny's, and Gerry's putdowns. As I repeat the words of the Our Father, I think how Gerry may be right—at home, I'm not funny.

A long gown is a statement. The white satin floor-length gown makes me feel like a queen of a tiny, nameless kingdom. In his rented white tuxedo jacket, John Burke looks handsome in a green-eyed, jet-black-hair way, his Aqua Velva competing with my Shalimar. To my eye, the prom theme of "Younger than Springtime" (what does that mean?) boils down to little more than scores of pastel-colored crepe flowers randomly tacked on the cafeteria columns. Posing for pictures in front of an imported wooden trellis, John and I stand stiffly, like soldiers at a drill inspection. When the oily-haired photographer urges us to stand closer to each other, we joke that no nun had hired him. Although I have known John since second grade, technically this is our first date. An hour before the prom, his older sister, Joan, had been waltzing him around their living room, he had said, and he let it slip that his mother and Joan were more excited about his going to the prom than he was—a sting almost as bad as bumping into Cornelius (now Neil) Cleary and Pat Smith out on the crowded dance floor. The truth is my wooden dancing is just a shade better than my singing, but, like Jean, I have great enthusiasm for it, and John pretends he does too. As we leave the cafeteria before the committee-planned chicken dinner at the Oaks Inn, each of us lifts a pink crepe paper rose. "As a souvenir," we tell each other.

After John has wiped traces of chicken fat from the corners of his mouth, folding his napkin with an unexpected delicacy, he wallows into the dreaded topic of Irish history. We bandy about military leaders and martyrs for a moment until I concede my winning the scholarship may have been a fluke. Was the award connected to my dad's death? A pity scholarship and a pity date, for suddenly I am aware that John is going to the beach after the prom. He has invited me to the prom, but the invitation abruptly ends there. I'm three years old again and watching my playmates parade by in their pastel-colored dresses headed for Linda Wheeler's party. I'll get though it—I have before—but inside I am wobbling and pain-red like strawberry jelly. Picking at the brownie sundae dessert, we, smile-weary, are left with little to say, the exact date of the Easter Uprising dousing any embers of romance between us. But prom night wheezes on, and when a little after midnight John plants me with a pre-planned good-night kiss at the back door, I can only wonder if he practiced this ritual with his sister as well.

Up in my room, I crumple the crepe paper rose and throw it across the room, aiming for my desk. Monica's dress I hang carefully on the back of my door and stand to gaze out the window. Tonight there is no moon sleeping in the black starless sky, as if the sad ritual of romance were too much for the Old Man to make even a sliver of an appearance. Four days from now, I am sure I will graduate, but when will I ever fall in love? When will I be invited to the beach party? When will I be writing love letters in the sand?

THE NUCLEAR OPTION

TIME: The present.

(Carole picks up the cell phone in her hotel room and dials. Gerry O'Malley answers. In the following conversation, there are pauses and hesitations, and laughter between questions and answers. Certain words are empha-sized. The Brian mentioned is Joey's oldest son.)

GERRY: Hey, what's up, Carole?
CAROLE: You love that caller-ID feature.

GERRY: I do. I do. I played the answering machine and heard you have a question about Mary. She's physically fine, in and out mentally. More out than in.

CAROLE: So the question is. . . .

GERRY: Go ahead, Carole. Get it out.

CAROLE: Why didn't we stand up to Mary?

GERRY: (*Smugly.*) Oh, that's easy. The Nuclear Option.

CAROLE: The Nuclear Option? And what would that be?

GERRY: Her threatening to leave us all the time. Any time there was any kind of major dispute—it was "I'm out of here. I'm leaving." Any time there was any kind of controversy, or problem that erupted into disagreement—"I'm gone." Get it?

CAROLE: (*She smiles.*) I get it. I get it. The Nuclear Option. How often do you remember Mary's threatening to leave? Every ten days? Once a week? Every two weeks?

GERRY: As far as I was concerned it happened too often, but I would say about once a month.

CAROLE: I'd say more like every two weeks.

GERRY: The worst was the craziness and not knowing just when it would hit. She was a ticking time bomb—not knowing when she was going to erupt, we were walking on eggshells all the time. So you could never really feel comfortable. You had no control over it anyway, but in such a large family you could be minding your own business and somebody else could be having a bad day, say something slightly controversial, and boom, you're still caught in the crossfire.

CAROLE: Did anybody ever call her on it? Maybe Joey?

GERRY: We wanted to avoid controversy. At least I did.

CAROLE: You can add my name to that list.

GERRY: None of us wanted to be in that position where she might make good on her threat. With our parents dying and all the other issues, I think we wanted to be as normal as possible.

CAROLE: Just blend in.

GERRY: Remember how she would erupt and explode and always take off in her car somewhere? Sometimes it would be for about an hour, maybe more. And, of course, the longer she was gone, the higher the anxiety level was. OK, is she out of here for good? What's going to happen to us? I'd wonder.

CAROLE: Did you ever talk about her threatening to leave to Joe, Steve, Bob, Tom?

GERRY: No, everybody was aware of what it was like. You knew it was a miserable situation. It was sort of like picking a scab—why would you want to continue to pick it?

CAROLE: I remember trying to figure out if there was any way I could take care of everybody if she did take off.

GERRY: Yeah, there you are, sixteen years old. It was all part of her threatening game that she played. To try to maintain power.

CAROLE: She was all-powerful.

GERRY: A god.

CAROLE: Speaking of God, what about her "take no prisoners" Catholicism?

GERRY: I think it was legitimate.

CAROLE: But I used to think, how could she be so judgmental about morality or whatever her definition of goodness was? And then she would turn around and behave with such cruelty. How many times did she slap you across the face?

GERRY: Jeez, I don't know, I'd say five to ten times. Probably closer to five. Maybe.

CAROLE: You got off easy. No, I take that back—none of us did.

GERRY: I think what was worse than the hitting was the constant anxiety about her eruptions. When is she going to fly off the handle? How long is it going to last? What is she going to do?

CAROLE: I timed one of her rages once. I still remember sneaking a look up at the kitchen clock. The fit lasted twenty minutes, but it seemed so much longer. Yet the aftermath could linger for days. How about Mary's revisionist history? Her saying she never hit us? Talk about denial. She's like an eastern European dictator.

GERRY: Eight witnesses could say otherwise.

CAROLE: What do you think you missed not having a mother? Or do you think you don't even know what you missed?

GERRY: I think you're jealous of other people if they have two parents and they were properly nurtured. What you miss is the nurturing . . . the times you want to seek out a parent's advice, or they gave you advice you wanted or not, and years later you would say they were right. Or maybe they weren't. A lot of little things like that. Being there on special occasions . . . I mean, how proud would our parents have been at, say, West Point—Brian's graduation? It would have been a special moment . . . it would have been a more complete experience. And, then, there's the tremendous sense of abandonment.

CAROLE: A friend who grew up on Hungry Hill told me how her mother thought that Mary was a saint. Meanwhile, when I stop to think about it, we treated her better than a lot of parents are treated. She had such a charming public face.

GERRY: She was like one of the people you work with that you would rather be on their good side, because any time they can turn on you . . . go crazy on you. Did you have time to go see Mary today?

CAROLE: Yes. I'm still in shock. She sounded really genuinely happy to see me although she went in and out of knowing who I was. When I was leaving, she said, "So lovely to see you." She said that last time, too.

GERRY: I know, today she is a completely transformed individual.

CAROLE: Do you think it's the Alzheimers or senility?

GERRY: Whatever it is, her personality has changed. She went from bad to good. She's on medication, and the last time I went up there for a meeting with her health care people, I said, "Whatever medications she's on, keep her on them. Don't tweak the meds at all, OK?!"

CAROLE: Today she said to me, "You know, those kids aren't really mine. I never had a child of my own."

GERRY: Yeah, she's said that before.

CAROLE: There was a thread of the old Mary when she was talking about bread. She's down on whole wheat, wants white bread on her sandwich. How tough the whole wheat is, not much taste to it, and I thought, better bread than me. But there was none of her old venom and energy. That's a comeuppance.

GERRY: I agree. I absolutely agree. I was out at Heritage yesterday, and I called Tommy on the cell phone. I put the cell on speaker phone so she could hear it, but I could also hear the dialogue between the two, and Tommy was so nice to her. You know there are some people up there who never get any visitors.

CAROLE: You are the candidate for sainthood here, overseeing her medical care. I am so grateful to you for that.

GERRY: How's Dave doing?

CAROLE: (*Laughing.*) Good. Mary asked me that four times.

GERRY: She will.

CAROLE: Do you remember her criticizing you?

GERRY: She might have, I don't recall.

CAROLE: (*In disbelief.*) I can't believe you can't remember being criticized.

GERRY: (*Chuckling.*) I don't want you to get the impression that I'm her advocate.

CAROLE: Well, she decimated me with her criticism. She criticized everything about me.

GERRY: Yeah, but you were her number one enemy.

CAROLE: Because—why?

GERRY: You were female, there were seven boys, she probably viewed you . . . especially after Dad died and you were left with a lot of responsibilities for the household, she saw you as a junior woman.

CAROLE: Yes, surrogate spouse, junior woman. I was always the mother in some way, or I thought I was.

GERRY: I think everyone was denied, somewhat, a childhood because she didn't have the proper nurturing that goes along with being a parent.

CAROLE: Any comments from her ever about school?

GERRY: No. No.

CAROLE: Any attempts to discipline or to encourage you?

GERRY: No. I don't think she had a great deal of time to get involved at a personal level.

CAROLE: Do you remember doing any chores?

GERRY: (*Pause.*) Not too many. (*Both laugh.*)

CAROLE: I'm tired of talking about her.

GERRY: Once her fuse was lit, you couldn't put it out.

CAROLE: Even if you agreed with her. Told her she was right.

GERRY: There was going to be an explosion.

CAROLE: And, then, there was always the Nuclear Option.

GERRY: (*Confirmingly.*) The Nuclear Option.

(*They chat a few more minutes and hang up. Carole puts the cell phone in her handbag and laughs.*)

55. We'll Remember Always
Graduation Day

THE COLISEUM AT the Eastern States Exposition grounds, an ice rink for hockey games in winter, is packed with camps of parents and relatives squinting to find their soon-to-be graduates. For the graduation ceremony, the girls in white caps and gowns—purity?—and the boys in purple—royalty?—are separated by sections. The sea of relatives sits behind me, my back is to them, and I imagine my parents are just late to my graduation, scrambling for seats in the last rows, craning their necks to find me. My father, handsome in his tan summer suit, adjusts my mother's mink stole, and his hand behind her sheathed back gently ushers her into a seat.

Although half a dozen bobby pins secure the mortarboard on my slippery, just-washed hair, I picture my cap sliding off when Sister Mary Eugene hands me my diploma. During Suzanne Kean's impassioned salutatory address, practically a eulogy on last week's death of Pope John XXIII, I stare distractedly at the tips of my white sixteen-dollar Thom McCann high heels, the prom and graduation choice of the twins and Jean, representing yet another Forbes and Wallace paycheck for me. When graduation is over, I think how I'll almost be relieved to return to my penny-pinching ways. I fiddle with the program's purple tassel, using it to underline my name, *Carole Marie O'Malley, and wonder if my dad would have chided me for the star, *Miss Honors Graduate,* or would my mother have praised me? Next at the podium, John Riordan, our valedictorian, drones on about nuclear disarmament and America's commitment to the space race. Knowing his plans to study nuclear physics at MIT, I relax a little, worrying less about the Russians rapping at my kitchen door hustling communism. My mind hurtling, I catch a word of John's every now and then, but wish the speeches had been printed in the program so I could read them.

When I line up to cross the stage, in an odd flash, I can almost hear my parents' voices ordering me to hold your shoulders back, Carole, hold your shoulders back. Approaching the dais, I try to walk slowly, aim for the coveted West Point posture. Sister Mary Eugene hands me my diploma and shakes my hand firmly, but she does not let go. "Carole, I am proud of you. Keep up your good work," she says in her firm, clear voice. "Thank you, Sister," I murmur as John Riordan looks up, surprised as I am at Sister's unexpected compliment.

The hard metal of the folding chair comforts my hands, gives them something to hold. Why should Sister's words, her *atta girl,* make me feel as if I'm falling down a flight of velvet stairs? Make my eyes a puddle of silken tears? To survive this ceremony—and I know I am almost at its end—I must keep myself from facing that my mother is dead and my father is dead. I bite down hard on my lip, overwhelmed by a deep loneliness, my efforts at pretending no longer working. I space out, play with my hands, but my raw-boned mood is jangled a moment later by the sound of music. Cued by the exhausting heartiness of Father Sears, our musical director, my classmates and I, the graduates of the Class of 1963, rise in perfect precision for the last time to sing, "with gusto," "The Royal Purple."

Half an hour later, shielding my eyes from the sun, I linger outside an entrance to the Coliseum, searching for Mary and my aunts and uncles. Freed, at last, from the shackles of the Sisters of Saint Joseph, my classmates mill about, shouting congratulations at one another, setting up plans, reading diplomas, masking waves of relief and uncertainty. I shrink a little when I watch some of my friends crying and hugging as if they will never see each other again. Won't we all be at East Longmeadow Friendly's tonight? As families hoot at finding one another, there are more tears, more hugs, more kisses, and more posing for cameras. Parents are popping pictures and shoving bouquets of roses into their daughters' arms. It seems as if there are bouquets everywhere. At this moment, surrounded by my classmates' mothers and fathers clinging to their embarrassed graduates, I feel uneasy and apart, like a leaf in a sea, even as my relatives encircle me.

Planting a kiss on my cheek, Mary says, "Well, this certainly is a big day for you, isn't it, Carole?" In her voice, there is a blurred edge of resentment. Ducking her question, I am saved by my uncle's draping his burly arm around my shoulders.

"Hey, Katsy, what is this about the honors? I'd say, kiddo, congratulations are in order." My uncle easily matched the bluster of Father Sears. "Let your old uncle give you a hug." After we hug, my aunt Mad steps closer to me as if she is waiting for a quieter moment, his wind to subside. With the fake smile I am so good at, I hide a growing dull emptiness inside me and begin to pray silently. Please, God, let me get through this, let me be OK. Let me not think, not feel while my well-trained uncles press cards into my hands, murmuring words of congratulations.

"Carole, I had no idea graduation would run this long. I have an appointment with Dr. Baltrucki in Hartford for these splitting headaches I've been having lately," Mary says, pointing to her watch. "Your aunt and uncle will drive you home." If she leaves now, why, she can't pull a scene, I think, suddenly warm with relief. But my thoughts—Where am I? Will I be OK? Will Mary stay? Could I manage? What is next? There is no proud parent for me—dance like the dry, yellowed blades of sea grasses flailing in a winter wind. As the crowd thins out, I see groups with fathers and mothers like sculptured bookends on either side of their child drifting away from me. The image of these tidy trios sets off a sense of loss in me as if they, these proud, these simpering, these television-perfect families are somehow forcing me into finally facing that everything I do, I do alone. Forget the Hammerstein lyrics, "You'll Never Walk Alone." I do walk alone. Maybe I always did.

There is a touch, a pull on my winged sleeve. Aunt Madeline is whispering to me. "Carole, if your father were alive, he would be so proud of you today. And he would have seen to it that you had a huge bouquet of roses."

The End

Epilogue
FADE OUT

MY FATHER LABELED me a "tough cookie," and I never thought to question his definition. And Aunt Madeline urged me, "Carole, be strong for your brothers." I never thought to ask, well, what about me?

The loneliness, the hurt, the secrecy, the isolation, the shame, I stuffed down into the pits of my brick-hard soul.

As an adult, I twice sought psychiatric help and was twice dismissed as highly functioning, as if not being so were somehow the only measure for help. These psychiatrists either glossed over or did not ask about my childhood credentials, the abandonment of my early orphanhood, "The Girl Whose Mother Died," and then "The Girl Whose Father Died," and my scarred status as the child of an alcoholic. I found my way into Al-Anon. At an Al-Anon meeting, a woman repeated a remark her therapist had made in a session that struck me as both wise and perceptive. I followed this stranger out of the room and, overcoming my fear of asking for what I need, asked for her therapist's phone number. She generously gave me the number, and that is how I found Sherrye Everett, a therapist who specializes in the treatment of active alcoholics and adult children of alcoholic families. Sherrye knew my game: let me fit in, let me blend, let me be flawless, let me be perfect—which, of course, allowed me no humanity, made me a stick figure. Although I was reluctant, I raked up the pain of my childhood so that I might learn what behaviors I took from that troubled time into my adult life. Insisting that I talk about me, Sherrye gave me the beginner's guide to feelings: mad, sad, glad, lonely, or scared, later adding shame and guilt. I still have her faded handout on defense mechanisms.

In the rookie stages of my recovery, I became a proselytizer, a messianic preacher of self-help programs, a cartoon-like role I gradually abandoned. My daughters grew up in a Skinner box—"I will not share my feelings with that mean girl"—but that is the material for their memoirs.

In my opinion, we have all been injured, but for today, six of the eight O'Malleys are sober, an extraordinary fact. While I accept the genetic pre-disposition to alcoholism, try to understand also that we, the O'Malleys, knew nothing else: no hobbies, no interests, no athletics as a family, no stopping for sunsets, no walks in the woods; instead we knew dimly lit bars and a whiskey bottle on the counter.

While I am not included in the annual Cape Cod "brothers only" fish-ing trip and I vocalize the resentment, we gather for graduations, high school and college, and weddings. In December 2003, we held a Pizzeria Uno family gathering in Springfield next to the Basketball Hall of Fame to honor Joey and Peggy's sons, Captain Brian O'Malley and Lieutenant Christopher O'Malley, before their deployment to Iraq. In March 2005, the O'Malleys and the Gaunts again gathered to celebrate their return.

Madeline O'Malley Quilty, my father's sister, died on March 10, 2005, at the age of 83. I remained close to her, thereby incurring Mary's dis-pleasure. She religiously attended O'Malley family functions, traveling to New Hampshire for Abby's college graduation, her last road trip from Springfield. She remembered each of our birthdays with a card. Whenever I mentioned the word "alcoholic," my aunt would bristle, but in the last year of her life she conceded that, as I had long suspected, my father had lost the will to live and drank himself to death. For me her admission felt like a moment of truth.

Michael is a retired postal worker. "Isn't that dignified, right?" He also has a thirty-year-old landscaping business. Michael's response to my writing a memoir was, "Why do you want to dredge that up?" and he suggested I write a book like Harry Potter instead. He lives in Springfield and is very generous to me and my daughters.

Danny is a Ph.D. candidate in psychology and a counselor in the Hampden County prison system. He is the father of Michael O'Malley.

Gerry, a retired social studies teacher, is married to Faye and the father of Gerry, Jr. Sixteen years ago, he started an alcohol and drug prevention club in Agawam Middle School which continues today. He and Faye became grandparents in July 2006. He still zings me whenever he can. They live in Westfield, Massachusetts.

Joey, a manager for an elevator company, is married to Peggy and has three grown sons, Brian, Christopher, and Joey, Jr. He and Peggy live in Chicopee, Massachusetts. He named his boat *Caitlyn,* after his granddaughter.

Steve, an investor, is married to Mary Ellen and has two teenaged sons, Steve and Tom. They occasionally ask for my advice and follow it. Victoria and I are delighted that their son Steve will be following Victoria to the same college next year. They live in Locust, New Jersey.

Bobby, a school custodian, is married to Elly and actively parented her two children, Kate and Josh. When he isn't fishing or landscaping, he can be heard calling into conservative radio talk shows that air on Cape Cod or needling the more liberal members of the O'Malley family. He and Elly live in South Yarmouth, Massachusetts.

*   *   *

Tom, a real estate developer, recently moved to Scottsdale, Arizona. "Say I'm in the witness protection program." He is married to Cathryn and the father of Rohan Joseph and Bridget Madeline. I try "not to take care" of him.

I am married to David Gaunt, a real estate investor, and the mother of three daughters, Abigail, Susan, and Victoria. As each graduated, we feted her with a formal restaurant lunch, followed by an informal family party at home, highlighted by a forced march in the living room to *Pomp and Circumstance.* At the ceremony itself, my husband handed each graduating daughter a bouquet of roses. The reality is that I am a "B" tennis player. I am taking steps to produce my nonautobiographical plays and have adapted my memoir, *Hungry Hill,* as a play. For many years, I volunteered as a group facilitator for an organization that helps parents in preventing drug and alcohol use with their children. Also, I served on the board of the Alcohol Council of New York for four years. My attendance at Al-Anon meetings has fallen off, but I continue to go, although sporadically, and am comforted in knowing it is always there. Like Caitlyn, I too have a power boat named after me, the *Carole Marie.*

We all have outlived our parents.

Acknowledgments

THE TROOPS who helped me "hold the fort": let me thank my brothers, Michael, Danny, Gerry, Joe, Steve, Bob, and Tom who, like me, cling to whatever scraps of memories of our father and mother we unearth along the way. I'm sure that, as Gerry has hinted, *Hungry Hill* misses much of the O'Malley joy, so I've left the joyful version to all of you. Although Michael discouraged me from "dredging" all that up, I thank him for his adjective "brutal" and his on-target assessment of that remarriage: "Not a sober minute." I am so grateful to my brother Gerry for his willingness to share his memories of our early years. That he oversees Mary's health care puts him on another celestial plane, and he is a hero in my eyes. I thank Gerry's wife, Faye, for sharing her recollections of Mary. To Tom, for his O'Malley support—always hold back a little—and his wife, Cathryn, for my best birthday gift ever, the tiara and the wand, and a special thanks for not getting the "really cheap one." The wand works. To Michael, Gerry, and Joe for making the "reunion" South of the Border restaurant lunch in Connecticut with our Hartford cousins. To my cousin Patricia Paggioli, classy as ever, for her good humor and, at times, chilling memories of my parents. To Sherrye Everett for helping me to chip away at a lifetime of defenses and not only to learn how to live but also to raise my children in a different way.

I am blessed by the generosity of friends. Norman and Marcia Kleinberg, our long-time friends, for persuading David and me to travel to Italy that first time, and a special thank you to Marcia for loaning me her high school cheerleading jacket. Vivian Gordon and Karen Hansen, event planners and traveling companions, for their ecstatic responses to my phone call from the airport tarmac. And then there are my fellow party animals: Mary Solomon, who offered to have a publishing party before there was a book. Mary Kelberg, who offered to have a party and had read pieces of the book. Gretchen Lengyel, who read a draft, did a line edit, and is planning yet another party when she isn't analyzing me. Joel and Leigh Turner-Ross for their encouragement, particularly Leigh for helping me decide which chapters Victoria recorded and her MBA prodding, "Remember, Carole, you have a product." To Joel, a former cheerleader at UPenn, I continue to wait for you and Leigh to create a cheer for *Hungry Hill.* Ginny Waldman, who saved my essay "Fashion Show," claiming it reflected her belief in me. Penny May, who has always been a "fan." Kathleen Heenan Olmstead, who would have been the darling of the Cathedral glee club, continues her efforts to make me into a "birder." Nancy Sander makes me laugh and is more willing to try anything new than even I am.

The nameless Sister of Saint Joseph who preserved and bound the back issues of the school newspaper, the *Cathedral Chronicle.* Terry Cosgriff of the Cathedral High School Alumni Office for her kindness in allowing me ready access to the old issues of the *Cathedral Chronicle* and sharing with me her childhood memories. Maggie Humbeston and Michele Barker of the Springfield Museums for pointing me to the origins of the name Hungry Hill.

My childhood and high school friends: Diane Thinel Matthews for sharing her sharp observations on my home: "It was always chaos and clear you ran the show," and for including me on family picnics to Look Park. Anne Sullivan Reade, whose calm good judgment steadied me, and for our endless pick-up basketball games and for tolerating my tennis. The twins, Monica Sullivan Parker and Veronica Sullivan Carroll, and to Ann Culloo for their sustaining friendship and memories of my mother. The late James Sullivan for always showing an interest in my writing, and the late Sally Sullivan, who insisted on my wearing Monica's gown and gloves to the prom.

Jean Phaneuf Zola, still, as ever, the "girl with the most enthusiasm," and to your grandchildren who brought you for a time to New York City. Dotty Homan Laughran for joining me on short notice, even by my standards, for our Gus and Paul breakfasts. Maria Scibelli DeAngelis for entrusting me with her junior prom dance program, her plastic bin of high school photographs, and for including me in our January potluck lunches. Sister Pat Smith, a missionary in Kenya, for her praying that God gives me what I need. God has. Giselle Gamache Varney for her spunk and for her willingness to make the follow-up phone calls. Margaret Sullivan, still willing and ready to get behind the wheel of the car, and for her insistence I recover my dining room chairs. Mary Ann Hosenfeld, who stayed still long enough to read the book. Pam Gardner Pollock for her many readings, finding more nuances than I had ever intended, for still starching her shoelaces, and for sharing her childhood secrets. My Kappa Alpha Theta "sisters": Betty Dadoly Weber, always a ready and willing reader of anything, even down to the grocery lists, I have ever written. I so love your father-daughter letter in the Tim Russert book. Marge Heap Lieber, for unearthing the same spirit and energy for *Hungry Hill* that she brought to her days scampering around Blunt Park and the Field House basketball court as a "Tech Tiger." Maureen Fitzgerald Hnatow and Sheila Fitzgerald Harrington for your shared excitement. Mary Bell Painten, also a regular at East Longmeadow Friendly's, for revealing her insights on surviving as a "maternal" orphan.

Steve and Carole Smith, my high-profile, glitzy Miami marketing team. The members of my former writing group Sande Berger, Beth Schorr Jaffe, and Bridget Casey Lopez for their careful early readings and much needed encouragement. Robert Reeves, the beleaguered director of the Southampton Writers' Conference, for publicly saying I was his "favorite." Chris Goff for his willingness to hype my earlier mysteries and his attempts to make lemonade of the rejections. Andrea Chambers, literary adviser and hand-holder. Jinny Ewald, who calmly told me what to cut from *Hungry Hill* and how to "improve" its structure. I am so grateful for your gifts. Janice Billingsley, writer and literary confidante, always there for me on those lonely, bleak days. Christine Schutt, literary helpmate, for giving practical publishing advice and for putting me in touch with Abby Weintraub. Abby Weintraub, whose jacket designs have left me moved and humbled. Tom O' Brien for deftly placing *Hungry Hill* into Bruce's capable hands. Bruce Wilcox, whose steady, patient support and gentle shoves inched *Hungry Hill* along on its journey to publication. Kay Scheuer for her careful editing and gentle "comments" that made me dig still deeper when I was unsure whether there was any coal left to mine. Sharon Paradiso, Reader A, for disclosing her secret identity to me and her insistence on the cameo appearances of the adult "Carole." (I am still looking into the Dodge commercial.) My legion of assistants: Meri Sulcer, who was with me at the beginning and was always seeking work; Page Travelstead, who was with me in the middle and whose scene analysis helped me to complete the play and screenplay; and Agustine Welles, who, along with Meri, guidelines in hand, helped me finish *Hungry Hill*. His upbeat attitude must be noted by theatrical casting agents.

Abigail, Susan, and Victoria, my Gaunt Women Rule traveling companions and proudest productions. I am singing to you in my off-key monotone, "I'll love you forever, I'll like you for always, As long as I'm living, my babies you'll be."

David who still can make me chuckle and who hired the Precisions for my birthday party. What a guy . . .

To the girl I was and to the woman I became.